Egalitarian Moments

Bloomsbury Studies in Continental Philosophy presents cutting-edge scholarship in the field of modern European thought. The wholly original arguments, perspectives and research findings in titles in this series make it an important and stimulating resource for students and academics from across the discipline.

Breathing with Luce Irigaray, edited by Lenart Skof and Emily A. Holmes
Deleuze and Art, Anne Sauvagnargues
Deleuze and the Diagram: Aesthetic Threads in Visual Organization, Jakub Zdebik
Derrida, Badiou and the Formal Imperative, Christopher Norris
Desire in Ashes: Deconstruction, Psychoanalysis, Philosophy, edited by Simon Morgan Wortham and Chiara Alfano
Ernst Bloch and His Contemporaries, Ivan Boldyrev
Why there is no Post-Structuralism in France, Johannes Angermuller
Gadamer's Poetics: A Critique of Modern Aesthetics, John Arthos
Heidegger, History and the Holocaust, Mahon O'Brien
Heidegger and the Emergence of the Question of Being, Jesús Adrián Escudero
Immanent Transcendence: Reconfiguring Materialism in Continental Philosophy, Patrice Haynes
Merleau-Ponty's Existential Phenomenology and the Realization of Philosophy, Bryan A. Smyth
Nietzsche and Political Thought, edited by Keith Ansell-Pearson
Nietzsche as a Scholar of Antiquity, Helmut Heit
Philosophy, Sophistry, Antiphilosophy: Badiou's Dispute with Lyotard, Matthew R. McLennan
The Poetic Imagination in Heidegger and Schelling, Christopher Yates
Post-Rationalism: Psychoanalysis, Epistemology, and Marxism in Post-War France, Tom Eyers
Revisiting Normativity with Deleuze, edited by Rosi Braidotti and Patricia Pisters
Towards the Critique of Violence: Walter Benjamin and Giorgio Agamben, Brendan Moran and Carlo Salzani

Egalitarian Moments

From Descartes to Rancière

Devin Zane Shaw

Bloomsbury Academic
An imprint of Bloomsbury Publishing Plc

BLOOMSBURY
LONDON · OXFORD · NEW YORK · NEW DELHI · SYDNEY

Bloomsbury Academic
An imprint of Bloomsbury Publishing Plc

50 Bedford Square	1385 Broadway
London	New York
WC1B 3DP	NY 10018
UK	USA

www.bloomsbury.com

BLOOMSBURY and the Diana logo are trademarks of Bloomsbury Publishing Plc

First published 2016
Paperback edition first published 2017

© Devin Zane Shaw, 2016

Devin Zane Shaw has asserted his right under the Copyright, Designs and Patents Act, 1988, to be identified as Author of this work.

All rights reserved. No part of this publication may be reproduced or transmitted in any form or by any means, electronic or mechanical, including photocopying, recording, or any information storage or retrieval system, without prior permission in writing from the publishers.

No responsibility for loss caused to any individual or organization acting on or refraining from action as a result of the material in this publication can be accepted by Bloomsbury or the author.

British Library Cataloguing-in-Publication Data
A catalogue record for this book is available from the British Library.

ISBN: HB: 978-1-47250-544-6
PB: 978-1-35003-787-8
ePDF: 978-1-47250-967-3
ePub: 978-1-47250-821-8

Library of Congress Cataloging-in-Publication Data
A catalog record for this book is available from the Library of Congress.

Series: Bloomsbury Studies in Continental Philosophy

Typeset by Fakenham Prepress Solutions, Fakenham, Norfolk NR21 8NN

Dedicated to the memory of Ruth and Robert Shaw

Contents

Acknowledgements ix
Introduction: Philosophy and Equality 1

Part I: Subjectivity

1 The 'Good Sense' of Cartesian Egalitarianism 25
   1.1. 'a history or, if you prefer, a fable' 25
   1.2. Descartes's egalitarianism and the problem of separation 29
   1.3. The rationality of a wrong 35
   1.4. Woman as other, woman as subject 37
   1.5. Toward collective egalitarianism 42

2 The Nothingness of Equality: Rancière's 'Sartrean Existentialism' 51
   2.1. Marked by Sartrean existentialism 51
   2.2. The politics of equality 56
   2.3. Between the practico-inert and the party 60
   2.4. Subjects of contingency 65
   2.5. The politics of impossible identification 72

Part II: Aesthetics

3 Modernity, Modernism and Aesthetic Equality 85
   3.1. Disagreement and misunderstanding 85
   3.2. From mimesis to aesthetics 92
      3.2.1. Breaking with mimetic norms 94
      3.2.2. Mute speech and literary equality 97
   3.3. Artistic autonomy and sociology in Greenberg 102
   3.4. Benjamin's 'archaeomodernism' 109
      3.4.1. The politics of art and technology 111
      3.4.2. Archaeomodernism and metapolitics 114
   3.5. Fragmentary emancipation, common sense, and aesthetic equality 117

4 Aesthetics, Inaesthetics and the Platonic Regime of Art 127
   4.1. The return from exile 127

4.2. Between aesthetics and inaesthetics   135
4.3. Between aesthetic education and the absolute   146
    4.3.1. Aesthetic emancipation and policing   149
    4.3.2. Schiller's aesthetic freedom   153
    4.3.3. Schelling on artistic production and practical reason 158
4.4. Monuments and micropolitics   161
4.5. Heterotopias: One world divides into two   167

Conclusion: The Politics of *Aisthesis*   175
Bibliography   187
Index   201

Acknowledgements

Parts of this book were previously published and have been reproduced, in revised form, with the permission of their respective publishers:

- 'Inaesthetics and Truth: The Debate between Alain Badiou and Jacques Rancière', *Filozofski vestnik*, 28, 2 (2007), 183–99.
- 'Alain Badiou, The Century', *The Radical Philosophy Review*, 11, 1 (2008), 81–5.
- 'Alain Badiou', in Miško Šuvaković and Aleš Erjavec (eds), *Figure u pokretu. Savremena zapadna estetika, filozofija i teorija umetnosti*. Belgrade: Atoča (2009), 645–57.
- 'Jacques Rancière, The Politics of Literature', *Marx and Philosophy Review of Books* (2011): http://marxandphilosophy.org.uk/reviewofbooks/reviews/2011/344.
- 'Cartesian Egalitarianism: From Poullain de la Barre to Rancière', *Phaenex*, 7, 1 (2012), 101–29.
- 'The Nothingness of Equality: The "Sartrean Existentialism" of Jacques Rancière', *Sartre Studies International*, 18, 1 (2012), 29–48.

I also presented portions of this book at the Society for European Philosophy and the Forum for European Philosophy in 2006, the North American Sartre Society in 2011, and the Society for Existential and Phenomenological Theory and Culture in 2013. My participation at these various conferences would not have been possible without the travel grants I received from the Association of Part-Time Professors of the University of Ottawa.

This list of publications and conference presentations only tells part of the story of writing this book. Although I didn't know it at the time, the research for this book began in 2006, when, due to my interest in his work on poststructuralist anarchism, I invited Todd May to give the keynote address to our graduate student conference at the University of Ottawa. May graciously accepted and told me that the topic would be 'Difference and Equality in the Thought of Jacques Rancière'. Having only read Rancière's *The Names of History* (in a way that, in retrospect, seems to have been inattentively), I rushed, for better or worse, to read *Disagreement* and *The Philosopher and His Poor* in preparation for his talk and the interview we planned to publish in the department's graduate journal. Since then, I've accumulated a great many debts while writing this book, having benefitted from the patience of my editor, Frankie Mace, the suggestions of several anonymous reviewers, and the conversations with and comments of the following friends and colleagues: Ian Beeston, Mark Raymond Brown, Penny Cousineau-Levine (who invited me in 2012 to discuss Rancière in her graduate seminar, 'Art and Cultural Theory'), Andrea Fitzpatrick, Wes Furlotte, Peter Gratton, T. Storm Heter, Bill Martin, Patrice Philie, Jeffrey Reid, Jeff Renaud, Tzuchien Tho and Jason M. Wirth. I would be remiss if I concluded this list without signalling the constant support of my family, and, especially, Kylie.

Not in Utopia, subterraneous Fields,
Or some secreted Island, Heaven knows where,
But in the very world which is the world
Of all of us, the place in which, in the end,
We find our happiness, or not at all.
William Wordsworth, *The Prelude* (1805, lines 140–4)

Introduction: Philosophy and Equality

Supposing equality

As an epigraph to *The Philosopher and His Poor*, Jacques Rancière reproduces a scene from Adrien Baillet's *La Vie de Monsieur Descartes* that recounts how Dirk Rembrantsz, a shoemaker by trade and autodidact mathematician and astronomer by avocation, sought out to confer with a certain René Descartes about important matters. Twice rebuffed by the philosopher's attendants, on the third visit he was received by Descartes, who recognized Rembrantsz's 'competence and merit on the spot, and wanted to repay him with interest for all his troubles'. Descartes, Baillet adds,

> was not satisfied in instructing him in all manner of difficult subjects and in imparting his Method to rectify reasoning. He also counted him as one of his friends: despite the lowliness of Rembrantsz's estate, M. Descartes did not regard him as beneath those of the first rank, and he assured Rembrantsz that his home and heart would be open to him at all hours. (quoted in Rancière, 1983, xxiii; Baillet, 1691, II: 554–5)

The question is: how do we interpret this story of an unlikely friendship between philosopher and cobbler? Certainly, it shows Descartes exhibiting that 'key to all the other virtues', which is generosity (Descartes, XI: 454). But there is obviously more to the story. It is also perhaps a tale of perseverance, as Baillet notes that Rembrantsz had often cultivated his knowledge of mathematics at the expense of his livelihood. Today, some of our contemporaries might lay emphasis on how the shoemaker became 'one of the foremost astronomers of his century' (in Baillet's words) and see in this story a testament to Rembrantsz's ability to pull himself up by his bootstraps. Which means that we may as well say it is a fable of luck or chance. Yet these interpretations do not yet tell us why the story prefaces *The Philosopher and His Poor*. One of Baillet's contemporaries, Antoine Boschet, may be of assistance. As Geneviève Rodis-Lewis points out, Baillet was attacked by his contemporaries upon 'the appearance of his *Vie de R. Descartes* [sic], which was judged ridiculous for the importance granted to mere valets and women'; as Boschet writes, 'There is no sex ... no condition, no social rank, no profession, whom Baillet does not honor by placing them in his work' (Rodis-Lewis, 1995, xiii). The scandal is that Baillet populates the pages of the life of the philosopher with those whose task it is to work and not to think. But for Descartes, there is no hierarchy of intelligences that makes it natural or obvious that some people work and others do astronomy or philosophy. 'Good sense' (*bon sens*), the *Discourse on the Method* begins, 'is the best distributed thing in the world' (VI: 1), though we need not truncate this observation with Montaigne's irony.[1] Instead, Descartes draws the consequence that there is an equality of intelligences and abilities shared by all human beings:

> the power of judging well and of distinguishing the true from the false – which is what we properly call 'good sense' or 'reason' – is naturally equal in all men, and consequently that the diversity of our opinions does not arise because some of us are more reasonable than others but solely because we direct our thoughts along different paths and do not attend to the same things. (VI: 2)

It is this equality of intelligences – of good sense, reason, or the power of judgement – that Descartes opposes to the established authority of the schools, their arguments, and their disputations. However, were we to visit Egmont, perhaps, we would discover much wider social consequences of the equality of intelligences: a cobbler doing astronomy, letters from a princess corresponding about philosophy, and a philosopher practising a variety of sciences.[2] This equality of intelligences, as Baillet's contemporaries had seen, disrupts a social order premised on hierarchies of sex, rank, birth, profession, and wealth. Political philosophy, perhaps, had trained them well. Were they familiar with Plato, they could retort that in a just city each person is allotted one task; had they read Hobbes, they could note that unfettered intellectual equality gives rise to an 'equality of hope in the attaining of our ends' that produces a state of enmity and war (Hobbes, 1651, II: 100).

Descartes's egalitarian gesture stands in sharp contrast to Plato or Hobbes. And we see in this episode from *La Vie de Monsieur Descartes* a hint of Rancière's singular thesis: equality is not only disruptive, insofar as it challenges the contingent hierarchies of social distinctions, but that equality is emancipatory. Indeed, for Rancière, equality is the impetus for politics. He defines egalitarianism as 'the open set of practices driven by the assumption of equality between any and every speaking being and by the concern to test this equality' (Rancière, 1995, 30/53). Political praxis is egalitarian and emancipatory, he argues, when it creates new ways of doing, being and speaking, reconfiguring the roles and places that organize society, that is, when it introduces what he calls a new 'distribution of the sensible' (*partage du sensible*). The principle of equality, or more specifically, the supposition of the equality of intelligences and abilities of anyone and everyone, combats the prejudice of political philosophy that social organization requires experts and elites to guide mass participation, from Plato's city, through Althusser's 'ossified Leninism' (in Alain Badiou's words), to today's societies of consensus. Intellectual equality, as James Swenson summarizes it, 'implies that people generally know perfectly well what they do and say, that the world is not – must not be – divided between those who think and those who need someone to think for them or to explain what they really want' (Swenson, 2009, 258). Thus Rancière's definition of equality challenges both the liberal assumption that the distribution of equality is merely a problem of governmental protections and the orthodox Marxist claim that equality is merely an ideological mask that veils the inequalities of capitalism. Instead of thinking politics as an interaction of individuals, political institutions, and governmental expertise, Rancière argues that equality is both the means and the end of political struggles to produce both forms for the organization of material life that overturn the logic of capital and places of collective praxis that break the monopoly of the governmentality of expertise.

Egalitarian politics, on Rancière's account, is disruptive, subversive, and emancipatory, although it is also transitory and rare, for politics is a momentary suspension of the inegalitarian relations that structure society. He opposes egalitarianism to the inequality that is produced by what he calls policing. By referring to the 'logic of policing' or the police, Rancière does not only mean cops – in the way that we understand that cops are one part of a larger penal apparatus. Policing is a set of procedures that organize society, distributing roles – such as the rights and duties of those who rule and those who are ruled – and legitimating the concomitant inequalities that are part of these procedures. As Rancière writes in *Disagreement*,

> The police is thus first an order of bodies that defines the allocation of ways of doing, ways of being, and ways of saying, and sees that those bodies are assigned by name to a particular place and task; it is an order of the visible and the sayable that sees that a particular activity is visible and that another is not, that this speech is understood as discourse and another as noise. (1995, 29/52)

While acknowledging his specific debt to Michel Foucault's analyses of the apparatuses of power/knowledge, Rancière stipulates that policing is defined less by techniques of discipline than by modes of inclusion and exclusion within a given set of social relations – distinctions between the visible and invisible, speech and noise, as well as public space and private space. As an example of how policing apparatuses patrol modes of visibility and speech, let us return to Baillet's account of Rembrantsz's efforts. Baillet acknowledges the social constraints that condition Rembrantsz's reception among Descartes's attendants, the social constraints that link a mode of visibility to a lack of speech. After first being rebuffed

> as an impudent peasant ... Rembrantsz returned in the very same suit of clothes and asked to speak to M. Descartes ... . His appearance did not help him win a better reception than the first time. When the attendants brought word to M. Descartes, they portrayed him as an importunate beggar who, in search of alms, asked to speak to M. Descartes about philosophy and astrology. (quoted in Rancière, 1983, xxii, tm; Baillet 1691, II: 554)

Appearing at the door in a peasant's outfit meant to Descartes's attendants that Rembrantsz could not speak about philosophy and astronomy, but rather that philosophy and astrology were but a ruse by which to collect alms. A peasant speaks about work or poverty or astrology, but not philosophy or astronomy. And, while we might find this particular story quaint, in our times there are similar forms of policing that govern *who* can speak about *what*, and *where* one can speak.

From this point on, we will mean by politics the enactment of the logic of equality through a process of political subjectivation that emerges through disagreement, challenging a wrong committed by a given regime of policing. Rancière argues that political disagreement (*la mésentente*) 'occurs whenever contention over what speaking means constitutes the very rationality of the speech situation'; disagreement concerns what is counted as speech and what is noise, who counts as one who speaks, and who counts as addressee, and who is excluded from the declaration of speech (1995, xi/13). Therefore, politics introduces, through disagreement, new ways of speaking, being, and doing.[3] Rancière argues that politics in this sense and policing are 'entirely heterogeneous' (1995, 31/55).[4] Thus Rancière insists that politics is a radical break with apparatuses of policing or power/knowledge; he notes that while 'Foucault uses the term biopolitics to designate things that are situated in the space that I call the police ... he was never drawn theoretically to the question of political subjectivation' (Rancière, 2000, 93).

Political philosophy: Archipolitics, parapolitics and metapolitics

We will examine Rancière's account of political subjectivation below. But first we must address the radical difference between Rancière's definition of politics and what is so often called political philosophy. The conventional ways of thinking about political issues – even in parliamentarian forms of so-called democracy – reflect upon techniques of policing, not politics in Rancière's sense of the term.[5] In fact, far from being egalitarian, political philosophy functions to persuade us that there are principled, even necessary, reasons to accept inequality. As Rancière argues, politics and police are heterogeneous. Political philosophy, by contrast, eliminates this heterogeneity by identifying politics with police procedures for 'determining the distribution of the sensible that defines the lot of individuals and parties' (1995, 63tm/97). In short, political philosophy seeks to substitute some principle or *arkhê* for the 'ultimate contingency of equality' (1995, 17/38) or 'egalitarian facticity' (1998a, 171).

Rancière identifies three paradigmatic forms of political philosophy: archipolitics, parapolitics, and metapolitics. Plato's *Republic* presents the exemplar of archipolitics, which suppresses the lack of foundation of politics and elaborates a project 'founded on the complete realization, the complete awareness (*sensibilisation*) of the *arkhê* of community' (Rancière, 1995, 65tm/100). Plato's city is organized according to techniques that account for each member of the community according to his or her function. Having a part in the city is having a function or occupation. For Plato, 'the image of justice', as Rancière writes in *The Philosopher and His Poor*, 'is the division of labor' (1983, 25). The division of labour, however, is not a moment of class conflict, but the realization of the so-called 'natural' aptitudes of individuals and parts of society, where each practises the virtue appropriate to his or her function and does not meddle with others'. In an archipolitical project, there is neither a supplement nor void in society, neither democratic excess nor the nothingness of equality that could challenge a wrong or an apparatus of domination. Instead, the 'egalitarian anarchy' of the *demos* is identified with a regime – democracy – or a modality of the corruption of the city, in which 'full of freedom and freedom of speech' (557b) of anybody and everybody inverts the roles and functions that order the well-governed city and equality reigns between 'equals and unequals alike' (558c): the ruled behave like rulers, rulers behave like the ruled, while citizens and slaves and foreigners, children and adults, as well as men and women, behave as equals. Even domestic animals are more free in a democratic city (563c).

By contrast, in Plato's city all parts of society are governed by the justice of doing one's own task and no other: having a part in the community is defined by one's function in society and practising one's particular virtue: 'it is right for someone who is by nature a cobbler to practice cobblery and nothing else, for the carpenter to practice carpentry, and the same for the others is a sort of image of justice' (443c; Rancière, 1983, 25). According to Plato, the cobbler has an occupation in society, but she has no part in any other activity, let alone deliberating about the governing of the city. For the worker whose capacity to reason is 'naturally weak', there is no harm in being ruled by a superior (590c–d). As Peter Hallward writes, in 'Plato's *Republic*, to each kind of person there is but one allotted task: labour, war, or thought' (2009, 142). And to each there is but one allotted virtue: moderation, courage, or wisdom. Yet, as Rancière notes, with each individual identified with her function and virtue, her part or share, and with democracy but a regime of the corruption of the city, the possibility of egalitarian politics is suppressed.

In the *Politics*, Aristotle argues that Plato's archipolitical project is impractical. Submitting the entire city to the principle of unity empties the city of politics. Rather than tending toward unity, a city is 'by nature' a plurality. The question, for Aristotle, is to establish stability within plurality. While it is best for the most virtuous to rule, it is not politically possible, since the 'natural equality of the citizens' entitles them a share in ruling the city (1261b1). Since not all citizens can rule at once, it is necessary to allow for transitions in rule, with different citizens ruling at different times. Thus over time, each will have a share in governing.

In opposition to Plato's archipolitics, Aristotle introduces a model of parapolitics, which is an imitation or mimesis of democratic discord (Rancière, 1995, 75/111). On Rancière's account, politics occurs when political subjects enact egalitarian logic and praxis to challenge the inequalities of society; politics involves a conflict between two heterogeneous logics. Though he acknowledges the conflict at the centre of the plurality of the city, Aristotle nevertheless reduces the conflict between egalitarianism and policing into a conflict between the *interests* of different factions of society, 'transforming the actors and forms of action of the political conflict into the parts and forms of distribution of the policing apparatus' (Rancière, 1995, 72/108). Politics becomes a problem of government, the *demos* a faction within society, and conflict a matter of *interests*. The task of political philosophy and good government is to mediate between the interests of different groups, for the rich claim wealth is the principle by which rule is established in the city while the poor claim that rule is to be distributed according to freedom (1280a5–7). Aristotle's solution is that a form of government must adopt principles that limit (or at least appear to limit) their own interests in the name of stability: in a democracy (the rule of the many and the poor), the people must aspire to elect the best of citizens to office so that nobles are not ruled by inferiors, while in an oligarchy citizenship must be distributed widely enough to make 'the entire governing body stronger than those who are excluded' (1318b33–37; 1320b26–8).[6] Although Aristotle glimpses the 'egalitarian contingency' that undermines the archipolitical project, he reduces the wrong that defines politics – the conflict between heterogeneous logics and praxes – to a conflict of the interests of different factions (Rancière, 1995, 71/107).

A modern form of parapolitics can be found in the work of Hobbes, who, like Aristotle, reduces the opposition between the logics of equality and policing to the problem of differing interests. For Hobbes, though, interests are constituted by individuals rather than by factions in society. Hobbes suppresses the possibility of politics by placing it outside of the community, substituting for politics as the conflict of egalitarian logic and police logic two differing states of right: the state of nature, in which 'every man has a Right to every thing'; and the state of sovereignty, in which the individual right to meet ends and interests is alienated or transferred to the sovereign (Hobbes, 1651, II: 105). However, as Rancière points out, in the attempt to legitimate sovereign power through the 'fable of the war of all against all', Hobbes inadvertently demonstrates that 'there is no natural principle of domination by one person over another' (Rancière, 1995, 79/115–16). For Hobbes, natural equality is defined by intellectual equality rather than brute physical equality:

> as to the faculties of the mind … I find yet a greater equality amongst men than that of strength. Prudence, is but Experience; which equall time, equally bestowes on all men, in those things they equally apply themselves unto … For such is the nature of men, that howsoever they may acknowledge many others to be more witty, or more eloquent, or more learned; Yet they will hardly believe there be many so wise as themselves … But this proveth rather that men are in that point equall, than unequall. For there is not ordinarily a greater signe of the equall distribution of any thing, than that every man is contented with his share. (1651, II: 99–100)

But, like Aristotle, in Hobbes's parapolitics the equality that undermines all distinctions is reduced to interest: for Hobbes the equality of intelligences and abilities will not activate a moment of political disagreement, but rather results in the equal right of anyone to achieve his or her interests or ends.

The third paradigmatic form of political philosophy is metapolitics, which Rancière defines as a symptomology or ideology critique that aims to unmask the 'absolute wrong' structuring social inequalities, to show how politics (again, identified with policing apparatuses of the state) conceals real injustice. Metapolitical interpretation seeks to uncover the true scene of an absolute wrong that is misrepresented by politics. Rancière claims that the 'canonical formula' for this ideology critique is found in 'On the Jewish Question', where Marx argues that political emancipation – insofar as all parts of society would be treated equally before the law – does not result in human emancipation; rather political emancipation reveals the limits of politics, 'its powerlessness to achieve the properly human part of man' (Rancière, 1995, 83/120). Behind appeals to legal equality there lies the inequalities of private property and money (what Marx will later identify as the inequalities produced by the accumulation of capital through expropriation and dispossession). Rather than human emancipation, political emancipation gives way to the atomism and egoism of individuals pursuing private interests and whims irrespective of the community (Marx, 1843, 54). On the one hand, then, metapolitics denounces the gaps between words and things (Rancière, 1995, 85/123), while on the other hand, metapolitics also functions as a scientific complement of political struggle insofar as it isolates those forces of history of which politics is only an appearance. As Marx writes in the 'Preface to *A Critique of Political Economy*', the 'anatomy of civil society is to be sought in political economy' (1859, 389), that is, political superstructures must be traced back to their real foundations in the contradictions of the forces of production. Whether they are interpreted in vanguardist, scientistic, or economistic forms, these forces determine political superstructures until the victory of the proletariat and the destruction of capitalism brings 'the prehistory of human society to a close' (1859, 390).

Philosophy and equality

Reading Rancière, we are often left with the impression that philosophy is little more than a discourse and discipline that serves to legitimate inequality. The guiding thesis of this study is that it is possible to read and to do philosophy so that it does not serve to legitimate regimes of policing, that it does not assume that it is reasonable or natural to distinguish those whose task it is to think and those for whom their only occupation is work. But the questions guiding this approach to philosophy are different from many of the traditional questions of the discipline. To seek out egalitarian moments in philosophy requires looking at the ways that equality interrupts first philosophy – be it metaphysics, ontology, or ethics – and political philosophy. In the first chapter, for instance, I will argue that Rancière practises what I call Cartesian egalitarianism, which is defined by the way it conceptualizes political subjectivity rather than by Descartes's metaphysics; Rancière is more interested in Descartes's methodological commitment to the equality of good sense than substantial difference between thought and bodies. Rancière's refusal to prioritize ontology or some other form of first philosophy over the politics of equality defines his method (see Chambers, 2013, 18–21), and allows him to think through the question of equality in relation to a disparate set of theoretical frameworks. Much like Rancière's account of 'political moments' that challenge 'the obviousness of a given world', these egalitarian moments open new possibilities for thinking emancipatory practices (Rancière, 2009b, ix).

To search in those traditional domains of philosophy for egalitarian moments, to register the difficulties posed to philosophy by the egalitarian facticity that defines the being-in-common shared by those political animals we call humans, requires reading philosophy through what I will call 'philosophical misunderstanding'. By this term I mean something similar to Rancière's definition of 'literary misunderstanding' (q.v. Chapter 3), in which literature introduces new relations between bodies and meanings, words and things, introducing excess bodies and words to upset 'the paradigm of proportion between bodies and meanings, a paradigm of correspondence and saturation' (2006b, 41). However, whereas literary misunderstanding works on 'percepts and affects' (2006b, 43), what I call philosophical misunderstanding works on concepts and arguments. Perhaps it bears some affinities with what we call deconstruction, but like Rancière, I am not focused on a critique of the metaphysics of presence. Philosophical misunderstanding is much closer to what Miguel Abensour calls a 'hermeneutics of emancipation', for which 'the task of the critic is to interpret every political question so as to translate the particular language of politics in the more "general" language of emancipation' (1997, 36). In a similar vein, Rancière argues that 'the political processing of wrong never ceases to borrow elements from "political philosophy" to build up new arguments and manifestations of dispute' (1995, 78/115).

The impetus for reconsidering philosophy through philosophical misunderstanding is to open new possibilities for egalitarian thinking and acting. Rancière's radical redefinition of politics as egalitarian, which is at odds with the definitions of politics used by political philosophy, is meant to cast in stark relief the inegalitarianism of much of philosophy. And yet, his 'political' interpretation of philosophy also shows how the arguments and demonstrations to prove that inequality is reasonable nevertheless require accepting the supposition of equality. He writes: 'My practice of philosophy goes along with my idea of politics. It is an-archical, in the sense that it traces back the specificity of disciplines and discursive competences to the "egalitarian" level of linguistic competence and poetic invention' (Rancière, 2011b, 14).

In what follows, I will use the concepts and methodologies of Rancière's philosophy, politics, and aesthetics to reconsider several key figures and texts – though not necessarily *canonical* figures and texts – in the history of modern philosophy. This book is divided into two parts: Part I focuses on Rancière's account of the politics of equality and political subjectivation, while Part II contrasts Rancière's aesthetics with competing accounts of the history of modern art that rely on the concepts of modernity, modernism, and inaesthetics. While Part I deals with political subjectivation and Part II aesthetics, both focus on different practices of dissensus. Though the term dissensus is Rancière's, I will use it broadly to refer to the ways that philosophy, politics, and aesthetics interrupt and challenge established discourses and practices of a given distribution of the sensible. In this regard, my use is functional, as Rancière's is. In the book-length interview *La méthode de l'égalité*, he states that he introduced the term *dissensus* to 'translate' *la mésentente* (disagreement), which, in French, carries a set of connotations that makes the term a 'polemical knot between different meanings of "*entendre*" (to perceive, to understand, to agree), which epitomize the sensible and conflictual dimension of the political community' (2012a, 151). Given that these connotations do not necessarily translate into other languages such as English, Rancière chose to replace *la mésentente* with 'a Latinate word which nevertheless does not belong to the Latin language – dissensus: a word which loses the power of understanding that belongs to real languages in favor of the possibility of a functional definition' (2012a, 151). While he chose the term to translate or replace *la mésentente*, dissensus now names what politics and aesthetics share insofar as they challenge, interrupt, and transform relationships between discourses, practices, and affects. The 'functional definition' highlights one more crucial dimension of Rancière's use of dissensus: that the practices of political disagreement and aesthetic equality cannot be defined in advance, meaning that moments of dissensus open the possibility for unforeseen social, aesthetic, and political emancipation.[7]

In Part I, I argue that Rancière's account of political subjectivation provides an impetus for reconsidering Cartesianism and existentialism from an egalitarian standpoint. The difference between traditional philosophical questions and the hermeneutics of emancipation or philosophical misunderstanding should become evident with the interpretation of Descartes that I propose in Chapter 1. So often Descartes's legacy is evaluated according to the implications and consequences of the dualism that divides thinking substance and extended substance. I will not argue that this approach is wrong, for there is no doubt that Descartes would have wanted to be judged according to the strengths or flaws of the principles of his first philosophy. Post-Heideggerian philosophy has thus criticized Descartes for granting, through the *cogito*, primacy to presence while reducing being to a calculable, objective world. However, I do not think that this critique exhausts the significance of Descartes's thought. By focusing on the legacy of the very supposition that makes the system verifiable – the supposition of good sense – we will outline a genealogy of what I will call Cartesian egalitarianism, a current of political thought that includes the work of François Poullain de la Barre, Joseph Jacotot, Simone de Beauvoir, and Rancière. These Cartesian egalitarians are less interested in adhering to Descartes's metaphysics than they are with thinking through the socio-political implications of the intellectual equality of good sense.

Therefore, in Chapter 1, I outline three characteristics of Cartesian egalitarianism. First, these Cartesians think political agency as a practice of subjectivity. Second, like Descartes, they maintain that intellectual equality is the basis of the subjectivity. Finally, they politicize the egalitarian subject. While Descartes makes the egalitarian subject one of the central principles of his philosophy, he circumscribes the consequences of his critique of the prejudices of intellect, authority, and habit to epistemological and metaphysical questions. In this sense, Descartes himself is not a fully committed Cartesian egalitarian. Beginning with Poullain, Cartesian egalitarians conceptualize politics as a processing of a wrong, meaning that politics initiates new practices through which those who were previously oppressed assert themselves as self-determining political subjects. As we will see, these Cartesian egalitarians – from Poullain, through Beauvoir, to Rancière – are all critics of Descartes's metaphysics. Nevertheless they maintain that good sense is the basis of emancipatory political subjectivation.

In Chapter 2, I reconsider the relationship between Sartre's existentialism and Rancière's egalitarianism. Despite his critique of Sartre's later work in *The Philosopher and His Poor*, I argue that Rancière owes several important intellectual debts to Sartre. First, I suggest that Sartre's analysis of the practico-inert – that is, his account of how identity, interests, and exigencies are operations of seriality – anticipates Rancière's account of how policing stratifies and classifies members of a given society according to roles, places, and occupations. If identity is a function or operation of oppressive or exploitative social relations, then both Rancière and Sartre contend that political praxis emerges through a dynamic of disidentification, whereby political subjects reject or disrupt the roles, occupations, and identities that are ascribed to them. Nevertheless, I show that there are significant differences between Rancière and Sartre. In *The Philosopher and His Poor*, Rancière argues that Sartre's account of political praxis is hyper-instrumentalized, that is, praxis is always submitted to the exigencies of either the practico-inert or the dialectic of organizing and totalizing that introduces both stability and inertia into group praxis. By contrast, in *Disagreement*, Rancière proposes an account of politics that emphasizes the disruptive and transformative effects of the supposition of equality. Politics and policing, he argues, are heterogeneous: while policing structures interests, identities, and exigencies, politics is a paradoxical praxis that has neither interest nor end other than momentary emancipation.

Second, I argue that Rancière's use, in *Disagreement*, of the terms freedom, contingency and facticity to characterize egalitarian political praxis is indebted to Sartre's *Being and Nothingness*. This does not mean that Rancière holds the ontological commitments of Sartre's existentialism. Instead, I think that Rancière appropriates these concepts in order to think egalitarian praxis historically. First, he appropriates them to show how the formation of subjectivity through freedom is a dynamic that introduces new ways of speaking, being, and doing, instead of being a mode of assuming an established identity. Rancière says as much when he states that his 'own rejection of identitarian fixations (*fixations identitaries*) was first satisfied in Sartrian [sic] freedom, its rejection of fixed identities, and the opposition it establishes to Being of doing things and making oneself' (Rancière, 2012b, 207). Although this claim is retrospective, and although it discusses his intellectual formation even before encountering Althusser, it remains instructive. Reading Rancière with Sartre amplifies the dynamic character of political subjectivation, which insofar as it is transformative, must be what it is not and not be what it is. Second, Rancière uses the concepts of freedom, contingency, and facticity to demonstrate the historical contingency of any situation or social order, a contingency that is the possibility of egalitarian praxis. Therefore these concepts provide a minimal theoretical structure to think politics historically.

Part I concludes with the observation that politics is, on Rancière's account, rare. When he concedes that politics – as an event that interrupts policing – is rare, this concession could leave the impression that, absent politics, a regime of policing and the operations by which it organizes a given distribution of the sensible are relatively static or overwhelmingly practico-*inert*. In Part II, I argue that what Rancière calls the politics of aesthetics is a micropolitics that takes place in the interval of the heterogeneity of politics and policing. By stipulating that aesthetics is a form of contestation and transformation that operates at the micropolitical level, it is possible to cast a stark contrast between Rancière's aesthetics and the theorists of modernity, modernism, and inaesthetics that he critiques. Ranciere's account of aesthetics does not, however, assume the historical validity of concepts such as modernity and modernism. Instead, he contends that there are three major regimes of the identification of art and the arts: the ethical regime of images, the representative regime of the arts, and the aesthetic regime of art. Concepts such as modernity, modernism, and inaesthetics are subsequently evaluated in relation to this classification of regimes.

I have set two tasks for Chapter 3. First, I outline Rancière's account of the historical emergence of the aesthetic regime of art. Then I examine his critique of Greenberg's sociologization of the politics of modernism and Benjamin's messianic critique of modernity. Rancière argues that the aesthetic regime emerges through a literary or aesthetic revolution that dispenses with the norms that govern the representative regime of the arts. The norms of the representative regime govern the production and reception of acceptable and successful forms of artistic mimesis. However, mimesis does not merely mean the adequate artistic and technical representation of an art's subject matter. Instead, Rancière contends that, within the representative regime, mimesis names a set of norms or principles that bind artistic values and hierarchies to social values and hierarchies. Thus when the representative regime distinguishes between genres and arts, these distinctions are defined by the subjects that each art or genre can appropriately represent.

Broadly speaking, the representative regime is a poetics of the great deeds of great men, regulated by norms that establish a 'causal rationality of action' modelled on speech (Rancière, 2006b, 9). This model of efficacious speech is structured by the 'will to signify', a relationship of address and mode of intelligibility that establishes a causal relation between the will of the speaker and the will of the addressee that must act in turn; this address both drives the plot of the work while inculcating the norms of the 'world of action' that direct what is appropriate for an audience to think and to feel (2006b, 14). For example, Aristotle – whose *Poetics* invents the paradigm of the representative regime – argues that tragedy effectively produces catharsis when those of 'great reputation and prosperity' fall into misfortune due to ignorance or error (1453a10). While comedy can imitate those who are worse than ordinary people, tragedy must represent those who are more noble; it would lack cathartic effects if it portrayed the noble falling into misery, the ignoble attaining happiness or the already undeserving falling from happiness to misery. The norms of mimesis that govern the representative regime require that characters' actions are appropriate to their social standing.

The aesthetic regime dispenses with these norms; it 'strictly identifies art in the singular and frees it from any specific rule, from any hierarchy of the arts, subject matter, and genres' (Rancière, 2004b, 23). The aesthetic regime is a historical set of practices and discourses of visibility and intelligibility that are defined by artistic novelty and social change whereby any part of the everyday world could become prosaic and aesthetic. Rancière argues that the aesthetic regime art is a domain of socially lived experience that provisionally inscribes and reinscribes the boundaries of art and non-art, that contests the social divisions that govern what and who are portrayed in, and who produces, art. While the representative regime is a form of policing the arts, the aesthetic regime produces forms of micropolitics that open new possibilities of aesthetic emancipation by producing art that is either imbricated in everyday social life or separated out from life as an autonomous domain that is heterogeneous to the imperatives of the canons of taste and circulation of commodities.

Given that the terms art and aesthetics name a regime that is both provisional and historically contingent, Rancière criticizes the teleological aspects that define – for different reasons – prevalent accounts of modernity and modernism. We will look first at Greenberg's account of modernism. He argues that the autonomy of each art is guaranteed by the unique opacity of its medium. By virtue of the interrogation of the opacity of a medium – for instance, painting interrogates the flatness and two-dimensionality of pictorial space – an art produces an experience that is irreducible to any other experience. But Greenberg's account is not merely descriptive of one approach to art. Instead, he traces a seeming historical teleology from Manet to 'American type' painting (Jackson Pollock, Willem de Kooning, Barnett Newman, Mark Rothko, Clyfford Still) whereby modern art arrives at abstraction: 'it seems to be a law of modernism … that the conventions not essential to the viability of a medium be discarded as soon as they are recognized' (Greenberg, 1958, 208). Such a teleological account – the outcome of modern art is a politics of resistant form – seems to relegate the practices that attempted to revolutionize art and life by abolishing their separation to a liminal space between serious, modernist art and kitsch.

Rancière's critique of Greenberg extends beyond the latter's narrow description of the history of modern art; he also attacks Greenberg's sociologization of art for producing a form of intellectual and aesthetic stultification. Indeed, in a recent interview, Rancière contends that the modernist paradigm elaborated by Greenberg is a 'liquidation of the dominant tendency of the aesthetic regime, which is to abolish the boundaries between "mediums", between high art and popular art, and ultimately between art and life' (Rancière and Davis, 2013, 204–5). Greenberg denies the possibility of aesthetic equality. Instead, he argues that the modernist avant-gardes are tasked with preserving living culture against bourgeois philistinism and proletarian kitsch. More specifically, he claims: first, that the modernist avant-garde is necessary because the masses by definition lack the leisure, time and knowledge necessary to appreciate high culture; but second, that the proletariat's demand for culture and entertainment, ultimately satisfied by kitsch, poses one of the greatest threats to living culture. On Rancière's account, Greenberg's modernist avant-garde plays a role similar to that described of communist intellectuals in *The Communist Manifesto*. The division of *aisthesis* between those who have leisure and those who do not, in Greenberg's account, ultimately stultifies and forecloses on what Rancière considers to be the emancipatory possibilities of the politics of aesthetics.

If Greenberg's politicization – sociologization – of modernism is both anti-egalitarian and anti-aesthetic (insofar as it liquidates the aesthetic regime of art), then Rancière should have more in common with the hermeneutics of emancipation that guides Benjamin's analyses of politics, history, and art. Benjamin's discussions of the 'literarization of the conditions of living' anticipate in part Rancière's account of the revolution of literature (Benjamin, 1934b, 742). This process of the literarization of life, according to Benjamin, subverts the distinctions that classify the differences between genres, between culture and politics, and between writer and reader. Nonetheless, Rancière critiques Benjamin on two points. First, he avers that Benjamin's work overstates the role of technology and technical means in making possible new forms of emancipatory artistic practices. Second, and more importantly, Rancière argues that Benjamin's 'weak messianism' submits politics and art to the historical teleology of redemption. On Rancière's account, a teleological account of the history of politics and aesthetics traps the struggle of the oppressed between the catastrophe of progress and an always approaching redemption, meaning that the political task of the present is to decipher – through a kind of messianic symptomology – and bear witness to the fragments of a past that once redeemed will 'become citable in all its moments' (Benjamin, 1940, 390). To the messianic Benjamin, Rancière opposes the archivist Benjamin who gathers the materials that could link the history of social practices to a history of subjectivation while simultaneously reflecting on the conditions of its own archival construction, disentangling its emancipatory aims from teleological and symptomological motifs (Rancière, 1996a, 39–40). In other words, to messianic redemption, Rancière opposes a micropolitics of fragmentary emancipation, misinterpretation and literary misunderstanding.

In Chapter 4, I continue to test the hypothesis that Rancière's politics of aesthetics designates micropolitical practices that interrupt the practico-inert structures of everyday life. In addition, I take up his claim that the emergence of the aesthetic regime of art does not foreclose on the possibility of the historical existence of other regimes of art (Rancière, 2004b, 50), to contend that both the aesthetic regime and what I call the Platonic regime of art become possible when the mimetic rules that structure the representative regime lose their normative force. Acknowledging the conflict of historically possible regimes serves to detotalize Rancière's account of the aesthetic regime – which he sometimes treats as a general historical apparatus of artistic production and reception and at other times as a praxis of staging a particular type of aesthetic experience – in order to underline how today the politics of art remains an open question.

The Platonic regime is not equivalent to what Rancière calls the ethical regime of images. This ethical regime, as it is set out in Plato's *Republic*, judges images according to the way that they affect the community. Hence the arts of painting and poetry are evaluated as any other craft – how they imitate a model or Idea. The arts of painting and poetry, which are imitations of crafts that imitate models, are twice removed from knowledge. But Plato's condemnation of art (if we may use an anachronistic term here) is not merely that art imitates truth. As Rancière points out, Plato also condemns poets and painters for transgressing the Idea of justice predicated on the supposition that each member of the city has but one occupation. Indeed, the poet is a double of the philosopher whose task it is to deliberate upon all human affairs, virtue and vice, and the nature of the gods – but where the philosopher legislates by means of reason, the poet persuades by means of images and rhetorics that appeal to an audience's unruly desires. Insofar as she produces merely the appearance of truth and uses these appearances to upset the order of the city, the poet is the artisan of injustice.

Chapter 4 is dedicated to showing how the Platonic regime of art – as it is constructed in the works of F. W. J. Schelling and Badiou – differs from the ethical regime of images and the aesthetic regime of art. While Schelling and

Badiou require, like Plato, the ontological verification of art in relation to the Idea, they both maintain that art is an autonomous domain that bears on truth. Since art is an autonomous domain that relates to truth, it cannot be evaluated like just any other craft (that is, evaluating art as an imitation of a craft that is produced in accordance to the knowledge of a model or Idea). Instead, to say that art relates to the Idea means that philosophy formulates a 'relation of rupture' (Noys, 2009, 385) that separates artistic events from a given state of a situation. Schelling names this Idea of the relation of rupture totality, which means that art exhibits thought in its totality as the identity or indifference of freedom and necessity, self and nature, subject and object. The totality of the artwork breaks with the fragmentary and mechanistic relations that govern contemporary society and points toward the possibility of a new mythology that would unify a people within an organic community. For Badiou, the relation of rupture is the Idea of subtraction, by which art makes visible the 'monumental construction, projects, the creative force of the weak, [and] the overthrow of established powers' that democratic materialism declares inexistent (Badiou, 2004, 133). Art is monumental by virtue of subtracting itself from the circulation of commodities and the levelling force of consensus.

I argue, then, that the irreconcilable difference between the Platonic regime and the aesthetic regime concerns the scope of the politics of art. For Schelling and Badiou, art must be monumental or eventual, while for Schiller and Rancière, the politics of art is micropolitical. As Schiller writes:

> In the midst of the fearful kingdom of forces, and in the midst of the sacred kingdom of laws, the aesthetic impulse to form is at work, unnoticed, on the building of a third joyous kingdom of play and of semblance, in which man is relieved of the shackles of circumstance, and released from all that might be called constraint, alike in the physical and in the moral sphere. (Schiller, 1795, 215)

The monumental concept of the politics of art, I conclude, is not problematic in itself. That is, we should not dismiss the possibility of monumental art – I can't help but think here of Vladimir Tatlin's ambitious project, the *Monument to the Third International* (1919–20) – despite the fact that such monumental projects seem to be relics of the past. Instead, the Platonic account of monumental art is flawed because it dismisses the micropolitical possibilities of artistic production and aesthetic experience. As Badiou writes, 'It is better to do nothing than to work formally toward making visible what the West declares to exist' – as if an artwork's current inscription within a given distribution of the sensible exhausts its potential intelligibility (Badiou, 2004, 148). Art, from Badiou's Platonic standpoint, must be monumental, or it will not be at all – it will be merely culture or kitsch. By contrast, one could construct a micropolitical account of aesthetics while remaining attentive to the possibility of an art exhibiting a monumental relation of rupture. Both Schiller and Rancière affirm that the micropolitics of aesthetics takes place in the interstices of the practico-inert structures of a given distribution of the sensible, and that this micropolitics interrupts and transforms established forms of visibility, intelligibility and place. Politics is rare, as Rancière notes, but the micropolitics of aesthetics, which happens in the intervals between policing and egalitarian politics, works to transform everyday life.

In the Conclusion, I examine the valences of Rancière's references to everyday life or social life in *Aisthesis*. While the present study considers Rancière's politics of equality and his account of aesthetics in turn, these concluding remarks allow us to reflect on the practice of writing as a political and aesthetic form. As he notes, in *The Politics of Aesthetics*, 'a theoretical discourse is always simultaneously an aesthetic form, a sensible reconfiguration of the facts it is arguing about' (Rancière, 2004b, 65). Therefore I will ask what, in *Aisthesis*, Rancière's repeated use of *life* as a metonymy for the politics of aesthetics makes visible and what it occludes. In *Aisthesis*, he argues that the aesthetic regime of art undermines the forms of social causality and social stratification that govern the other regimes of art (the representative regime and the ethical regime) and Greenberg's sociologization of modernism. Aesthetics opens a field of free play and free appearance that, in contrast to the models of social causality, allows anyone and everyone to 'do nothing'. In other words, *life* names both the emergence of a regime of *aisthesis* whereby aesthetic equality becomes available to anyone and everyone and a practice of artistic production whereby 'anyone can grab a pen, taste any kind of pleasure, or nourish any ambition whatsoever' (Rancière, 2011a, 51). Rancière's *Aisthesis*, concerning these theoretical points, is consistent with his other works on aesthetics. However, I will conclude by noting that the political scope of aesthetics has changed. In *Aisthesis*, Rancière outlines the politics of aesthetics – the politics of the *aisthesis* of *life* – in relation to the other regimes of art and Greenberg's modernism. In effect, aesthetics is a politics that affirms the emancipation of words, bodies, and affects by virtue of being neither the representative regime of the arts nor the ethical regime of images. But, as I have argued, and as Rancière contents in his other works on aesthetics, the micropolitics of aesthetics names a constellation of discourses and practices that intersect – that is, by turns affirm, interrupt, and contest

– with the many ways that lived experience is socially mediated: other regimes of art, the apparatuses of policing, and the emancipatory politics of equality.

In what follows, I consider equality, in its political and aesthetic forms, as a significant problem within the history of philosophy from Descartes to Rancière. The purpose of this study is to outline an egalitarian frame of reference for rethinking modern philosophy after Descartes. The following analyses of a number of egalitarian moments in philosophy are meant to engage Rancière's terse and sometimes polemical historical shorthand. For example, he insists that political subjectivation is modelled on Descartes's '*ego sum, ego existo*', and in Chapter 1, I aim to make historical and conceptual sense of this claim. But what follows is not an exegesis or explanation of Rancière's – or anybody else's – work.[8] There is, for example, no discussion of Rancière's work on film. Nor do I intend for this study to be comprehensive.[9] Instead, I place Rancière's work in a historical context of considering equality as a political, philosophical, and aesthetic question, while reading the history of modern philosophy from an egalitarian standpoint. Using Rancière's concepts and arguments to reconsider the history of philosophy while using this counter-history of egalitarian moments to situate Rancière's work amounts, perhaps, to a hermeneutic circle or, as he would say, a historical fiction. But it is no more of a historical fiction than the way that the predominant frameworks of continental philosophy – such as post-Heideggerian phenomenology and deconstruction, psychoanalysis, and post-Marxism – formulate historical or genealogical accounts of thinking their present problematics. What counts is whether or not Rancière's work and this history of egalitarian moments offer new and compelling possibilities for thinking our present engagements with politics and art.

The present study has been motivated by the fact that evaluating Rancière's work using the assumptions and methods of these established frameworks in some way occludes important aspects of his thought. If one supposes that politics – or the political (which is something other than politics) – must be grounded in political ontology or the deconstruction of the metaphysics of presence, Rancière's work might seem retrograde or even incoherent. Likewise if one expects his politics to decipher in the surfaces of political discontent the true demands of radical struggle. In what follows, however, I do not attempt to adjudicate the differences between Rancière's egalitarian method and these established theoretical questions and frameworks. Instead, by tracing a provisional – and let me stress that it is provisional and non-exhaustive – account of a history of egalitarian moments in philosophy, I hope to show how Rancière, in ways unforeseen by other approaches in contemporary continental philosophy, asks compelling questions and makes compelling claims about equality. More importantly, though, I hope to draw attention to previously overlooked concepts and arguments that could still be taken up as new forms of dissensus.

Notes

1. The source of this passage is probably Montaigne (see Rodis-Lewis, 1990, 170), who writes in his *Essays*, in the chapter 'On Presumption', that 'It is commonly held that good sense is the gift which Nature has most fairly shared among us, for there is nobody who is not satisfied with what Nature has allotted him' (II, XVII, 746). Note also how Hobbes's discussion of intellectual equality echoes Montaigne's remarks.
2. Though some of these experiments, such as those involving vivisection, are reprehensible.
3. There have been various translations of Rancière's term *subjectivation* (see Rockhill's 'Glossary' in Rancière, 2004b, 92). In *Disagreement*, Julie Rose translates the term as 'subjectification', and in previous publications I had adopted this translation. I have since decided to translate *subjectivation* as subjectivation. As Samuel Chambers argues, this distinguishes subjectivation from *assujettissement* (subjectification), a term used by the early Foucault – not to mention Lacan and Althusser – to designate forms of interpellation within networks of power/knowledge (Chambers, 2013, 98–101). I have silently modified subsequent quotations to accord with this translation choice.
4. Strictly speaking, Rancière differentiates between 'equality' and 'politics'. Equality is a principle that 'is in no way in itself political', but it becomes political when collective practices of political subjectivation challenge, through dissensus, regimes of policing (1995, 31–32/55).
5. Todd May argues that conventional debates on equality focus on what he calls 'passive equality', which he provisionally defines as 'the creation, preservation, or protection of equality by governmental institutions' rather than any concept similar to Rancière's radical or 'active' equality (May, 2008, 3). On this point, see Chapter 2.
6. For Aristotle, the legislator 'must not think the truly democratical or oligarchical measure to be that which will give the greatest amount of democracy or oligarchy, but that which will make them last longest' (1320a1–4).
7. There are numerous other terms that Rancière uses functionally, insofar as the meaning of these terms is at stake in dissensual practices. These terms include, but are not limited to: society, political life, community, a common world, and being-in-common.

8   Here I will point the interested reader to a number of books with a more direct focus on Rancière (May 2008, Davis 2010, Tanke 2011, Chambers 2013), to an edited volume on Rancière's key concepts (Deranty 2010a), and to two in-depth engagements with Rancière's politics (May 2008, Chambers 2013).

9   Indeed, each chapter could be read as a reflection or commentary that builds upon a work or small number of works of Rancière's: in Chapter 1 it is *The Ignorant Schoolmaster*, in Chapter 2 *Disagreement, Hatred of Democracy*, and *The Philosopher and His Poor*, in Chapter 3 *The Politics of Literature* and *The Politics of Aesthetics*, and in Chapter 4 *Aesthetics and Its Discontents* and *The Emancipated Spectator*. Further study of egalitarian moments that also addresses Rancière's relationship to post-Heideggerian thought, Marxism, and psychoanalysis could begin with, for instance, *On the Shores of Politics, Althusser's Lesson*, and *The Aesthetic Unconscious*.

Part I

Subjectivity

Argument

French philosophy – in its post-Heideggerian, structuralist and poststructuralist iterations – has undertaken a critique of the subject. In *The Order of Things*, Michel Foucault contends, against Sartre's anthropology, that if 'the archaeology of our thought easily shows, man is an invention of recent date', it is just as possible that for historically contingent circumstances the figure of man – as a epistemological and practical agent and target of analysis – could someday disappear 'like a face drawn in sand at the edge of the sea' (1966b, 387). In an interview published the same year as *The Order of Things*, Foucault states that the '*Critique of Dialectical Reason* is the magnificent and pathetic effort of a man of the 19th century to think the 20th century' (1966a, 569–70). Decades later, Jean-Luc Nancy introduces the anthology *Who Comes After the Subject?* by noting that, 'since the close of the Sartrean enterprise', the 'critique or deconstruction of subjectivity' is one of the 'great motifs of contemporary philosophical work in France' (1991, 3–4). And yet several recent philosophers working from within the framework of contemporary French philosophy – such as Alain Badiou, Jacques Rancière, and Slavoj Žižek – argue that political subjectivation is central to conceptualizing radical political practice. In Part I, I propose that Rancière's account of egalitarian political subjectivation gives us good reason to reconsider the legacy of Cartesian and existentialist theories of the subject.

1

The 'Good Sense' of Cartesian Egalitarianism

1.1. 'a history or, if you prefer, a fable'

For Jacques Rancière, politics is, in part, a conflict over social rationalities or logics. Far from reverting to a kind of idealist revanchism, aiming to interpret the world rather than change it, Rancière argues that politics is a moment of conflict between two ways of thinking and organizing – theorizing and practising – social relations. Politics begins when the supposition of equality interrupts the logic of policing and introduces new forms of speaking, being, and doing. The conflict of these two logics or rationalities and practices is the basis of any set of social relations. Every account of politics as speech or rationality (*logos*) is also a count of what speech or rationality is: political conflict 'forms an opposition between logics that count the parties and parts of the community in different ways' (Rancière, 1998e, 35).

Let us examine a paradigmatic form of treating the double count and account of *logos*, where Aristotle defines the human animal as political:

> Nature, as we often say, makes nothing in vain, and man is the only animal whom she has endowed [*hexei*] with the gift of speech [*logos*]. And whereas mere voice [*phônê*] is but an indication of pleasure and pain, and is therefore found in other animals (for their nature attains to the perception [*aisthesin*] of pleasure and pain and the intimation of them to one another, and no further), the power of speech is intended to set forth the useful and the harmful, and therefore likewise the just and the unjust. And it is a characteristic of man that he alone has any sense [*aisthesin*] of good and evil, of just and unjust, and the like, and the association of living beings who have this sense makes a household and a city. (Aristotle, 1253a9–18tm; see Rancière 1995, 1/19)

With a touch of irony, Rancière states in his 'Ten Theses on Politics' that 'nothing could be clearer' than Aristotle's deduction: a human and thus political animal is an animal endowed with *logos* and an *aisthesis* of justice and injustice, good and evil, as well as the useful and harmful (1998e, 37). These political animals share not only the capacity to indicate pleasure and pain, like all other animals, but they also share in common a sense of justice, the useful, and the good. And yet, Rancière notes, it is not obvious how 'language expresses a shared *aisthesis*' (1995, 2/20). While *logos* and an *aisthesis* of justice, the useful, or the good may be shared, this *logos* is not possessed by all. A slave, Aristotle argues, is he who 'by nature' apprehends (*aisthesis*) speech but does not possess (*hexis*) it (1254b24–25). Women are similarly dispossessed of *logos*. At the beginning of the *Politics*, Aristotle claims that women are made only for the purpose of the reproduction of the species and are thus inferior to men.[1] Later, he argues that women are free (1259a40) but are incapable of ruling, for just as the rational part of the soul rules over the irrational, so does a man rule over a woman – who possesses reason without authority (1260a14). Although Aristotle argues that the possession (*hexis*) of speech is unique to human animals and indicates that they are part of the political community, there are nevertheless those, such as women and slaves, who have or possess no part in the community. Though Aristotle might not consider it as a wrong, his account or count of how human beings are political animals implies that there is a part of the human community without a part, what Rancière refers to as 'the part of those who have no part' ('*la part des sans-part*').

Politics, for Rancière, turns on a count of what there is in common in social life, what he calls a distribution of the sensible, the distribution of social relations and the ways in which bodies, places, practices, and visibilities are made intelligible. What separates the logic of the police and egalitarian logic is the count of the parts of the distribution of the sensible. The police counts the parts of society as parties with specific interests that can be represented according to customary forms of intelligibility, with no possibility that there is a void or supplement in society, a part which has no part, a part which is neither represented nor counted (Rancière, 1998e, 36). For Rancière, politics takes place when a part of those who have no part, through political subjectivation, contests the policing of social relations in order to introduce new ways of speaking, being, or doing.

In contrast to the political philosophy of the ancient Greeks, which serves to justify inegalitarian regimes of policing, Rancière explicitly links his account of political subjectivation to René Descartes, to whom little political philosophy, let alone egalitarianism, is often attributed. In *Disagreement*, Rancière argues that:

> Politics is a matter of subjects, or, rather, modes of subjectivation. By *subjectivation* I mean the production through a series of actions of a body and a

capacity for enunciation not previously identifiable within a given field of experience, whose identification is thus part of the reconfiguration of the field of experience. Descartes's *ego sum, ego existo* is the prototype of such indissoluble subjects of a series of operations implying the production of a new field of experience. Any political subjectivation holds to this formula. It is a *nos sumus, nos existimus*. (1995, 35–36/59)

A political subject introduces within a given distribution of the sensible new ways of being, doing, and speaking premised on the supposition of equality. But how does this account relate to Descartes, with his 'provisional moral code' (*Discourse on the Method*, VI, 22–8), his general reluctance to engage socio-political questions, and his attempts to restrict the method of doubt to epistemological and metaphysical considerations (*Meditations*, VII, 15)? What do Descartes's *cogito* and Rancière's account of political subjectivation have in common?

I will argue in this chapter that Rancière's thought is indebted to a specific tradition of Cartesian egalitarianism that runs from the often-neglected work of François Poullain de la Barre to Simone de Beauvoir. It is possible to identify three overarching features of this tradition. First, Cartesian egalitarianism thinks political agency as a practice of subjectivity, even if its proponents differ on how political practice is subjectively engaged (whether, for instance, this engagement begins with individuals or collectives). Second, Cartesian egalitarians share the supposition that there is an equality of intelligences and abilities shared by all human beings. This supposition follows from the beginning of Descartes's *Discourse on the Method*:

> Good sense (*bon sens*) is the best distributed (*partagée*) thing in the world: for everyone thinks himself so well endowed with it that even those who are the hardest to please in everything else do not usually desire more of it than they possess. In this it is unlikely that everyone is mistaken. It indicates rather that the power of judging well and of distinguishing the true from the false – which is what we properly call 'good sense' or 'reason' – is naturally equal in all men, and consequently that the diversity of our opinions does not arise because some of us are more reasonable than others but solely because we direct our thoughts along different paths and do not attend to the same things. (VI: 1–2)

Looking past the ironic posturing of the first sentence, Cartesian egalitarians such as Poullain de la Barre or Joseph Jacotot take this '*bon sens*' as Descartes's fundamental idea: 'there are not several manners of being intelligent, no distribution between two forms of intelligence, hence between two forms of humanity.

The equality of intelligences is first the equality of intelligence with itself in all of its operations' (Rancière, 2005a, 412). The equality of intelligences has one other crucial consequence: if there is no hierarchy of intelligences, then there is no natural or inevitable hierarchy between those who rule and those who are ruled.

Third, Cartesian egalitarians conceptualize politics as the processing of a wrong through the practice of dissensus. As Rancière writes, 'politics becomes the argument of a basic wrong that ties in with some established dispute in the distribution of jobs, roles, and places', initiating 'conflict over the very existence of something in common between those who have a part and those who have none' (1995, 35/59). Politics is not concerned with those who already possess speech or visibility, nor is politics about power, consensus, or better or worse regimes. These are, in fact, problems of policing. When Rancière argues that politics turns on a wrong, he claims political practice for those who have been marginalized or excluded; political subjectivation is always a moment of dissensus that challenges the structural inequalities of a given regime of policing, when those without speech begin to speak, when the uncounted offer an account of themselves, when the previously invisible occupy a visible place.[2]

In this chapter, I will examine how these three features of Cartesian egalitarianism emerge from the work of Descartes. Although subjectivity (as *cogito*) and intellectual equality are central components of his philosophy, Descartes nevertheless limits his critique of the prejudices of intellect, authority, and habit to the epistemo-metaphysical problem of separation. After reconstructing how egalitarianism functions in Descartes's system, I will show how Poullain reconceptualizes the problem of separation in a socio-political context, transforming it into the problematic of a wrong. He uses Descartes's dualism to show that there are neither natural qualities of the mind nor of the body that justify the inequality of the sexes. Women have been wronged, Poullain argues, because there are no clear and distinct reasons for their subjugation. Instead, women have been denied the capacity of fully exercising their reason due to the political self-interest of men and the force of social convention.

After examining Descartes and Poullain, I will shift the discussion to the philosophy of Beauvoir. Though this has the unfortunate effect of setting aside many other developments in the historical relationship between Cartesianism, egalitarianism, and feminism, Beauvoir's conception of the relationship between political subjectivity and the processing of a wrong foreshadows several of Rancière's concerns.[3] I will argue that Beauvoir's account of a wrong – which occurs, for instance, when a woman is forced to assume, and thus limit, her freedom as an 'other' rather than a 'subject' – marks a significant advance over

Sartre's individualist ethics of the 1940s. Because Beauvoir focuses on those whose agency has been historically marginalized, her account of political subjectivity avoids the pitfalls that have so often plagued many strains of Marxism, which amplify the teleological character of the proletariat's historic mission. For Beauvoir, it is not possible to subordinate one struggle to another; a historic mission, as it were, can only be built out of practices of solidarity, and not out of the hierarchization of demands, abilities, and intelligences.

Thus I focus on Beauvoir because her Cartesian egalitarianism is an important precedent to Rancière's. Since Rancière does not, to my knowledge, extensively discuss the work of either Poullain or Beauvoir, I do not intend this as an explication of Rancière's work, but rather as 'a history or, if you prefer, a fable' (Descartes, VI: 4) that provides an overview of a longer tradition of egalitarianism than is typically acknowledged. I will conclude by showing, through a focused reading of his book *The Ignorant Schoolmaster*, how Rancière's understanding of Cartesianism emphasizes the egalitarianism of Poullain and Beauvoir rather than Descartes's metaphysical or epistemological commitments. In the *Principles of Philosophy*, Descartes writes that the 'last and greatest fruit of these principles is that they will enable those who develop them to discover many truths which I have not explained at all' (IXb: 18). Though we will be telling a history or fable, revisiting the work of Descartes and his successors will outline a much richer history of Cartesian egalitarianism.

1.2. Descartes's egalitarianism and the problem of separation

We do not typically consider Descartes an egalitarian. He is more often interpreted, in the post-Heideggerian tradition of philosophy, as an epochal figure of the modern destiny of metaphysics. On this account, Descartes introduces the metaphysical ground of technicity by dividing all beings between thinking subjects and objects of a calculable objective world.[4] Or, following Antonio Negri, he is considered an architect of a 'reasonable ideology' that expresses the class compromise constitutive of the formation of bourgeois class power after the 1620s: whereas Descartes formulates his philosophy as the production of human significance (and practical utility) in its separation from the world, the bourgeoisie affirms its position in civil society at the same time that it accepts a temporary class compromise with absolutism (Negri, 1970, 295–6).

Recently, however, several prominent radical thinkers have laid claim to the legacy of the Cartesian subject. For example, Alain Badiou, Rancière and

Slavoj Žižek all hold that the emergence of subjectivity in political praxis is irreducible to the reconfiguration of Cartesian thought as instrumental rationality, whether it is considered as a moment of technological enframing or as a moment of bourgeois compromise.[5] Yet the Cartesianism of Badiou and Žižek does not imply the supposition of equality. Instead, their commitment is largely programmatic. Žižek, in *The Ticklish Subject,* proposes that the Cartesian subject is a revolutionary alternative to what he considers to be the hegemony of 'liberal-democratic multiculturalism', a category into which he throws things as unlike as new age obscurantism and postmodern deconstruction (Žižek, 1999, 1–4). For Badiou, Descartes is a paradigmatic materialist dialectician, insofar as he maintains that truths are eternal against the general presumptions of both 'democratic materialism,' which counts only bodies and languages, and Nietzsche's and Heidegger's 'aristocratic idealism,' which, despite its overwhelming sense of resignation, aims to preserve the poetic event against modern nihilism (2006b, 1–6).

In contrast to these interpretations, I will argue that Descartes's work wavers between egalitarianism and the constraints of method. On the one hand, the Cartesian project, even for Descartes, requires the supposition of equality in order for its method to be verified. That is, rather than appealing to tradition, convention, or authority to establish the validity of his system, Descartes calls for the well-considered and reasonable judgements of his readers. And yet, on the other hand, Descartes makes persistent appeal to the necessity of method to prevent the egalitarianism of his appeal from encouraging a thoroughgoing critique of all social conventions. Instead, his system is directed toward epistemological and metaphysical questions, which are structured by the problem of separation.

Let us begin with Descartes's supposition of equality. Despite his programme of searching out the self-foundational moment of a system, his philosophy is nevertheless conditioned (but not necessarily determined) by its historical situation, or the distribution of the sensible within which it was elaborated. When Rancière speaks of a distribution of the sensible, it includes the relations between subjects, objects, and places, and the ways of speaking, doing and being that make these relations intelligible. While policing, in Rancière's terms, is a process of hierarchically arranging these relations and enforcing them, we should not consider a distribution of the sensible as static until politics intervenes; instead, the intelligibility of these relations is also dynamic, which can change, enter into periods of stability, and undergo crises from which a politics of dissensus can emerge (or not).

Though it is not a moment of politics in Rancière's sense, Descartes's thought inaugurates a new way of thinking the relations between subjectivity, habit, and intelligibility within an intellectual milieu in transition, in which Scholasticism and Renaissance philosophy have been challenged by a renewed sense of scepticism. This conjuncture is not unique to philosophy, but is itself enmeshed within a series of socio-political upheavals. Negri, for instance, points to the recomposition of class power after the European economic crisis of 1619–22 and the condemnation of Galileo (1970, 112–26; 140–55). Moreover, as Susan Bordo argues, the renewal of scepticism is not only of philosophical interest, but also an expression of the 'epistemological implications of cultural difference' brought on by advances in European techniques of travel (to, for instance, China) and the conquest of the Americas (Bordo, 1987, 40–1). She cites, for example, Montaigne's remark that 'every man calls barbarous anything he is not accustomed to; it is indeed the case that we have no other criterion of truth or right-reason than the example and form of the opinions and customs of our own country' (Montaigne, I, XXXI, 231).

In the *Discourse*, Descartes makes a similar remark: 'It is good to know something of the customs of various peoples, so that we may judge our own more soundly and not think that everything contrary to our own ways is ridiculous and irrational, as those who have seen nothing of the world ordinarily do' (VI: 6tm).[6] He draws two conclusions from this diversity of customs: first, 'not to believe too firmly anything of which I had been persuaded only by example and custom' (VI: 10), and second, that the knowledge of cultural difference helps justify the supposition that opens the *Discourse*, that good sense or reason is 'naturally equal in all men' (VI: 2).[7] From these two conclusions Descartes proposes a new relationship between subjectivity, habituation, and intelligibility. This new relationship is founded on the *cogito* or thinking being, which emerges from a method of doubt directed toward habits or practices derived from custom and a discourse of intelligibility established on the authority of the schools. The significance of this critique of convention turns on whether it is conceived as a project of intellectual emancipation, or as the metaphysical and epistemological problem of separation.

It is possible, beginning with the *Discourse*, to read Descartes's project as an exercise in intellectual emancipation. Starting from the premise of the equality of intelligences and abilities, Descartes delineates his method of directing his reason as an example of 'self-instruction' for the reader to judge as to whether it is a worthy example for imitation or improvement (VI: 4). It is not a necessary order of reasons, as it is in the *Meditations*, or an attempt at 'teaching', but an account of how Descartes had 'tried to direct [his] own' reason (VI: 4). By stressing the egalitarian aspect of this work, we can see that the validity of the subject as thinking being is verified by the capacity for the direction of reason to be repeated through each reader's self-instruction. The emergence of the *cogito* transfers authority from the customs of the schools to all those to whom reason or good sense is distributed – a lesson in the practice of thinking learned from Descartes's travels rather than the schools (VI: 5–6). The intelligibility of the new philosophy – and its foundation, the *cogito* – is verified through the free use of the reader's own reason, rather than doctrinal authority.

Nevertheless, the socio-political consequences and the gestures toward a broader vernacular culture found in the *Discourse* are absent from the *Meditations*. The contingent emergence of the *cogito* as a response to a crisis in intellectual authority within the sciences is instead given a metaphysically necessary status, and philosophical inquiry becomes a problem of ascertaining the proper epistemological and metaphysical foundations for physics. The egalitarian moment of the *Discourse* is now restricted to the problem of the separation of self and world.[8] Once we enter into the order of reasons of the *Meditations*, the situation becomes, as Sartre argues, that of 'autonomous thought which, by its own power, discovers intelligible relationships between already existing essences' (1947, 499tm).

Let us look at the way that the *Meditations* recasts the relationship of subjectivity, habit and intelligibility. The 'First Meditation' begins with Descartes's acknowledgement that he has been accustomed since childhood to a method of making judgements that has led to numerous falsehoods, which leads him to suspect that the basis of those judgements – information 'acquired either from the senses or through the senses' – is doubtful (VII: 18). This passage carries a double significance. In fact, Descartes wavers between two different accounts of the basis of the judgements he has discovered to be doubtful. Both share the same starting point – the prejudice of relying on the senses has a basis in the habits acquired in childhood – but they differ on how these habits are acquired. One, which I will call the 'prison of the body' account, identifies the body as the cause of the prejudices that prevent the proper use of reason.[9] In the subsequent history of Cartesian egalitarianism, this metaphysical account of the origin of prejudices is rejected in favour of the second account, which focuses on the socio-political critique of convention, such as the criticism of Scholasticism.

In the *Discourse*, we find a socio-political critique of the prejudices of childhood. One accepts teaching based on authority and explication, rather than according to reason. Descartes recounts that from 'my childhood I have been nourished upon letters, and ... I was persuaded that by their means one could acquire a clear and certain knowledge of all that is useful in life' (VI: 4). Books – 'letters' – would have taught him the basic premise of Scholastic philosophy, that *'nihil est in intellectu nisi prius fuerit in sensu'*, that 'nothing is in the intellect unless it was first in the senses' (Carriero, 2009, 12ff.). Rather than understanding the immediacy and intelligibility of the sensible as a naïve standpoint, we could understand it as a product of a determinate (and by Descartes's time, reified) historical production of knowledge, that is, of Scholasticism. In this case, the method of doubt and the emergence of the subject of the *cogito* become a challenge to one particular historical system of knowledge, though a persistent vigilance is required to prevent Descartes's thought from being reified into a teaching based on authority, a vigilance evidenced by his repeated references to needing to inculcate new habits of thought against the lures of custom. This is how, broadly speaking, the Cartesian egalitarians will take up his thought.

On the other hand, Descartes also faults the body itself for propagating the habits and prejudices of childhood; the body is, on this account, the prison of the soul.[10] In the *Principles of Philosophy*, Descartes writes:

> In our childhood the mind was so immersed in the body that although there was much that it perceived clearly, it never perceived anything distinctly. But in spite of this the mind made judgments about many things, and this is the origin of the many preconceived opinions which most of us never subsequently abandon. (VIIIa: 22)

On this account, Scholasticism's reliance on the senses as the foundation of knowledge serves to reinforce the prejudices of the body. The task for thinking, for Descartes, is to obtain through the method of doubt a reflexive distance from what we take to be the immediacy of the senses to allow the intellect to mediate our judgements. The task is to separate thinking substance, the *cogito*, from the mechanisms of the body through a method that makes it possible to discover clear and distinct ideas of 'already existing essences,' as Sartre puts it – of, for instance, thought, extension, substance, and God (1947, 499tm). Of course, as many commentators have pointed out, it is difficult to see how Descartes can establish a measure to test the truth of a judgement after the introduction of hyperbolic doubt. Even if he can demonstrate the truth of the *cogito* as a thinking being, it is still possible that he is being deceived about other kinds of knowledge. To overcome the evil genius hypothesis, Descartes proceeds in the 'Third Meditation' to attempt a proof of his dependence on a supremely perfect being. This supremely perfect being functions, in the system, as the guarantor of the knowledge that Descartes establishes throughout the rest of the *Meditations*, gradually returning into his grasp the fields of mathematics, physics, and everyday sense experience – as long as these things are conceived 'clearly and distinctly'. With thought and extension clearly and distinctly separated, and with their correspondence guaranteed by God, the reconstruction of philosophy from the *cogito* allows Descartes to introduce a physics that explains bodies and movements according to the general rules of mechanics and mathematics, rather than the Scholastic – or childlike (VII: 437–9) – cognition of universals from particular qualities derived from the senses (see Carriero, 2009, 16–17; Garber, 1986, 84–8). By establishing the 'already existing' essential validity of the separation of thought and extension, Descartes limits the possibility that doubt toward the sensible could open into a socio-historical critique – that is, that knowledge could be historically situated.

Instead, Descartes suggests that Scholasticism lends the errors of the body an artificial veneer of rationality. In the unfinished dialogue 'The Search for Truth', Descartes juxtaposes the 'natural' use of reason to the 'artifice' of Scholasticism. In this text, the greatest threat to knowledge is not the separation of thought and extension and of self and world, because in his system God guarantees that they have an intelligible relationship; the greatest threat is that the good sense of the meditator is captured by the artifice of authority and the schools, that, as in the case of Epistemon the Scholastic, one is lulled into the 'habit of yielding to authority rather than lending [one's] ear to the dictates of reason' (X: 523).[11] By contrast, Descartes claims that his method begins, through the use of doubt, by inculcating 'a judgment which is not corrupted by any false beliefs and a reason which retains all the purity of its nature' (X: 498). The whole rhetorical staging of 'The Search for Truth' relies on Eudoxus being able to direct Polyander (a character who has never studied but possesses 'a moderate amount of good sense') in this 'natural' use of his reason with the aim of discovering the true principles of (Cartesian) philosophy (X: 514). Yet if Cartesianism lays claim to being the 'natural' use of reason, then it risks, despite Descartes's protests that he is not attempting to 'teach' anyone, repeating the problems that he had identified with Scholasticism: the naturalization of doctrine through the reification of a historically situated knowledge. In Rancière's terms, the intellectual emancipation promised by the Cartesian *ego sum, ego existo* is subordinated to the intellectual policing of method.

1.3. The rationality of a wrong

The social and political consequences of Descartes's thought were not lost on his contemporaries, especially in the conflicts over the equality of the sexes.[12] His account of the egalitarian distribution of reason stands in stark contrast with the Aristotelianism of the Scholastics.[13] As we have seen, while Aristotle defines humans as rational animals, he nevertheless proceeds to dispossess slaves and women of *logos*. Women are doubly dispossessed, with bodies created for the 'single use' of reproduction (1252b1–5) and a capacity for the use of reason for which they possess no authority.

Poullain de la Barre appropriates Cartesian philosophy to show, in contrast to Aristotle, that patriarchal social forms possess authority without reason. In *On the Equality of the Two Sexes*, Poullain notes that:

> if something is well established, then we think it must be right. Since we think that reason plays a role in everything men do, most people cannot imagine that reason was not consulted in the setting up of practices that are so universally accepted, and we imagine that reason and prudence dictated them. (Poullain, 1673, 54)

Using the results of Cartesian philosophy, Poullain argues that the inequality of the sexes – that is, the subjugation of women – is founded on the prejudices of habit, custom, and political self-interest rather than well-founded reasons. Though we have seen that Descartes restricts his system to the epistemological and metaphysical problem of separation, Poullain uses Cartesian philosophy to conceptualize the wrong at the basis of the inequality of the sexes: both popular opinion and scholarly learning dispossess women of subjectivity and the capacity to reason. Poullain's task, then, is to demonstrate how the part of those who have no part – women as they are socially excluded and subjugated – can lay claim to a political subjectivity that they have been denied. This claim begins with undermining the foundations of long-standing prejudices that justify inequality. This process of critique can open the possibility of a more egalitarian distribution of the sensible, in which women are recognized as thinking and speaking subjects, not merely passive objects of men's possession, and as agents who are just as able as men to make public use of their reason.

In *On the Equality of the Two Sexes*, Poullain argues – in a passage that later appears in paraphrase as an epigraph to *The Second Sex* – that the historical and intellectual record shows that:

> Women were judged in former times as they are today and with as little reason, so whatever men say about them should be suspect as they are both judges and defendants. Even if the charges brought against them are backed by the opinions of a thousand authors, the entire brief should be taken as a chronicle of prejudice and error. (1673, 76)

To overturn these judgements, Poullain criticizes both 'popular' and 'learned' prejudices against women. There are, he argues, no natural reasons for the 'chronicle of prejudice and error', but only the 'reason' of political self-interest. The oppression of women has been enforced by the physical strength of men, and policed by naturalizing a gendered division of labour within the distinction of public and private domains (see his 'historical conjectures' at 1673, 56–60). This situation is reproduced, he argues, when in both ancient and modern times intellectuals have generally taken 'their prejudices with them into the Schools' and worked to give reasons for the subjugation of women (1673, 79).

Poullain appropriates Descartes's distinction between thought and the body to show that there are neither intellectual nor physical inequalities between men and women. Customary prejudice, he notes, holds that women cannot exercise reason as well as men, often pointing out how women are more passionate or intemperate, how their use of reason is less independent of the body. Poullain turns this argument around to claim that those who maintain this customary prejudice have themselves provided reasons that do not consider the faculties of the mind independently from the body. For, he claims, given that thought is a substance other than body, the mind has no sex, and if the mind has no sex, good sense or reason is equally distributed to both men and women. Moreover, if equality is indeed the case, there is no natural basis for an intellectual division of labour. From the standpoint of well-considered reasons, his misogynist opponents have confused nature and custom: the perceived intellectual flaws of women are the product of their exclusion from education. In addition, the intellectual stultification of women, Poullain notes, also has a political basis: those who deny that the 'scope of reason is boundless and has the same influence over all people' do so out of self-interest, fearing that ending a gender- (and class-) based intellectual division of labour will devalue the prestige and authority that comes with learning (1673, 95). Given the numerous prejudices of intellectuals, Poullain even suggests that the exclusion of women from education could work to their eventual advantage because they would be able to direct their natural reason without the artifice of the schools (1673, 62–5).[14]

That the mind has no sex, and that good sense or reason is equally distributed among all humans, are the positions of Poullain that are closest to Descartes.

It is more difficult to use the Cartesian system to establish that inequality is not based on embodied differences, given that Descartes sometimes maintains that the body is the prison of the soul, that the confusions of the body produce many of our prejudices. The stakes are also elevated when one considers that the authoritative figures of Scholastic philosophy viewed the capacities of the body with some disgust – especially when it comes to women's bodies. Women were considered 'monstrous' by Aristotle and considered 'imperfect' or 'incomplete' men by others (Poullain, 1673, 118).[15] Poullain, then, cannot rely on Descartes's claim that the body is the origin of human prejudices about the world to show that there are no natural inequalities that can be discovered in the embodied differences between men and women.

Instead, Poullain, like several other Cartesians and *cartésiennes*, attempts to rehabilitate the body within the Cartesian system.[16] He argues that the reproductive functions are the only embodied differences between men and women; in all other ways the mechanisms of the body follow the same laws (1673, 82). Poullain emphasizes Descartes's *Passions of the Soul* over his 'prison of the body' conjectures.[17] In addition, embodied differences are not considered imperfections.[18] Instead, Poullain claims that 'God desired' to create the difference of the sexes so that human beings would be dependent upon each other, and that each body is 'perfect in its own way: both are presently constituted as they were intended' (1673, 104). This position, however, valorizes motherhood in a way that later feminists such as Beauvoir would openly challenge. Despite his precautions in other arguments, Poullain seems to rely on the assumption (especially given that he attributes it to 'God's desire') that maternity is a natural good that provides women with 'the highest purpose in the world, namely to bear us and nourish us in their womb' (1673, 104). Nevertheless, these arguments for the equality of two kinds of 'perfect' bodies contrast starkly with the depreciations of the body current during the seventeenth century. Despite the contingencies of his historical situation, Poullain's philosophy is a prototype for an emancipatory political thought that seeks to show both how all humans are capable of exercising their freedom, and how, as Beauvoir will write three centuries later, biology is not destiny.

1.4. Woman as other, woman as subject

As is well known, both Sartre and Beauvoir take the *cogito* as a starting point for interrogating the freedom of human being. In Beauvoir's words, the

'Cartesian *cogito* expresses both the most individual experience and the most objective truth' insofar as it affirms that human freedom is the basis of all values (Beauvoir, 1947, 17). As Sartre underlines, the basis of this 'most individual experience' is the democratic character of good sense.[19] He emphasizes that 'the famous assertion that good sense is the most widely shared thing in the world doesn't simply mean that every man has in his mind the same germs of thought, the same innate ideas', but that there is a free capacity of judgement shared equally by all humans (Sartre 1947, 505). To be more specific, Sartre reads this moment of freedom as the capacity to doubt, to negate all qualities other than freedom; the basis of the thinking subject is 'that nothingness, that little quivering of air that alone escapes the enterprise of doubting and is *nothing other* than doubt itself; and when it moves out of nothingness, it does so to become a pure assumption of being' (Sartre, 1947, 520). Cartesian freedom, emerging out of a moment of doubt, must be transformative, a projection into an open future. This much, I think, Sartre and Beauvoir have in common, but they diverge concerning how the freedom which is the basis of all value can be realized within the social life of the individual. Through the mid-1940s, Sartre largely remains focused on the problem of how an individual can act freely within a historical situation that is not of his or her own making, and many of his more hyperbolic comments imply that, as long as one is not in bad faith, all choices are equivalent as long as they are free (see Section 2.4).

Genevieve Lloyd worries that Beauvoir's commitment to the 'ideal of radical freedom' could add 'an extra burden of self-recrimination on those – male or female – who find themselves caught in oppressive situations' (Lloyd, 1993, 98). However, already in *The Ethics of Ambiguity* (1947), Beauvoir is attentive to the situation of the oppressed and marginalized in ways that Sartre would only recognize later: throughout her analyses of the existential attitudes that lead to bad faith or individualist ethics, she repeatedly claims that a subject's freedom must work toward the freedom of others.[20] For Beauvoir it is necessary that practices of freedom and the situations that they transform be understood as historically differentiated, so neither situations nor choices are equivalent. This requires Beauvoir to move from an individualist ethics to conceptualizing these concerns from their bases in social perceptions and relations designated as *l'expérience vécue*: the socially lived experience of giving an account of oneself within a historically concrete situation (see Simons, 1999, 41–54).

In *The Second Sex* (1949), Beauvoir frames the question of subjectivity more explicitly as a political problem, not just in the sense that she examines how a subject assumes her freedom within a historical situation, but also insofar as this question turns on what we have called a wrong: she pursues the consequences of the fact that, despite being an 'autonomous freedom', a woman 'discovers and chooses herself in a world where men force her to assume herself as Other' (Beauvoir, 1949, 17/1: 31). Like Poullain, Beauvoir rejects the thesis that there are biological data that necessarily determine, and form the 'fixed destiny' of, the subjugation of women within the social hierarchy of the sexes (1949, 44/1: 70). Instead, she argues that all situations are politically and historically conditioned, meaning that all possible biological data take on social values rather than intrinsically natural values that transcend a given situation.[21]

Beauvoir therefore turns to the investigation of the historical and political bases of the inequality of those who are able to assume their subjective freedom, and those who – depending on the situation, could be women, African Americans, the colonized, or other groups – confront a historical situation in which they are considered pejoratively as 'others'. It is a fundamental supposition of existentialism that all human beings have the capacity to exercise their freedom, because freedom is the basis of all social values, and yet in each situation they cannot exercise the full extent of their freedom.

Beauvoir politicizes the existentialist account of subjectivity and freedom by conceptualizing how a wrong is introduced into social distinctions between subjectivity and alterity. This wrong occurs because women are constrained by a situation in which men are subjects and women are others. The distinction between self (or subject) and other, she notes, is not necessarily the basis of a wrong. The category of the other 'is as original as consciousness itself' (1949, 6/1: 16). Beauvoir states that the distinction between self and other can designate a relationship of reciprocity (such as that between nature and culture) or opposition and antagonism (between, for instance, two different cultures). But it is quite possible that the well-travelled person can recognize the reciprocity of these two different cultures, which relativizes her concept of alterity – just as Descartes noted that visiting others can reveal how one's own customs are just as arbitrary and locally determined as another's. In such a situation, alterity is not a negative category, but one through which one's own values are questioned and reconsidered.

What is different about the situation of women is that the distinction between men and women carries with it a series of value-laden social judgements: a woman is defined against the standard of man and the man's attributes are given positive values, while women's attributes are considered negatively as flaws or insufficiencies. These values are reinforced because men arrogate to themselves the sole capacity to make such judgements. As Michel Kail writes, women are interpellated in 'a specific regime of alterity [that] shows that rulers control the meaning of the situation by setting the very conditions that make relationships possible' (Kail, 2009, 157). Beauvoir produces numerous examples to show how, in such situations, 'Humanity is male, and man defines woman, not in herself, but in relation to himself; she is not considered an autonomous being' (Beauvoir, 1949, 5/1: 15). This situation is prevalent in both social and intellectual life. Take, for instance, Emmanuel Lévinas's account of one's responsibility toward a transcendent Other: Beauvoir sardonically notes that his claim that 'alterity is accomplished in the feminine' forgets that a 'woman also is consciousness for herself' (1949, 6, n.3/1: 15 n.1).

Although much of *The Second Sex* is dedicated to diagnosing and cataloguing how a woman is defined against a masculine standard, Beauvoir also points toward the possibilities of women's emancipation. First, she argues that subjective practice must be socially transformative: the reified social structures that commit a wrong against a marginalized or oppressed group must be challenged and interrupted by the free creation of new social values. A wrong occurs, she argues, when one's freedom is denied within a given social situation, such as when the values of 'patriarchal femininity' – such as the myth of the 'Eternal Feminine' – are created or upheld by men and utilized to police the 'proper' places or practices for a woman.[22] While the values that underlie patriarchal femininity are often inconsistent, they function to treat femininity as an absolute alterity, which dispossesses women of their subjective freedom. As Beauvoir writes:

> to the dispersed, contingent, and multiple existence of *women*, mythic thinking opposes the Eternal Feminine, unique and fixed; if the definition given is contradicted by the behavior of real flesh-and-blood women, it is women who are wrong: it is said not that Femininity is an entity but that women are not feminine. (1949, 266/1: 383)

Although Beauvoir's use of the term *wrong* is not exactly equivalent to Rancière's, they are nevertheless analysing the same type of oppression: the values of patriarchal femininity function to dispossess women of their freedom, their speech, and their capacity to give an account of themselves. In addition, Beauvoir argues that it is not enough to reverse the polarities of the values and distinctions of patriarchal femininity, in the way that the mystic identifies with the absolute alterity of the feminine – or celebrates, rather than denigrates, women's proximity to nature in contrast to the artifice of masculine culture; as Mary Wollstonecraft points out, there is no reason to lend credence to 'prejudices that give a sex to virtue' (1792, 75). Again, to affirm the social character of women's struggle, Beauvoir holds that attempts at 'individual salvation' such as mysticism, love, or narcissism 'can only result in failures' (1949, 717/2: 517); a wrong must be challenged by a socially transformative engagement that undermines the judgements and distinctions of patriarchal femininity through the free creation of social values.

Second, Beauvoir's politics are universal and egalitarian. She argues that the recognition of some people as subjects and the social exclusion of some people as others is the fundamental basis of inequality. Be it the distinction between men and women, Americans of European descent and African Americans, or the bourgeoisie and the proletariat, 'whether it is race, caste, class, or sex reduced to an inferior condition, the justification process is the same' (1949, 12/1: 24). In each case those who rule attempt to demonstrate that there is some natural reason for inequality: 'one of the ruses of oppression,' she writes in *The Ethics of Ambiguity*, 'is to camouflage itself behind a natural situation since, after all, one can not revolt against nature' (1947, 83). Thus a crucial task for politics is to demonstrate that these so-called natural differences are based on social relations. But the dual lesson of Beauvoir's critique of Marxian economism must not be forgotten. First, all struggles emerge from, and are conditioned by, their local and historical situation, which means that they use varied approaches to emancipatory practices. Hence second, the emancipatory aspirations of a people cannot be subordinated to another group's aspirations. One cannot argue that the historical mission of the proletariat requires that, for instance, women subordinate their demands and practices to those of the proletariat. However, despite the rejection of a teleological concept of historical struggle, one should nevertheless maintain, like Beauvoir, that women's liberation requires the end of their economic exploitation. These various struggles can only be strengthened and reinforced by what Beauvoir calls reciprocity – by practices of freedom and solidarity that do not reproduce the social hierarchies that these groups are combating.

While Sartre's existential appropriation of the *cogito* marks him as a Cartesian, Beauvoir is a Cartesian *egalitarian*. Her conceptualization of political subjectivity follows Descartes and Poullain insofar as it affirms that reason or good sense is equally distributed to all people – far from a world of sovereign subjects and their inferiors, she proposes a politics that instils the reciprocity of practices of freedom. Her existentialism begins with the individual, but it demands that the individual aims toward accomplishing practices of reciprocity and freedom that expand 'toward an indefinitely open future' (1949, 16/1: 31).

1.5. Toward collective egalitarianism

This history or fable of the egalitarianism that leads from Descartes to Beauvoir shows that Cartesianism cannot be reduced to several of its more prominent conceptual commitments, such as mind–body dualism, the technicity of its mechanistic physics, or even, as we will see with Rancière's critique, the so-called rigours of the method. Cartesianism is also defined by its egalitarianism: the formation of a political subject from the supposition of the equality of intelligences. This subject is political insofar as its praxis turns on the processing of a wrong, an egalitarian challenge to the inequalities of any social order. As we have seen, Cartesianism from Poullain to Beauvoir constitutes a direct challenge to the claim that there is a hierarchy of intelligences.

If egalitarianism is a key component of this kind of Cartesianism, then it becomes possible to see why Rancière argues, in *Disagreement*, that 'Descartes's *ego sum, ego existo* is the prototype of such indissoluble subjects of a series of operations implying the production of a new field of experience' (1995, 35/59). This new field of experience – what we could call, following Beauvoir, a collective reciprocity of equality – is opened when the part of those who have no part engage in political practice, challenging a social distribution that counts them as inferiors or subordinates, such as the count, challenged by Poullain and Beauvoir, that women are others and not subjects of freedom. Without this aspect, it is difficult to see why Rancière lays claim to the Cartesian legacy, for he directly challenges, through a discussion of Joseph Jacotot, many of Descartes's epistemological and metaphysical assumptions.

In fact, Rancière's work does not contain an extensive interrogation of Descartes's thought. As we have seen in the Introduction, Rancière reproduces as an epigraph to *The Philosopher and His Poor* a passage from Baillet's *La Vie de Monsieur Descartes* that gives an account of the friendship between Dirk Rembrantsz, a Dutch peasant shoemaker and autodidact astronomer, and Descartes, in which Descartes embraces a man of lower social standing because of their common interest in astronomy (1983, xxii–xxiii). Baillet's story provides a counterpoint to the ways – criticized by Rancière – in which Plato, Marx, Sartre, and Bourdieu treat the poor in their respective philosophies. But there are other moments when Cartesian egalitarianism surfaces in *The Philosopher and His Poor*. At one point, Rancière contrasts Descartes's supposition of the universality of 'good sense' to Plato's distribution of the virtues within the parts of the city. Though each part of the city is organized around its full realization, coordinating functions and virtues:

only a government of philosopher-guardians can give the first order its own virtue, wisdom (*sophia*) ... There is no virtue or education that belongs to the laboring people. Their 'own' virtue – moderation, common 'wisdom' (*sōphrosunē*) – must come to them from outside. There is no 'self-mastery' that the inferior can claim as its own virtue since, by definition, mastery presupposes a superior. The 'wisdom' of the people cannot be either a 'good sense' or a 'common sense' shared equally by the most educated and the least educated; nor can it be a quality specific to inferiors. It is simply the submission of the lowest part of the state to its noblest part. (Rancière, 1983, 24–5; on Kant's aesthetic common sense, see Section 3.5)

According to Plato, of the three classes in the city, only the philosopher has the capacity to contemplate and assign virtues. With the artisan, the superior part of the soul is ruled by a weaker part, and thus 'to insure that someone like that is ruled by something similar to what rules the best person, we say that he ought to be the slave of that best person who has a divine ruler within himself' (590c), as to be ruled by a superior does not wrong the inferior. To Plato's division of labour, Rancière opposes the supposition of the Cartesian 'good sense' shared equally by all human beings in order to isolate a wrong: artisans, relegated to one function, and dispossessed of the capacity to deliberate about the city, must submit to a virtue chosen by those (self-)entitled to the mastery of thinking. This virtue of *sōphrosunē*, often translated as 'moderation', means that each member of the community is to stay in his or her place (Rancière, 1983, 25–7; 1995, 67/101–2). The Platonic division of labour is not a natural structure of the city, but a relation of domination. As Rancière argues elsewhere, the equality of intelligences undermines all claims to 'natural' or 'just' orders of submission. First, for one to command and one to obey, there must be something in common between the two: 'you must understand the order and you must understand that you must obey it. And to do that, you must already be the equal of the person who is ordering you. It is this equality that gnaws away at any natural order' (1995, 16/37). Moreover, the supposition of the equality of intelligences means that an individual cannot be identified with any one function; since all individuals reflect on their position in the social order, 'it is impossible for shoemakers to just make shoes, that they not also be, in their manner, grammarians, moralists, or physicists' (1987, 34).

Rancière develops a more extensive engagement with Cartesian egalitarianism in *The Ignorant Schoolmaster*, where the figure of Descartes intermittently emerges in the discourse of Joseph Jacotot, who argues that the *cogito* is 'one of the principles' of intellectual emancipation (quoted in Rancière, 1987, 35; Van de Weyer, 1822, 23). As James Swenson notes, Rancière's 'free indirect style' poses several interpretative challenges with *The Ignorant Schoolmaster*, where Rancière adopts Jacotot's vocabulary, 'rigorously avoids any anachronism in his references', and refrains from differentiating his position from that of Jacotot (Swenson, 2009, 266). This produces some uncertainty concerning 'where the voice of Jacotot stops and Rancière's begins' (K. Ross, 1991, xxii). With these precautions in mind, I will focus on Rancière's discussion of Jacotot's reading of Descartes. More specifically, I will argue that Rancière's reference in *Disagreement* to Descartes's *ego sum, ego existo* as the prototype of political subjectivation is an appropriation of Jacotot's reading of Descartes.

In *The Ignorant Schoolmaster*, Rancière contrasts the emancipatory teachings of Jacotot to the stultification of the teachings of the 'Old Master', whose primary function is to explicate knowledge to those who do not possess it.[23] Jacotot presents – or, perhaps, discovers – a method of teaching that emphasizes the equality and reciprocity of intelligences, and thus realizes that the pedagogue must teach that he or she has no expertise to teach (Rancière, 1987, 15). Rather than transmission and expertise, the ignorant schoolmaster interrogates and verifies that the student is attentive (1987, 29). Rancière argues that the division of labour between the 'Old Master' and the family, between instruction and moral teaching, reinforces social order: the student draws from science what is not his own, and he draws from moral education what his place *is* (1987, 35). Using a free indirect style that quotes Jacotot, Rancière writes:

> Emancipation is precisely the opposite of this; it is each man becoming conscious of his nature as an intellectual subject; it is the Cartesian formula of equality read backwards. 'Descartes said "I think, therefore I am"; and this noble thought of the great philosopher is one of the principles of universal teaching. We turn this thought around and say: "I am a man, therefore I think." The reversal equates 'man' with *cogito*. Thought is not an attribute of the thinking substance; it is an attribute of *humanity*. (Rancière, 1987, 35–6; cf. Van de Weyer, 1822, 23)

Jacotot, for Rancière, turns Cartesian thought around twice. Jacotot's Cartesian egalitarianism privileges the supposition of equality that begins the *Discourse on the Method*: given that reason is equally distributed to all, each meditator thinks. Hence there is no hierarchy of intelligences, and each human activity 'is the practice of the same intellectual potential' (1987, 36). In addition, the equation of 'man' and '*cogito*' is telling. As we know, after the *cogito* is demonstrated in the 'Second Meditation', Descartes rejects the inference that the *cogito* is a 'man' or 'rational animal' (VII: 25-6). As much as this equation might upset Descartes, Rancière or Jacotot are not interested in metaphysical disputations. Instead, they aim through philosophical misunderstanding to underline the importance of the Cartesian supposition of equality: to say '*ego sum, ego existo*' is the initiation of a new field of experience for speaking beings, rather than one step in an orderly method. Method, Rancière argues, is one way to restrain the equality of intelligences, by ranking the capacity for inquiry by setting out a series of steps that must be duplicated, lest the student go astray. Recall that in the 'Fourth Meditation', Descartes argues that the will is the cause of error because its powers extend beyond those of the understanding, but by restraining the will to clear and distinct knowledge – built upon the order of method – it is possible to avoid error. By contrast, Jacotot argues that intellect without will is the cause of error, because willing is the activity that engages us with the world and with others (Rancière, 1987, 54–5). Jacotot's second formulation of Descartes's principle underlines the practical interpretation of the *cogito* over an epistemological interpretation:

> Descartes said: to think is to live; I exist, I am man, therefore I think. Yes, all men think, all men feel [*sent*]; but not all men know how to express their thoughts, nor communicate their sentiments [*sentiments*] ... But to feel is nothing, to think is nothing, if we do not know how to express our thinking. (in Van de Weyer, 1822, 25)

Descartes, who relies on an orderly method, can bracket this engagement with the world and build an epistemological system of truth, while for Jacotot, the subject is thrown immediately into a social situation where intellectual equality and good sense must engage a variety of activities by which 'we direct our thoughts along different paths and do not attend to the same things' (Descartes, VI: 2), which requires the will to direct the attention of the intellect. Thus Jacotot and Rancière introduce a second turn of Cartesian thought by rejecting the structured order of reasons of method.

Following Jacotot, Rancière argues that once the supposition of equality is accepted, emancipation can begin from anything that individuals have in common. For Rancière, this supposition is not just a concern of pedagogy, but of politics itself. To underline the Cartesian import of this supposition, let us look at another intellectual source for his concept of a wrong. It is without doubt that this concept of a wrong is in part derived from the young Marx's account of the proletariat: the proletariat has a universal character because its revolution marks the dissolution of all classes when it overthrows the bourgeoisie which has perpetrated an 'unqualified wrong' in its oppression of all other classes (Marx, 1844, 38; cf. Rancière, 1995, 18). Yet there is a tendency within Marxism that subordinates all other 'particular wrongs' experienced by others (such as those experienced by women or by the colonized) to the historico-teleological mission of the proletariat, and this tendency is explicitly rejected by Cartesian egalitarians such as Beauvoir or Rancière, who argue that *emancipatory* struggles cannot be subordinated to one another, but must be reinforced through solidarity, by whatever they have in common.

A Marxist analysis would certainly note that Cartesianism in general stakes its validity on an individual's perception of the social world and an individual's practice. Rancière – like Beauvoir before him – sees the limitations of individualism, and that is why he transforms the subjective *ego sum, ego existo* into the reciprocity of the *nos sumus, nos existimus*, with the latter designating a new field of collective political practice. *How* Rancière conceptualizes collective political practices is the focus of the next chapter. Thus let us conclude by underlining that the Cartesian 'prototype' has two positive aspects. First, like Marx, Poullain and Beauvoir conceptualize politics as the processing of a wrong. But second, and in contrast to the teleological tendencies of Marxism, there is no privileged subject, no finality that drives history, but only the persistently renewed struggle against all forms of social inequality. Emancipation is not an end point of a historical continuum. Instead, emancipation is only possible through the efforts of those who combat inequality and oppression through practices of reciprocity and solidarity. In this sense, Rancière is a Cartesian egalitarian.

Notes

1   Giuseppina Mecchia argues that 'one could easily say that according to the classics' that politics is not 'rooted in the equality of speech but … in the hierarchical ordering of the *oikia* or household' (2009: 75). I do not think it so easy; even if the household is discussed before the definition of what the city shares in common, Aristotle nevertheless argues that the city 'is by nature clearly prior to the household [*oikia*] and to the individual, since the whole is of necessity prior to the part' (1253a19–20tm).
2   The phrasing of this point was developed in dialogue with Jason M. Wirth, who gave a commentary on an earlier draft of what has become Chapter 2.
3   For accounts of the relationship between Cartesianism, egalitarianism and feminism, see Atherton 1993, Harth 1992, Rodis-Lewis 1990, 169–80, and with

discussions of Poullain's predecessors, Delon 1978 and Stuurman 2004, 52–86. Atherton argues that seventeenth-century feminism was motivated in part by 'the concept of reason that could be found in Descartes' rather than, as later feminism would be, by 'any general beliefs about equal human rights' (Atherton, 1993, 20).

4 Heidegger claims that 'Descartes does not doubt because he is a skeptic; rather, he must become a doubter because he posits the mathematical as the absolute ground and seeks for all knowledge a foundation', that is, the *cogito*, 'that will be in accord with it' (1962, 103).

5 Badiou argues that a Marxism 'sutured' to the scientific condition of philosophy (read: Althusser) dovetails theoretically with Heidegger when it reduces the subject to 'a simple operator of bourgeois ideology'. The scientific Marxist, then, would say: 'for Heidegger, "subject" is a secondary elaboration of the reign of technology, but we can see eye to eye if this reign is in fact also the bourgeoisie's' (1989, 92). It should be noted that Negri is more ambivalent than Badiou's typical 'scientific Marxist'; he seems to admire the revolutionary character of Descartes's thought even if he reproaches what he sees as its fundamental compromise.

6 Later in the *Discourse*, Descartes writes: 'I have recognized through my travels that those with views quite contrary to ours are not on that account barbarians or savages, but that many of them make use of reason as much or more than we do' (VI: 16).

7 Aimé Césaire, in his *Discourse on Colonialism*, invokes the principles of Cartesianism against the false universality of the colonial legacy (its science, politics, and sociology), which denigrates the non-European to the benefit and 'glory' of Western bourgeois society. He argues that 'the psychologists, sociologists *et al.*, their views on "primitivism", their rigged investigations, their self-serving generalizations, their tendentious speculations, their insistence on the marginal, "separate" character of non-whites', rest on 'their barbaric repudiation, for the sake of the cause, of Descartes's statement, the charter of universalism, that "reason … is found whole and entire in each man", and that "where individuals of the same species are concerned, there may be degrees in respect of their accidental qualities, but not in respect of their forms, or natures"' (1955, 56).

8 This egalitarianism would also be troubled by the exclusion of the figure of madness from the valid and considered reasons for doubt. Even Descartes's correction of Arnauld – the reason of madmen is not 'extinguished' but 'disturbed' (VII: 228) – will not ameliorate this exclusion (see Foucault, 1972).

9 This name is derived from a passage in Descartes's letter to Hyperaspistes, dated August 1641, where he states that if an infant's mind were 'released from the prison of the body', it would discover innate ideas within it (III: 424).

10 Descartes's conjectures on the 'prison of the body' are especially problematic given that they are not sustained by his *Passions of the Soul*.

11 See also Descartes's letter to Voetius, dated May 1643, where he contrasts the use of reason for 'education' with scholastic 'learning', through which students 'lose the use of their natural reason and put in its place an artificial and sophistical reason' (VIIIb: 43).
12 Harth discusses responses to Descartes from several now neglected seventeenth-century *cartésiennes*: Anne de la Vigne, Marie Dupré and Catherine Descartes (niece of René), as well as Princess Elisabeth of Bohemia (1992, 64–106).
13 Not to mention the Platonic gestures of Philo and Augustine. On this point see Lloyd, 1993, 18–37.
14 Note that this claim echoes Descartes's critique of scholastic artifice and, intentionally or not, suggests the 'gallantry' that Poullain derides elsewhere (1673, 49; see also 69–72 for other passages that suggest a gallant discourse).
15 The editors source Aristotle's claim to *Generation of Animals*, 737a27-8. The claim that women are imperfect men is attributed by Poullain to Philo, and by Beauvoir to Aquinas (1949, 5/1: 15).
16 Again, see Harth 1992, 64–106.
17 See Poullain, 1674, 227. Stuurman argues that the *Passions of the Soul* 'gives us only a physiological explanation and a general taxonomy of the passions. The theory cannot explain why particular people are more strongly affected by some passions than by others' (2004, 87–8).
18 It is also interesting to note that during his reconstruction of the Cartesian system in his *On the Education of Ladies*, Poullain follows the proof for the existence of the *cogito* with a proof for the existence of the body: 'I concluded just now that I exist, I who think, because I act. There being a thing from which I cannot be separated which brings me pleasure and pain without any contribution on my part, and sometimes even despite myself, then this thing that I call my body must really exist' (1674, 178).
19 This democracy of judgement, according to Sartre, also underlies the democracy of 'universal suffrage' (1947, 505).
20 It is the subject's relation toward others that gives content to freedom: the subject 'can will itself only by destining itself to an open future, by seeking to extend itself by means of the freedom of others. Therefore, in any case, the freedom of other men must be respected and they must be helped to free themselves. Such a law imposes limits upon action and at the same time immediately gives it content' (Beauvoir, 1947, 60). Note that 'helping' others, as it were, must take place through reciprocal engagement rather than through an intervention from the outside of their respective projects (see 1947, 88–9, and Beauvoir's comments on charity at 1947, 86).
21 For Beauvoir, childhood plays a crucial role in the habituation of social roles, values and prejudices. In *The Ethics of Ambiguity*, she writes that 'Man's

unhappiness, says Descartes, is due to his having first been a child' (1947, 35), but her reading of Descartes in this respect bears more similarities to Poullain, who challenged the reification and 'inevitability' of social convention, than to Descartes, who wavered between faulting as the origin of prejudice and habit either social reification or the natural composition of the body itself. In *The Second Sex*, Beauvoir criticizes both the Freudian determination of penis envy from an anatomical lack (1949, 287/2: 18) and (implicitly) Sartre's bizarre claim that a woman's existence 'in the form of a hole' is first grasped in the infant's 'ontological presentiment' of sexuality (Sartre, 1943, 782/660), because childhood must also be historically situated.

22 Toril Moi coins the term 'patriarchal femininity' to refer to feminine qualities as defined by patriarchal societies (1994, 192).
23 In another gesture that opposes ancient Greek political philosophy to Cartesian egalitarianism, Rancière argues that the 'Socratic method is ... a perfected form of stultification' (1987, 29).

2

The Nothingness of Equality: Rancière's 'Sartrean Existentialism'

2.1. Marked by Sartrean existentialism

We have established, thus far, the Cartesian egalitarianism of Jacques Rancière. This commits him to an egalitarian concept of subjectivity without entailing adherence to other Cartesian principles, such as the often criticized dualism that splits thinking substance from extended substance. That is to say that Rancière maintains the principle of intellectual equality, the good sense supposed at the outset of the *Discourse on the Method*, without committing to Descartes's metaphysics. Rancière appropriates this supposition of good sense from Descartes, though, as we might say, he directs it along different paths.

In this chapter, I will examine how Rancière develops a dynamic and collective account of egalitarian subjectivity through a critique of the work of Jean-Paul Sartre. I will argue that reading him with and against Sartre contributes to delineating Rancière's concept of political subjectivity, which emerges as a collective subject, a *'nos sumus, nos existimus,'* in opposition to policing. Whereas the standpoint of Cartesian egalitarianism begins with the individual and her relations to other individuals through forms of reciprocity and solidarity, Rancière's politics of equality – especially as it is outlined in his landmark text, *Disagreement* – begins with the disruptive and irruptive power of a collective subject, a people, a *demos*.

Initially, it might seem that Rancière's egalitarianism and Sartre's existentialism – even with their respective commitments toward outlining an account of political subjectivity – have very few features in common. In his most extensive engagement with Sartre in *The Philosopher and His Poor*, Rancière concludes that Sartre reaffirms the Platonic injunction that each member of society must remain in a place where he or she must stay.[1] In particular, he finds that Sartre persistently claims that workers' fatigue, lack of time, and frustrations with the mute solidity of the practico-inert are obstacles to the formation of an active group out of their seriality. The problems of fatigue and lack of free time could point to the possibility of a critique of leisure time and the imposition of work under capitalism, but Rancière interprets Sartre's iteration of this critique as the rejection of 'the elastic intervals of autodidact freedom...in the disoriented space of pathways and dead ends where people searched not long ago for what rebellious workers and dreamers called "emancipation"' (Rancière, 1983, 147). Consequently, these obstacles of the practico-inert prevent workers' self-organization and necessitate an external *puissance*, an external activity or power, to catalyze the passive masses. The philosopher of freedom and 'continuous creation' requires, on Rancière's account, a historical vanguard such as the party to forge the goals to be realized by mass politics. This verdict echoes that of *Black Skin, White Masks*, where Frantz Fanon argues that Sartre betrays his own principles when, in 'Black Orpheus' (1948a), he considers African struggle a tributary of the proletariat's, as if the 'historic chance' of black struggle is a meaning already there to be taken up, rather than self-created and self-organized in lived praxis, when he forgets 'that consciousness needs to get lost in the night of the absolute, the only condition for attaining self-consciousness' (Fanon, 1952, 112).

Just as this is not Fanon's last word on Sartre, neither is it Rancière's. More recently, in several interviews and short texts, Rancière has made reference to Sartre's work while summarizing his basic philosophical commitments.[2] These comments reveal Rancière's engagement with not only the later, political (that is, Marxist and anti-colonial) works such as the first volume of the *Critique of Dialectical Reason* (1960; hereafter referred to as the *Critique*), but also the earlier, existentialist-phenomenological philosophy of *Being and Nothingness* (1943). Admittedly, Rancière's comments are both retrospective and schematic, but they are, I will argue, nonetheless instructive. They provide an impetus to reconsider Sartre's work – from *Being and Nothingness* to the *Critique* – in light of Rancière's politics of equality. This reconsideration is in order for two reasons. First, both Sartre and Rancière propose accounts of emancipatory political subjectivation in which subjective praxis emerges as a radical break with a given set of oppressive and exploitative social relations. Just as Rancière argues that politics is heterogeneous to policing, for Sartre, the free activity of praxis is absolutely opposed to the passive and alienated experience of the practico-inert – as he writes, 'the free development of a praxis can only be total or totally alienated' (Sartre, 1960, 395). This common emphasis on the *subjective* aspect of praxis distinguishes Sartre and Rancière from many of the more prominent poststructuralists, including those who work within post-Heideggerian French thought (Jean-Luc Nancy and Giorgio Agamben), Michel Foucault, and the 'Spinozism' of Gilles Deleuze and Antonio Negri.[3] Establishing Rancière's relationship to Sartre could, then, contribute to our understanding of their differences with these poststructuralist thinkers.

Nonetheless, there are important differences between Sartre's and Rancière's accounts of political praxis. Before discussing these differences, it is important to underline the second reason for reconsidering Sartre's influence on Rancière: both conceptualize identity as a function or operation of oppressive or exploitative social relations, and thus, for both Rancière and Sartre (in both the *Critique* and *Being and Nothingness*), political praxis involves a disidentification with one's previous identifications and interests. In terms of the organization of this chapter, after outlining Rancière's egalitarian politics (in Section 2.2), I will contrapose Rancière's criticisms of Sartre's philosophy to Sartre's critique of the seriality of identification, and then proceed to a reading of *Being and Nothingness*. Let us look first at the *Critique*. There, Sartre argues that identity is a serial classification of massified individuals, meaning that identity is an 'abstract generality' that characterizes individuals in their exteriority and separation (Sartre, 1960, 260). For Rancière, identity functions as a categorization of classes, groups, and occupations within a regime of policing. For both thinkers, politics involves a radical rupture with these established identities; as Rancière writes, echoing Marx: if classification is a crucial function of policing, politics is 'the dissolution of all classes' (Rancière, 1995, 18/39).

An important difference between Sartre and Rancière turns on how they conceptualize disidentification. Rancière, in *Disagreement*, thinks politics as a paradoxical and non-instrumental praxis, an activity with neither end nor interest other than the disruptive and transformative effects of the supposition of equality, by which he means 'the open set of practices driven by the assumption of equality between any and every speaking being and by the concern to test this equality' (Rancière, 1995, 30/53). In this sense, Rancière's account is consistent with his earlier criticisms of Sartre found in *The Philosopher and His Poor*, where he argues that Sartre's account of activity results in the hyper-instrumentalization of praxis: 'if the world's matter is to bear the history of liberation, it must be traversed entirely by technique' (Rancière, 1983, 155). Freedom becomes a 'super technique,' always turned to an ultimate end that forecloses on the intervals of autodidactic freedom that structure, on Rancière's account, emancipatory politics. This hyper-instrumentalized praxis never escapes from either internal or external exigencies – whether Sartre is discussing the exigencies of the practico-inert, the pledged group, the organization, or ultimately, the party (1983, 140, 154).[4] Rancière's critique of Sartre turns on locating that point in revolutionary struggle that is, properly speaking, emancipatory. In short, he argues that Sartre's dialectic of politics emphasizes the emergence of stability, organization, and the totalization of free praxis rather than that moment of disruptive emancipatory power. Therefore, Rancière's politics of equality maintains the *collective* aspect of Sartre's political subjectivity while rejecting its dialectic.

After examining Rancière's reading of the *Critique*, we will turn to Sartre's critique of identity found in *Being and Nothingness*. To my knowledge, Rancière's only references to *Being and Nothingness* are at best oblique and cursory. Given that it establishes the tenets of Sartre's existentialism – when Sartre considered existentialism a philosophy and not merely an ideology (Sartre, 1957b, 8) – it must be the work to which Rancière refers when, in response to a question about identity politics posed to him during an interview with the Quebecois journal *Possibles* in 1999, he states that 'I must have been marked during my youth by Sartrean existentialism, meaning that every identity locks us into a role' (Rancière, 1999, 105). Years later, he reiterates his youthful 'Sartrean existentialism' when he recalls that his 'own rejection of identitarian fixations (*fixations identitaires*) was first satisfied in Sartrian [sic] freedom, its rejection of fixed identities, and the opposition it establishes to Being of doing things and making oneself' (2012b, 207). Though Rancière does not provide the following examples, these brief remarks conjure, to a reader familiar with Sartre, the characters exemplifying the 'Patterns of Bad Faith' in *Being and Nothingness*, such as the man who while labouring with the 'typical gestures' of the café waiter is never closer to this role than an actor to Hamlet (Sartre, 1943, 103/95). Or, take the example of the woman on a date who refuses to see the double entendres of her suitor's advances. She engages in a denial of a network of significance within – as we will know better after Simone de Beauvoir's *The Second Sex* – a woman's situation.[5] Words and bodies are treated as they *are*: his words are then only addressed to her personality, her intellect and her 'full freedom'; her actions aim to be 'what is respectful and discreet in the attitude of her companion,' and her hand in his, when he makes his move, is 'divorced' from her intellect and treated by her as an inert thing rather than a gesture towards an amorous decision (Sartre, 1943, 96/90).

And yet isn't comparing this woman and this waiter-actor with the highly politicized examples cited by Rancière discordant? What does the waiter have to do with Auguste Blanqui, who, when asked to state his profession by a court magistrate during his trial in 1832, professes that he is a proletarian? What does the woman on the date have to do with Olympe de Gouges, who, to challenge the distinctions of public and private space that exclude women from collective social practices, declares that the woman who has the right to mount the scaffold 'must equally have the right to mount the rostrum' (de Gouges, 1791, 91; Rancière, 2005b, 60)? What relationship can there be between *Being and Nothingness*, that distended manual on the courage to walk the narrow paths of freedom in a world of bad faith, absurdity, and failure, and the work of Rancière, who places the equality of intelligences and abilities at the heart of an insurgent politics that challenges the contingency of the regimes of representation that police ways of doing, being, and speaking? One might object that Rancière's suggestion that he must have been marked by Sartrean existentialism is made in jest.[6]

Let us look again at the objections leveled at Sartre by Fanon and Rancière. They are based on the fact that, in certain cases, Sartre does not pursue the consequences of existentialism – that workers or Africans are considered as they *are*, rather than as subjects oriented toward a free or emancipatory project. Through collective practices, a people is thrown into a situation in which it must be what it is not and not be what it is. In this phrasing, I have deliberately echoed Sartre's description of consciousness: that it 'must necessarily be what it is not and not be what it is' (Sartre, 1943, 120/110). This describes a dynamic through which consciousness surpasses its facticity through transcendence. The patterns of bad faith are modes of avoiding the consequences of freedom by reifying either transcendence or facticity. As Sartre states,

> bad faith seeks to affirm their identity [that of transcendence and facticity] while preserving their differences. It must affirm facticity as *being* transcendence and transcendence as *being* facticity, in such a way that at the instant when a person apprehends the one, he can find himself abruptly faced with the other. (Sartre, 1943, 98/91)

The man who plays at being a waiter who *is* his facticity is confronted by transcendence as if it comes from without, while the woman who *is* her transcendence is confronted by her facticity (her embodiment) from without. With this in mind, we can return to Fanon's and Rancière's objections to Sartre – that workers or Africans are treated according to their facticity by Sartre (that is, workers *are* their fatigue, Negritude *is* its particularity), meaning their free project comes from without, from either the party or the proletariat.[7]

After addressing Rancière's critique of Sartre, I will propose a constructive reading of Sartre and Rancière that sheds a new light on both of their respective projects.[8] On the one hand, Rancière's appropriation of Sartre's *Being and*

Nothingness in his politics of equality can contribute to a reading of Sartre that reconstructs his project in terms of freedom and equality rather than that of authenticity. On the other hand, reading Sartre's work will accent how Rancière's egalitarianism utilizes the concepts of freedom, contingency and facticity. Most importantly, Sartre's account of consciousness demonstrates that subjectivation is a dynamic and not a mode of identification – precisely as Rancière argues when he claims that politics is a dynamic of subjectivation that constitutes new ways of speaking, being and doing. To this end, in Section 2.4, I will read *Being and Nothingness* with a focus on the relationships between freedom, contingency, and facticity, using Sartre to demonstrate the importance of these concepts for Rancière's egalitarianism. I will conclude, in Section 2.5, that Rancière's claim that politics involves an 'impossible identification' is proposed as an alternative to Sartre's account of praxis. In short, Rancière's paradoxical politics involves a political subjectivation that undermines previous identities by momentarily identifying with a part of society that has no part, with this dynamic introducing new and more egalitarian ways of speaking, being, and doing into a given set of social relations.

2.2. The politics of equality

In *Disagreement*, Rancière contends that politics is a practice of equality. Whereas most forms of political philosophy consider equality as a problem of institutional guarantees, Rancière proposes that we must think equality as a practice of politics, as a transitory project that rests on the supposition of the equality of intelligences and abilities of anyone and everyone, rather than as a problem of entitlements. Todd May characterizes the difference between Rancière's egalitarianism and mainstream political theories of equality as a difference between 'active equality' and 'passive equality.' He argues that the discussions of mainstream Anglo-American political philosophy are limited to questions concerning 'passive equality': 'the creation, preservation, or protection of equality by governmental institutions' (May, 2008, 3). This institutional or distributive concept of equality, May notes, can be situated within what Rancière considers to be policing. By contrast, Rancière's politics involves the activation or declaration of equality; 'active equality' is a practice of dissensus premised on the equality of intelligences that (1) declassifies the presumed organization of roles and occupations within a regime of policing by (2) declaring that each of us 'possesses the quality of being able to consider and act upon our world in such a way as to create a life that has significance for us' (May, 2008, 57). Like May, I do not want to suggest that institutional correctives to inequalities of wealth, access, and rights do not have their place in social practices, as many of these 'correctives' are concessions won through mass social struggle. But, following Rancière (among other radical thinkers), I think it is clear that distributive efforts cannot address the inequalities that structure their political foundations. To reduce equality to a problem of entitlements concedes the foundational inequalities that perpetuate the very problems that these institutional corrections attempt to redress.

How, then, do we think equality outside of the parameters of institutions and entitlements? Rancière proposes that equality is *the* constitutive problem of politics. On the one hand, all social relations, all inequalities, are predicated on the supposition of equality – even in situations of domination, the dominated are still able to understand how they are dominated. People must be equal as speaking beings for some to command and others to obey.[9] It is worth noting, however, that theoretically speaking, the hegemonic political philosophies of these social relations – of policing – seek either to naturalize these inequalities or demonstrate their necessity, to show how the practical supposition of the equality of intelligences and abilities does not signal inclusion within the community. Recall Fanon's discussion of the way that colonialism destroys the history of the colonized in order to convince them that they *need* the colonizers, hammering 'into the heads of the indigenous population that if the colonist were to leave they would regress into barbarism, degradation, and bestiality' (Fanon, 1961, 149).

In classical political philosophy, Rancière argues, the necessity or nature of inequality is signified by the difference between speech (the use of *logos*) and voice (the expression of pleasure and pain). The distinction turns on the possession of *logos* rather than merely its comprehension. In articulating the differences between humans, slaves, and animals, Aristotle states that, as Rancière translates it, the 'slave is the one who participates in the community of language under the form of comprehension (*aisthesis*), not [under the form of] possession (*hexis*)' (Rancière, 1995, 17tm/38; Aristotle, 1254b20–21). Or, take Plato, who distinguishes between the *logos* of the philosopher and the *doxa* of the *demos* who can be so easily swayed by sophists or by poets (Rancière, 1995, 10/29; 1983, 46). In sum, Rancière argues that these political philosophies seek to find a principle or *arkhê* proper to the community, a principle that also works to deny politics, which occurs in the intersection of two opposed logics: police logic and egalitarian logic.

When Rancière distinguishes between political activity and what he calls a regime of policing, he explicitly points out that the choice of the term policing is non-pejorative, and he uses it to designate systems or social mechanisms that distribute roles and activities within a given set of social relations or a given distribution of the sensible. Thus, as I mentioned in the Introduction, techniques of policing are more extensive than those assigned to a police force or penal system. Rancière also argues that policing should not be considered as a state apparatus. To speak of a state apparatus, he argues, whether it is an ideological state apparatus or a repressive state apparatus as conceptualized by Althusser, presupposes an opposition between state and society in which state apparatuses impose or command order from above society (not to mention that for Althusser the subject is 'always-already' interpellated by ideological state apparatuses, which forecloses on the possibility of what Rancière calls political subjectivation – though 'science,' for Althusser, is outside of ideology) (Althusser, 1970, 175). Instead, Rancière's account recognizes that the policing of roles can be implemented or distributed in relatively fluid social relations, just as the destructive power of capital, through which 'all that is solid melts into air,' nevertheless maintains varying degrees of social stability in order to function – such as that particular unfreedom of the worker to sell her labour freely. Police logic, then, configures occupations, identities, and systems of legitimation, and organizes speaking beings according to differences while at the same time representing them as natural. Police logic is not political; instead, it is the denial of politics, insofar as it attempts to naturalize a contingent order and reduce antagonism to administration. This logic counts and orders all parts of society according to some measure or proportion, but Rancière argues that policing excludes the possibility that this count is premised on a fundamental miscount that denies that there could be a part of society with no part. Rancière names the logic of the 'part of those who have no part,' the logic of equality.

Egalitarian logic is the way that a collective challenges the distribution of roles and identities in society, the way that collective practice demonstrates the contingency of all regimes of inequalities. Rancière refuses the idea that there is one principle of the rationality (*logos*) of community. Instead, politics plays out at the intersection of two logics. Politics is the 'activation' (in May's words) of the principle of equality against the hierarchical organization of policing, a practice of disidentifying with the typical roles and representations that regulate social life.[10] Egalitarian logic challenges the social relations that produce these inequalities by initiating 'polemical situations' that contest how 'one of the partners [that is, the police] of the interlocution refuses to recognize one of its features (its place, its object, its subjects)' (Rancière, 1995, 56/86). Every activation of egalitarian logic then opens the political antagonism whereby the part of those who have no part contest the police order in the name of equality.

For a concrete example of such a polemical situation, we will return to the trial of Auguste Blanqui. Rancière writes:

> Asked by the magistrate to give his profession, Blanqui simply replies: 'proletarian.' The magistrate immediately objects to this response: 'That is not a profession,' thereby setting himself up for copping the accused's immediate response: 'It is the profession of thirty million Frenchmen who live off their labor and who are deprived of political rights.' The judge then agrees to have the court clerk list proletarian as a new 'profession.' (Rancière, 1995, 37/62)

Blanqui thus names a subject of a wrong, the proletariat, through subverting the accepted meaning of the word 'profession': while for the prosecutor 'profession' means a job or trade, for Blanqui it names 'a profession of faith, a declaration of membership of a collective' (Rancière, 1995, 38/62). Here, for Rancière, the proletariat is not a substantial class. To profess to being a proletarian names a wrong: that workers have been counted only as those with jobs or trades and not as equals of those who are not deprived of political agency or rights. On Rancière's account, Blanqui's testimony stages or activates the politics of dissensus (on the 'staging' of politics in Rancière, see Hallward, 2009). Blanqui's claim is not merely for juridical recognition; this moment of dissensus, as Oliver Davis notes, 'cannot be resolved by legal means alone, even if the law and statements of equality enshrined within it sometimes have a role to play' (Davis, 2010, 83). The disagreement between Blanqui and the magistrate stages the disjunction between the interests of a particular social group and political agency. There is a disjunction between being a worker (a sociological category) and enacting a form of political agency that aims to disrupt and dissolve these categories or identifications. Within the police logic, that a 'worker's *having a part* is strictly defined by the remuneration of his work' defines the workplace as a private domain not regulated by the functions of the public domain (Rancière, 1995, 29/52). Proletarian struggle attempts to transform the ways of work, to make of them collective practices rather than private transactions. The activation of egalitarian logic, then, opens new ways of speaking, being and doing. The part of those with no part are not purely excluded from the police order, but miscounted as being what they *are* (counted, for instance, as workers), not counted as equal participants in social life.

2.3. Between the practico-inert and the party

Rancière argues that the dynamic of political subjectivation begins when subjects disidentify with the roles, occupations and places assigned to them by the apparatuses of policing. While he acknowledges Foucault's influence on his concept of policing, I think a stronger case can be made for Sartre's. On the one hand, Rancière notes that while Foucault 'was never drawn theoretically to the question of political subjectivation' (Rancière, 2000, 93), Sartre attempts to explain how the practical activity of the individual, as it takes place within the field of the practico-inert, serves to reproduce the conditions of her exploitation *and* how the dynamic of the subjectivation of free praxis emerges out of these conditions.[11] On the other hand, Sartre characterizes identity as a form of seriality, just as Rancière argues that identity is a function of policing. Rather than conceptualizing identity as a constitutive moment of subjectivity (whether identity is conceived in metaphysical terms as the subject's substance or practically as the self-recognition of the self's practical activity), both argue that identity is an abstract generality or role assumed within an inert or reified set of social relations – the conditions of exploitation and domination of either the practico-inert or a regime of policing. Therefore, if identity is a feature of an exploitative and inegalitarian set of social relations, political praxis must pose a radical break with these relations through a process of disidentification.

Seriality, identity and interests – in Sartre's terms, exigencies – are all structures of what he calls the practico-inert. These structures arise as a response to scarcity, which, he argues, makes praxis intelligible. Human praxis, Sartre contends, is a negation of scarcity. In its basic form, scarcity is 'the contingent but fundamental relation of man to Nature,' but it is also a mediating relation of determinate historical and material conditions (Sartre, 1960, 260).[12] While human praxis is an attempt to negate the fundamental form of scarcity, it often produces and reproduces historical forms of scarcity: advanced capitalist countries, for example, have until recently generally minimized the effects of environmental scarcities within their borders while producing massive inequalities in wealth between the rich and the poor within and without. At a basic level, Sartre argues that all praxis is an attempt to transform the world by negating the needs arising from scarcity. However, in many cases, the means to overcoming scarcity are determined by the structures of the practico-inert, meaning that these means coerce the individual into reproducing the conditions of her exploitation or domination.

I say *coerce* because Sartre argues that individual praxis is, at the outset, constrained by a set of what he calls exigencies, which arise from the structures of the practico-inert field. To state the problem in Marx's terms from the *Economic and Philosophic Manuscripts*, the worker needs to negate her basic needs, and is thus forced to enter into social relations that dispossess her of her free praxis. An exigency is precisely a demand which arises on the basis of the possibilities of the practico-inert which takes on the character of a 'categorical imperative' without interiority (thus this imperative is far from Kant's concept of the categorical imperative), forced on the individual by the situation: 'the basic form of exigency lies in the inert expectation on the part of the instrument or material, designating the worker as the Other who is expected to do certain things' (1960, 187; 188). The individual's praxis is determined by the inertia of worked matter and by the inertia of others, but it is also important to underline that she enters into these practico-inert relations as an other, that is, her role is identified according to its 'abstract generality' and interchangeability.[13] More specifically, the interests of the worker are produced by structures of seriality – her interest 'is merely a specific form of exigency' (1960, 197).

Sartre attacks the view of classical economics that individual interests – even if they happen to be identical to the interests of other individuals – precede sociality. By contrast, Sartre argues that 'classical economics tried to define identical interests as if they existed equally in every individual member of a group, and it did not take account of the fact that this very identity was the result of a serial process' (1960, 205). On Sartre's account, identity is not self-identity, the interiority of a subject or individual; instead, identity designates the exteriority and interchangeability of an individual within a serial gathering. The place of an individual, for instance, in a queue, is determined by an arbitrary factor, such as the number on a ticket, rather than according to any 'intrinsic qualities' (1960, 261) of the individual. In a sense, a place in a line *is occupied* by an individual more than an individual *occupies* a place in a line. In other words, a common interest produces a 'practico-inert unity' in a gathering that is nevertheless not oriented, as it would be in a group, by common praxis or project. Instead, seriality is organized by material exigencies. Sartre gives the example of the nineteenth century capitalist who – insofar as he has taken on a role, as he 'is *already* his factory' – is led to automate parts of his factory: the capitalist's decisions are imposed by market factors such as competition with other capitalists, so what appears to be his interest is that of all other capitalists ('the interests of Others') as determined by material social structures (technical capacities, profit rates, worker unrest) (1960, 200–201). Likewise, in order to gain sustenance in a capitalist society, the worker must sell her labour-power as a commodity whose value is determined by the rate of socially necessary labour more than an individual's particular skill set; as Marx states, the 'value of labour-power is determined, as in the case of every other commodity, by the labour-time necessary for the production, and consequently also the reproduction, of this specific article' (Marx, 1867, 274). The value of labour-power is not determined by an individual's needs or abilities, but rather the average compensation required for the upkeep of the worker (see also Sartre, 1960, 207).[14] As Sartre argues, exigencies and interests work as negative pressures or constraints on individual projects – barring, until the emergence of group activity, the possibilities of free praxis. He writes: 'Being-outside-oneself as worked materiality therefore unites under the name of interest, individuals and groups by negation, always other and always identical, of each by all and of all by each' (1960, 202). Far from a form of group praxis, 'of each by all and of all by each' signals the formation of identity through exteriority and separation.

For both Sartre and Rancière, identification is a function of oppressive social relations, whether we call these relations policing or the practico-inert. The key political and philosophical problem, then, is formulating a praxis of disidentification. Rancière maintains that:

> Political activity is whatever shifts a body from the place assigned to it or changes a place's destination. It makes visible what had no business being seen, and makes heard a discourse where once there was only place for noise; it makes understood as discourse what was once only heard as noise. (Rancière, 1995, 30/53)

Politics is a moment of dissensus whereby the supposition of equality interrupts a given social order and demonstrates the contingency of the distribution of roles. In his short essay 'The Cause of the Other,' Rancière reiterates his concept of political praxis in terms similar to Sartre's account of seriality: political subjectivation breaks with the 'identity of the other' assigned to an individual by techniques of policing (Rancière, 1997, 32; see Section 2.5). Politics, then, is a disruption of how ways of being, speaking, or doing are distributed, counted, or identified – in a manner similar to the disruption of seriality and the practico-inert by group praxis. However, while both Sartre and Rancière conceptualize political subjectivation as a dynamic of disidentification, significant differences between them remain.

In *The Philosopher and His Poor*, Rancière contends that Sartre, despite his delineation of the various oppressive structures of the practico-inert, reinforces the distinction between those whose activity it is to think and those whose activity it is to work. Rancière reads Sartre's distinctions between activity and passivity and interiority and exteriority (the group is active interiority while seriality is passive exteriority) in light of Marxist distinctions between the roles of the intellectual and the party and the roles of the workers. Therefore, Rancière focuses on Sartre's thematization of workers' fatigue. Rancière argues that Sartre's account of fatigue slips from describing the situation of the workers to describing their being. In the terms of *Being and Nothingness*, Sartre identifies workers according to their facticity – they *are* their fatigue. Although, of course, he intends the following as a description of a situation that is to be surpassed by free praxis, Sartre comments that '*fatigue is being* in so far as it is distinct from knowledge and from praxis' (1960, 335). This distinction, for Rancière, reiterates the distinction between the party (the organization of knowledge and praxis) and workers, who are, like the practico-inert, passive matter to be transformed by praxis. Thus, on Rancière's account, Sartre precludes any possibility of workers' autonomous free praxis; they are, in effect, trapped between the passivity of the practico-inert and the activity of the party.

For Rancière, this point is illustrated by Sartre's account of 'the manifestation *par excellence* for revolutionary reminiscence – the storming of the Bastille,' which, in the *Critique*, is the paradigmatic moment when the practico-inert is liquidated by group activity (Rancière, 1983, 149). How Sartre interprets this moment of collective, emancipatory practice is, for Rancière, emblematic of the project of the *Critique*. From Rancière's perspective, one could search out how the praxis of the 'poor' produced an event that was unprecedented, and, while acknowledging its transitory temporality, trace its transformative effects on social life, how the 'Bastille' becomes a watchword – or even homonym – for emancipatory struggle. This would be to treat the storming of the Bastille as, in Rancière's terms, a political event. However, as Rancière argues, for Sartre, at this point in revolutionary praxis, the unity of the group in the Parisian crowd is constituted from without, and thus free, self-determined, revolutionary politics comes later. Rancière does not object that political praxis derives its tactics and strategies from its given situation, but rather he rejects Sartre's emphasis on the emergence of this praxis as a negation of – a reaction to – the royal decrees; that is, he rejects the idea that the 'poor' can only take the impetus for praxis from the outside. Sartre even suggests that the revolutionary group was 'alienated' into praxis: 'the political praxis of the government alienated the passive reactions of seriality to its own practical freedom' (Sartre, 1960, 355). Here, Rancière contends that Sartre's work dovetails with Marxist metapolitics:

the 'essential is already given. The power of royal praxis through which the group comes to be is of the very same nature as the power of worked matter or the power of the pure communist act;' each is a power over a proletariat that can never completely work out its passivity and alienation (Rancière, 1983, 150). The significance of the storming of the Bastille, of the unprecedented liquidation of practico-inert structures by practices of freedom, is constituted from without: Sartre's Parisian mob derives its impetus from the threat of royal decrees, and its revolutionary potential can be preserved from the threat of dispersion only by the exigencies of self-organization and hierarchization – which, Rancière argues, ultimately means the exigencies of the party.

Recall Sartre's claim that 'the free development of a praxis can only be total or totally alienated' (Sartre, 1960, 395). The difference between Sartre and Rancière can be summarized by the way each of them would interpret this passage. Sartre would place the emphasis on totalization: free praxis must totalize or else it disintegrates into total alienation. Hence Sartre's concern with structures – such as the pledge – that stabilize group praxis. Rancière, by contrast, would place the emphasis on the disjunction between free praxis and alienation – emphasizing their heterogeneity. The storming of the Bastille, then, would be a moment of disruptive emancipatory force that breaks with all forms of exigency.

Rancière contends, on this basis, that Sartre commits to a hyper-instrumentalization of political praxis, rendering freedom a 'super-technique' subject to the exigencies that emerge from within group praxis or from without (Ranciere, 1983, 156). While the emergence of the group breaks with the passivity and inertia of the practico-inert through a kind of spontaneous activity, it does not take on stability until the introduction of a pledge that legislates a relation of 'fraternity-terror' in response to external exigencies that threaten the group with dissolution (Sartre, 1960, 418–419; Rancière, 1983, 151). Though the pledge gives consistency to the group, as the individuals who make up the group become 'the same' in praxis, it is also the 'advent of self-imposed inertia' that reintroduces the creeping mechanisms of reification that constitute the practico-inert, which the group attempts to undermine through the heterogeneity (via the division of labour) that constitutes the organization (Flynn, 1984, 110). In the terms of Rancière's *Disagreement*, the dialectic that leads the group to the sameness of the pledge and the complexity and heterogeneity of the organization's division of labour – and eventually the exigencies of the party (see Ranciere, 1983, 140, which I think is based on a polemical reading of Sartre, 1960, 662) – leads also to the reintroduction of inequality and thus policing into group praxis. Even Sartre admits that as the group struggles to maintain its praxis, 'the organization is transformed into a hierarchy, and pledges give rise to institutions' (1960, 583). By the time of the pledge, in Rancière's view, politics is already over.

2.4. Subjects of contingency

Thus we cannot reconstruct Rancière's account of political subjectivation using the categories of group praxis established in the *Critique of Dialectical Reason*, though, as I have argued, the *Critique* contributes to grasping exigencies, interests, and identities as functions of policing. While both Rancière and Sartre hold that politics is a praxis that breaks with and disrupts regimes of identification, for Rancière political praxis does so in a non-instrumental way; politics does not aim to seize or exercise power, but introduces new ways of being, speaking, or doing via the supposition of equality (1998e, 27).

Nonetheless, Rancière's use of seemingly Sartrean terms in certain passages of *Disagreement* and *On the Shores of Politics* – especially freedom (*liberté*), contingency (*contingence*), and, less frequently, facticity (*facticité*) – suggests that a reconsideration of *Being and Nothingness* could contribute to our understanding of his concept of subjectivation, the *nos sumus, nos existimus* that is a subject of contingency rather than substance.

This does not mean that Rancière holds the same ontological commitments of *Being and Nothingness*, nor does it imply that Rancière necessarily intended to use these terms in a deliberately Sartrean manner.[15] Instead, I will argue that the way Sartre turns the nihilating activity of freedom against the substance of the Cartesian subject provides a model for Rancière's formulations such that 'freedom, as an empty property' (*liberté, comme propriété vide*), or as an 'inexistent qualitative difference' (*différence qualitative inexistent*), undermines all forms of inequality, or, that it is the 'empty freedom' (*liberté vide*) of the *demos* that demonstrates the contingency of all social order (Rancière, 1995, 8/27; 10tm/29; 15/35). Like Blanqui's proletarian profession, subjectivation inscribes a name that marks its difference with any part of the count of the community. Subjectivation opens up new ways of speaking, doing, and being, which can either be transitory or be reinscribed into the police order, but its dynamic is not part of this order. At most, the subjectivation of equality only leaves a 'reiteration of the pure trace of its confirmation' (Rancière, 1995, 34tm/58). The subject is not substance; instead subjectivation is a social dynamic that activates an 'empty freedom' within the contingencies of its situation. If, as Rancière phrases it, all speaking beings are equal in intelligences and abilities, their respective occupations and places in society could be otherwise.

The return to Sartre's *Being and Nothingness* might seem like a regression that forfeits the 'advances' of the consistency on poststructural critique of existentialism, such as Foucault's genealogical studies and Derrida's deconstruction of the priority of presence that operates within the Western philosophical tradition. From a poststructuralist perspective, Sartre's work reiterates the problem of presence through an interrogation of the being of consciousness. Yet Christina Howells has convincingly shown that, despite defining subjectivity as 'consciousness (of) consciousness,' Sartre's distinctions between the in-itself (*en soi*) and the nihilating activity of the for-itself (*pour soi*) problematize 'any easy understanding of the subject, casting doubt on all attempts at identifying it other than as self-divided and self-negating' (Howells, 1992, 334). Consciousness, according to Sartre, 'does not coincide with itself in a full equivalence'; it must 'necessarily be what it is not and not be what it is' (Sartre, 1943, 120/110). Thus subjectivation is a dynamic of consciousness that hollows out all substantial claims of the Cartesian subject. Just as subjectivity is the self-negating activity of freedom for Sartre, so equality is the disidentifying dynamic of politics for Rancière – the *nos sumus, nos existimus* is not a declaration of identity but its disintegration.

Therefore, we will focus on the way that Sartre develops the problematic of presence, facticity, and freedom in first two parts of Part II, Chapter 1 of *Being and Nothingness* (the 'Immediate Structures of the For-Itself'). By then, Sartre has already shown that consciousness is always wrenched away from its being by temporality, that is, by not being the past that it has been, while not yet being its future possibilities (Sartre, 1943, 72–73/70–71).[16] Temporality produces the structure by which consciousness must be what it is not and not be what it is, and in Part II, Sartre pursues the consequences of this structure for the emergence of the for-itself in the world.

He begins with the problem of presence, which has traditionally been conceived, in terms of consciousness or subjectivity, as a fullness of the self-presence, substance, or essence of being. For Sartre, however, the for-itself is presence in the mode of never coinciding with itself. Only being-in-itself, as he says, 'is what it is.' Contrary to the 'infinite compression' of the in-itself, the activity of the for-itself 'decompresses' being by always surpassing what it is (1943, 120–121/110). Presence to self is only possible because the for-itself is always distanced or different from itself. This has already been acknowledged by previous philosophers when the interrogation of consciousness (of) belief led them to a 'game [*jeu*] of reflections' between consciousness as reflection and consciousness as reflecting. While they have defined consciousness as an infinity, Sartre argues that this merely 'fixes' and 'obscures' the phenomena (1943, 122/112).[17] He proposes, instead, to approach the being-for-itself of consciousness as a dynamic activity. Then presence is only possible for being-for-itself as distance or difference; when we ask '*what it is* which separates the subject from himself, we are forced to admit that it is *nothing*' (1943, 124/113). Rather than being the revelation of essence or substance, presence is an 'inconsistency of being' (*inconsistance d'être*) which marks the nothingness or distance of being-for-itself: 'Nothingness is always an *elsewhere*' (1943, 126tm/114).

Hence being-for-itself cannot be its own foundation, inasmuch as all attempts to found itself in-itself end in failure. From this, Sartre encourages the cultivation of freedom of the for-itself while acknowledging its ultimate absurdity.[18] Both are responses to the contingency of the for-itself. While Ronald Aronson has called contingency, which he links to the failure of freedom that makes of a human being a 'useless passion,' one of the 'more somber, negative counterparts' to the positive propositions of Sartre's ontology (Aronson, 1980, 81), we will focus on how the contingency of all situations also opens the possibility that they could be otherwise. While Rancière would not accept Sartre's account of the 'fundamental project' of determining human reality as an In-itself-For-itself, contingency plays a dual practical role in Rancière's thought, opening the possibility that the world could be otherwise, while demanding, as May points out in connection with Foucault, 'a hyper- and pessimistic activism' (Foucault, quoted in May, 2008, 126). Indeed, Sartre's discussion of facticity and contingency deals concretely with the for-itself in its presence to the world, that is, the 'pure contingency' of the for-itself 'thrown into a world and abandoned in a "situation"' (Sartre, 1943, 127/115).

It is important to differentiate between contingency and facticity in this account, so that we do not mistake Sartre's point that things could be otherwise with the idea that they are not, in some way, historically conditioned. Despite his tendency to indulge in hyperbole concerning absolute freedom and absolute choice during the 1940s, the analysis of facticity shows that the free activity of being-for-itself takes place within a set of historical constraints that limits its possibilities.[19] Contingency means that, from the consideration of being, the being of the for-itself and its situation could be otherwise, which sustains the possibilities of surpassing the givens of any particular situation. But the for-itself *is* thrown into its situation, and this determines its possibilities. He returns to the example mentioned in the 'Patterns of Bad Faith' of the man who plays at being a waiter: in that situation, even if I play at the role of being a waiter, this 'contingent block of identity' is mine in a way that it would be 'vain for me to play at being a diplomat or a sailor' (1943, 131/119). It would be in vain because this play (at being a diplomat or sailor) transforms the waiter's previous mode of bad faith (identifying with his facticity) into identification with pure transcendence that no longer refers to a situation. Facticity is defined, if I may switch to the first person for a moment, by the way that a particular and ultimately contingent fact of a situation is *mine*. Nevertheless, a situation, and even what is *mine*, is fundamentally determined by others: 'It is my place, my body, my past, my position in so far as it is already determined by the indications of Others, finally my fundamental relation to the Other' (1943, 629/534).

The determination of the situation by others indicates that it is mine as an ostensive function, pointing toward aspects of my concrete facticity, rather than a possessive function. Thus the bad faith of pure transcendence acts 'as if I were to my self the truth of myself', which ignores the 'equal dignity' of being-for-others and being-for-myself (1943, 100/92).[20] While freedom wrenches me away from my situation and opens the possibility that I might change it, this fact does not eliminate the way that others saturate this situation with other determinations that render some of my possibilities vain. I am always situated between my freedom and my facticity. Hence Sartre writes:

> the for-itself is sustained by a perpetual contingency for which it assumes the responsibility and which it assimilates without ever being able to suppress it. This perpetually evanescent contingency of the in-itself..., without ever allowing itself to be apprehended, haunts the for-itself and reattaches it to being-in-itself. (1943, 131/119)

This concrete and ostensive facticity is what we mean when we say that being-for-itself *is*: to treat facticity as a transcendent that cannot be surpassed through freedom is to lapse into bad faith. But Sartre also argues that there is no way to eliminate contingency in order to take up a transcendent project of authenticity in the manner that Heidegger develops an ethics to 'reconcile his humanism with the religious sense of the transcendent' (1943, 128/116). Such a criticism suggests that taking up Sartre today requires abandoning the project of authenticity.[21] One possibility is to think his work in terms of its anti- and postcolonial resonances and with Rancière's politics of equality. If Rancière's work speaks to Sartrean existentialism, it is because human existence is absurd and contingent, as Sartre claims, except that it is also fundamentally egalitarian.

There are two critical questions that we will now pose to Rancière that I think

The Nothingness of Equality: Rancière's 'Sartrean Existentialism'   69

can be answered by reference to Sartre (the first is posed by Bosteels, 2009, the second by Hallward, 2009). First, how does Rancière reconcile his analysis of equality with the movements he cites in developing his political thought? More simply put: how can the principle of equality be thought historically? Second, we might ask how to register the effects of egalitarian logic on the order of policing, if equality cannot be institutionalized?

Let us begin with the first question, concerning historicizing the principle of equality, for, in Rancière's work, the opposition of equality to the police functions as a transhistorical structure of politics; that is, when there is politics, it is at the intersection of egalitarian practices and policing. This holds whether we are discussing the Athenian *demos*, plebian revolts on Aventine Hill, or workers' struggle in nineteenth-century Europe. It is notable that these examples share, on Rancière's account, a similar dynamic despite the differences of demands and practices, which suggests that accounting for these differences provides the impetus for historicizing egalitarianism. Very rarely, in his examples, do these movements demand equality directly. Instead, Rancière argues that 'every politics works on homonyms and the indiscernable' (Rancière, 1995, 91/130). This is, at first sight, a puzzling claim, as he is arguing that each politically contentious term, such as *the social*, *class*, or *profession*, is not a word with different meanings, but two words with different meanings but identical spelling and pronunciation. There is one word, defined and used within the regime of policing, and there is another, homonymous word that names the logic of equality. Although politics and policing are heterogeneous, politics is never 'pure'. Political subjectivation begins when the homonymous use of common terms produces dissensus. This is evident in Blanqui's subversion of the magistrate's articulation of profession. Class, Rancière adds, is a 'perfect example' of a homonym, which in police logic names the classification of parts of the social order, but which in egalitarian logic designates 'an operator of conflict, a name for counting the uncounted, a mode of subjectivation superimposed on the reality of all social groups' (Rancière, 1995, 83/121).[22]

Homonymy is also the case for *demos*. For Plato, the *demos* names the wrong that the people commit when they attempt to rule on the basis of *doxa* and 'appearances' rather than the *logos* and *arkhê* of community. As I mentioned above, Rancière turns the problem around and returns the *logos* of equality to the activity of the *demos*; they do not act irrationally, but out of the supposition that all Athenians are born free. This freedom of the *demos* is nothing other than the nothingness of equality: 'the freedom of the *demos* is not a determinable property but a pure facticity' (Rancière, 1995, 7tm/26).[23] Sartre has prepared us to interpret this passage. Freedom (here the name for equality) is not a positive attribute or substance of the *demos* but instead arises from *its* contingency – being born in Athens after enslavement for debt had been abolished. These homonyms share an egalitarian logic, which is a dynamic of subjectivation and not a creation *ex nihilo*. This means that while the terms are historically contingent (class, proletariat, the social), they name, at particular times, a dynamic of equality that surpasses their facticity toward new ways of speaking, being, and doing. Yet this example is less than sufficient, given that the freedom of the *demos* did rest in large part on the quality being a male citizen. It nevertheless stands out to Rancière for the 'threat' that classical political philosophy had felt from an equality that opposed qualifications of birth or wealth. Equality has had a long history since then, so let us look at one more example.

In *Hatred of Democracy* (2005b), Rancière analyses how the distinction between public and private spheres exercises police logic insofar as it works to organize society around the reinforcement of inequalities of wealth, institutional access, and rights, if not the reinforcement of relations of domination toward those who are excluded from these. This failure of the rights of man and the rights of the citizen to protect those who are excluded from social life has led a number of prominent critics, from Edmund Burke and Hannah Arendt to Giorgio Agamben, to denounce the duality of *man* and *citizen*. For these critics, if there are two principles, at least one must be illusory, if not both. For Burke and Arendt, according to Rancière,

> the rights of man are either empty or tautological…bare man, the man who belongs to no constituted national community, has no rights. The rights of man, then, are the empty rights of those who have no rights. Or they are the rights of men who belong to a national community. They are, then, simply the rights of the citizens of that nation, the rights of those who have rights, and hence a pure tautology. (Rancière, 2005b, 59)[24]

From this standpoint, equality becomes, or is returned to, a problem of passive equality, reduced to the logic of institutional access and constitutional guarantees, even though this critique concerns the failure of these guarantees. This critique remains at this level because none of these critics advocate mass politics, let alone of the 'trust in the people' demonstrated by Rancière's egalitarian politics.[25] By contrast, Rancière does not dismiss rights as the illusory guarantees of liberalism. Instead, as May notes, Rancière is careful to show that the politics of equality cannot be reduced to the contours of liberalism, and that where 'politics becomes passive is not in the recognition or embrace of rights; it is when rights come to structure the field of politics' (May, 2008, 34).[26] Rancière argues that critics such as Burke, Arendt, and Agamben are mistaken in seeking to *identify* the subject of rights and check his or her possessions (*having* rights), when the dynamic of subjectivation is 'always defined by an interval between identities determined by social relations or juridical categories' (Rancière, 2005b, 59).

For Rancière this interval has allowed political subjects to challenge distinctions between public and private life, citizen and man. Olympe de Gouges, in her 'Declaration of the Rights of Woman' (1791), challenges how these rights exclude women. However, for Rancière, this dissensus over rights does not turn on the *possession* of rights, but their activation through political practice. Here he reiterates Sartre's emphasis on activity over possession (Sartre, 1943, 558/475). But Rancière's formulation also echoes Sartre's account of the dynamic of subjectivation. Sartre, as we have already mentioned, writes that consciousness must necessarily 'be what it is not and not be what it is' (*d'être ce qu'elle n'est pas et de ne pas être ce qu'elle est*) (Sartre, 1943, 120/110). To formulate a third possibility that avoids the logical bind of the empty or tautological problem of rights, Rancière states that the dissensus over rights concerns 'the rights of those who have not the rights that they have and have the rights that they have not' (*les droits de celles qui n'ont pas les droits qu'elles ont et qui ont les droits qu'elles n'ont pas*) (Rancière, 2005b, 61/68). Both formulations reject the priority of being or possession and instead emphasize the differences between subjectivation and identification. This is an especially salient point for reconsidering Sartre's work, which has quite often been dismissed as a reiteration of consciousness as the identity of self-presence.

For Rancière dissensus over the 'rights of those who have not the rights that they have and have the rights that they have not' turns universality against the particular and contingent lines – those ramparts of inequality – that separate the public (universal) and private (particular) spheres. While the discourse on rights can be a moment of dissensus and politics, it is not necessarily so – rights can be reduced to questions of distributive justice and institutional guarantees, or far worse, invoked to justify imperialist interventions.[27] This should not be surprising: as Rancière states in *Disagreement*, politics is rare, just as Sartre notes that the anxiety that throws us toward the interrogation of being and of freedom is rare (Rancière, 1995, 17/37; Sartre, 1943, 73/70). But rights actively challenge policing in the name of equality when one polemically deploys the universality of one set of rights against the particularities institutionalized by the other. The universality of the rights of man can be activated to contest the exclusion of peoples from the 'privatizations' and privileges of citizenship, or the universality of the rights of the citizen can be used to contest the lines between public and private life. The movement for rights for workers, for instance, asserts the universality of public and collective decision making to oppose the presumption that work is a private transaction. Or, to return to the example above, Olympe de Gouges disputes the exclusion of women from French citizenship when she argues that the woman who has the right to mount the scaffold 'must equally have the right to mount the rostrum' (de Gouges, 1791, 91; Rancière, 2005b, 60). This is not to say that, for instance, de Gouges *has* the rights guaranteed under the rights of man, but not the rights of the citizen. Instead, her actions declare the rights that the law denies her.[28] For Rancière, it is clear that equality names a practice and a logic and not something that somebody has. In each case, political subjectivation works to produce homonyms out of the contingencies (freedoms, rights, classes) of social situations. Rights are not principles with a significance or guarantee 'in themselves,' but only become political (or become depoliticized) within engaged social practices.[29]

2.5. The politics of impossible identification

The question remains as to whether equality can become permanent within the police order. As we have seen, Rancière argues that the police and the politics of equality are two heterogeneous logics. The positive aspect of the distinction between two logics of social practice is that, against mainstream political philosophy, Rancière restores rationality to the practice of political dissensus. However, this move forecloses, it seems, on the possibility of egalitarian politics effectively transforming the policing of the social order. This is one of the major points of contention with Rancière's approach. Peter Hallward, for example, argues that it is 'far from clear that the resources of the *interval* as such can give effective analytical purchase on the forms of relation (relations of oppression, exploitation, representation, and so on, but also of solidarity, cooperation, empowerment) that shape any particular situation' (Hallward, 2009, 154). Rancière reinforces these doubts when he writes that the 'always one-off act of equality cannot consist in any form of social bond whatsoever. Equality turns into the opposite the moment it aspires to a place in the social or state organization' (Rancière, 1995, 34/58). The strict opposition between equality and the police suggests that egalitarian politics can only be temporary and cannot be sustained without introducing inequalities.

Rancière amplifies the heterogeneity of politics and policing when, in 'The Cause of the Other,' he describes political subjectivation as – in contrast to the techniques of identification of policing – a dynamic of 'impossible identification' (see also Rancière, 1998a, 112–125; and the discussion of the demonstrations of October 1961 in 1995, 138–139/187–188). Rancière's account of impossible identification is attentive both to forms of social inclusion and exclusion and how to combat them, for political subjectivation is oriented toward a relation to the other that is inclusive without being dominating and that is political rather than ethical. The result of this politics of the cause of the other is to transform the boundaries of inclusion and exclusion by combatting a wrong committed against others without speaking for them.

Rancière considers this politics of the other with a specific point of reference. He asks: what was at stake in the political praxis of those French citizens who opposed the actions of the French government in the Algerian war? He contends that this question was posed through 'two opposing Sartreanisms' (1997, 28). On the one hand, Sartre's preface to Fanon's *Wretched of the Earth* forcefully argues that this book is not addressed to the French; instead, the French appear as objects, as ruthless hypocrites whose system of colonialism betrays their humanist principles. In the language of the *Critique*, Sartre's preface establishes that there is no 'common activity' of group praxis possible between the French anti-colonialists and the Algerians. Sartre claims that through the revolutionary praxis (and its necessary violence) of the colonized, 'we, too, peoples of Europe, we are being decolonialized: meaning the colonist inside every one of us is surgically extracted in a bloody operation' (Sartre, 1961, lvii). Despite the anti-ethical stance of his preface, Rancière argues, Sartre's radical exclusion of the 'cause of the other' from the possibilities of the political praxis of the French who opposed the war results in 'a purely ethical and individualistic relationship with the [Algerian] war' reminiscent of the ethics of *Being and Nothingness* – or, I might add, 'Existentialism is a Humanism' (Rancière, 1997, 27–28). Thus Rancière contrasts Sartre's preface to *Wretched of the Earth* with Maurice Maschino's own Sartrean justification for desertion: 'If I am mobilized in a war, that war is my war. It is made in my image and I deserve it' (quoted in Ranciere, 1997, 28; cf. Sartre, 1943, 709–710). Nevertheless, what Rancière considers to be a 'truly political mobilization' inclusive of the cause of the other is an 'impossible identification' forged from these two opposed Sartreanisms: 'this war is *and* is not our war' (Ranciere, 1997, 28).

This Sartrean paradox, 'this war is *and* is not our war' demarcates a space of French opposition to the war. The response of the French activists and demonstrators opposed to the war (as shorthand I will henceforth refer to them as protestors) was constrained by the fact that, first, it was not their war. They could not identify directly with Algerian struggle in either Algeria, for there it was a matter of Algerian self-determination, or in France, where they would be speaking in the place of Algerians. Second, the Algerian war was their war, and to oppose it required disidentifying from the French state and its apparatuses of policing. The politics of the cause of the other, Rancière writes, produces 'a *people* different from the people seen, named and counted by the State, of a people defined by the wrong done to the constitution of a commonality that was constructing an other communal space' (Rancière, 1997, 29).

Rancière examines, as an exemplary case of this dynamic of political subjectivation, the protests that occurred in France after the brutal repression of a demonstration on 17 October 1961, called by the *Front de libération nationale*; aided by a news blackout, the French police proceeded to beat and drown numerous Algerians. The response of the protestors – 'our' response, Rancière writes – was a political response to the cause of the other, which has three characteristics (Rancière, 1997, 29). First, the protestors rejected, or disidentified with, the actions of the French state and the atrocities it committed in their name. Second, this political mobilization demonstrated that a wrong had been committed. Policing, as Rancière notes, operates through a count of parts of society, counting who is part of the community and who is not. Politics is a moment of making visible or making heard that part of society, the 'part of those who have no part,' which has not been counted. As Rancière states, due to the news blackout, 'it was impossible even to count the victims' of the massacre (1997, 28).[30] Thus, demonstrating a wrong did not rely on counting the victims. Instead, the protestors contested the operations of inclusion and exclusion that rendered Algerian struggles invisible and speechless. Third, there is an impossible identification with the cause of the other. The demonstrations forced the count of what was not counted by the French state – making Algerian struggles visible, making French atrocities visible – revealing how Algerians continued to be excluded from French public space, despite being granted French citizenship (the difference between French *subjects* and French *citizens* having been abolished in June 1958). This political subjectivation identified with the other, the part of those who have no part, who mark the difference between political citizenship and juridical citizenship, between a political people and a juridical people (Rancière, 1997, 29). Elsewhere, he will suggest that politics signals the difference between a *demos* and an identarian *ethnos* (Rancière, 2012b, 212).

Perhaps, Rancière writes, this impossible identification anticipated the 'exemplary formula' of May 1968: 'We are all German Jews': 'That impossible identification inverted a name that was meant to stigmatize by turning it into the principle behind an open subjectivation of the uncounted, but it did not politically confuse them with any representation of an identifiable social group' (Rancière, 1997, 30).[31] However, the politics of impossible identification is not, on Rancière's account, limited to these cases. As shown by the example of Blanqui, Rancière argues that an impossible identification is part of political subjectivation itself; it is always possible because the count of any policing regime is always a miscount, an inegalitarian distribution of roles and parts of society. Politics is possible because there is always a disjunction between particular identities or social categories and egalitarian political agency. Without the possibility of political subjectivation, Rancière claims, the worker, immigrant, or migrant worker is confined to the 'identity of the other, to being a mere object of pity or, more commonly, hatred' (Rancière, 1997, 32). To elaborate further, the immigrant becomes an object of pity when her struggle becomes a humanitarian cause (which seeks to ameliorate her suffering), and an object of hatred when she is considered as an other, a member of a social group, who does not belong to the national *ethnos*. In neither case is she a political agent. As Rancière argues, what makes the 'political identity of the "worker" or the "proletarian" operational [is] the disjunction between political subjectivity and social group' (Ranciere, 1997, 32). Here we re-encounter the Sartrean inflections of Rancière's account of identity, reminiscent of Sartre's investigations into the abstract generalities of the material forces and exigencies, the reified and passive identities, of the practico-inert. Politics, for Rancière, is possible because there is always a disjunction between the interests and identifications of social groups and political agency – that impossible identification with the cause of the other, with the part of those who have no part.

This account of the politics of impossible identification has not entirely answered the question of how equality might become a permanent feature within regimes of policing. At best, it demonstrates that the politics of dissensus contests and transforms the count of speech, the divisions of social space that demarcate who speaks and who makes noise, more than the quantity or number of those who speak, more that it initiates any stable mechanisms for guaranteeing that such speech is heard. Given the transitory and temporary irruption of politics, and given possibility that radical change can be subsumed by relations of domination and oppression, it can still seem like nothing has changed, though we should keep in mind that, at one point, Rancière states that politics is the 'name of nothing' (Rancière, 1995, 35/58).

We will conclude with a Sartrean suggestion that provides a clue into what Rancière means when he writes that politics is the name of nothing. In his discussion of sincerity in *Being and Nothingness*, Sartre draws a surprising conclusion: sincerity is a phenomenon of bad faith. The person who demands sincerity from another does not elicit the other's freedom or responsibility; instead he demands that his addressee identify herself as what she *is*, reifying her freedom. As we know, bad faith demands that we affirm our facticity to be transcendence and affirm facticity (*our* contingency) as transcendence, when the dynamic of subjectivation demands that consciousness must be what it is not and not be what it is. As Sartre writes, 'the essential structure of sincerity does not differ from that of bad faith since the sincere man constitutes himself as what he is *in order not to be it*' (Sartre, 1943, 109/100).

We have already drawn attention to the parallels between Rancière and Sartre, so let us sketch a preliminary reply to the problem of the opposition between egalitarian logic and police logic. Granting that equality can be a permanent feature of the social order suggests that we have finally *arrived* at equality, which means that it is no longer a problem of active struggle. In many ways, we already acknowledge that we will never arrive when, as critics, we recognize how political struggle has transformed social relations, and yet, more must be done. To say '*here* is an egalitarian institution' turns a dynamic into a *thing*, and, as we could say following Todd May, transforms an activity into the passive equality of distributions between institutions and entitlements. This response is not entirely satisfactory, but neither is it complete. As I will argue in Part II, Rancière conceptualizes aesthetics as a form of micropolitics that takes place in the interval of the heterogeneity of policing and politics.

Notes

1   To reach this conclusion, Rancière revises his position in *Althusser's Lesson*, where he defends Sartre against Althusser's criticisms by arguing that Sartre's thought must be evaluated in light of his political commitments: his support for anticolonial insurgency in Algeria, his engagement with the student uprisings of May 1968, and his alliances with Maoist militants that involved assuming the editorship of *La Cause du people* and participating in the Lens tribunal. Rancière asks: do these commitments 'not attest to some sort of convergence between Sartre's theoretical questions and the questions the Cultural Revolution raised' (1974, 19)? Do they not propose some new practices of interaction between intellectuals and the masses? In *The Philosopher and His Poor*, Rancière separates Sartre, the philosopher, and Sartre, the activist of the late 1960s and 1970s: 'To

speak and act in favor of the most disadvantaged, he will now fall silent *as a philosopher*. From Russell's tribunal to the tribunal of Lens, he will speak only in the register and space of *judgment*' (1983, 156).

2   In this chapter, we will focus on comments from three sources: 'The Cause of the Other' (1997), 'Politique et identité' (1999), and 'Work, Identity, Subject' (2012b). Note also his comments in Rancière and Davis (2013, 215): 'generally, I have found little interest in questions of interiority....This is my Sartrean side, if you recall Sartre's famous text [*The Transcendence of the Ego*] on Husserl and consciousness as that which is outside, a thing among things. That text shaped me a lot when I was young.'

3   For his critique of the 'epochal' claims about the end of metaphysics and about post-subjectivity that have emerged since, as Nancy phrases it, 'the close of the Sartrean enterprise' (Nancy, 1991, 3), see Rancière's 'After What' (1991). For Rancière's discussions of Foucault, see 'Biopolitics or Politics?' (2000, 93) and Chapter 3; on Deleuze, see the Conclusion; on Foucault's and Deleuze's account of the role of intellectuals, see Rancière and Rancière (1978, especially 87–100); on Negri see 'The People or the Multitudes?' (2002b, 84–90). We will discuss Agamben below.

4   For further discussion of Sartre's 'poor,' see Giuseppina Mecchia 2010.

5   To make this link clearer: Sartre is discussing in part how the woman denies her embodiment as a woman, which, as we know from Beauvoir, is done in bad faith: 'no woman can claim without bad faith to be situated beyond her sex' (Beauvoir, 1949, 4/1: 13). Of course, Beauvoir is more specific than Sartre about the gender inequalities present in a woman's situation. Note also Toril Moi's critique of Sartre's account: by 'refusing to take the different social conventions applying to the two protagonists into account, Sartre can only see [the woman's] refusal as a sign of her will to self-deception....The real problem in this passage is not the woman's interpretation, but Sartre's bland assumption that he *knows* more than the woman' (1994, 128, my emphasis).

6   Note, however, the parallel between Rancière's comments and those of Alain Badiou, who refers to Sartre as 'a man who was, when I was eighteen, my absolute master and the man who initiated me into the delights of philosophy' (2008, 191–192).

7   As we know, Sartre concedes much of Fanon's critique of 'Black Orpheus' by the time he writes the preface to *The Wretched of the Earth*.

8   This has been suggested, but not developed, by Todd May (2008, 65) and Peter Hallward (2009, 141).

9   See Rancière 1995, 16/37: 'There is order in society because some people command and others obey, but in order to obey and order at least two things are required: you must understand the order and you must understand that you

must obey it. And to do that, you must already be the equal of the person who is ordering you. It is this equality that gnaws away at any natural order.' Sartre makes similar claims about how structures of domination undermine themselves. In the *Critique*, in a passage on colonialism, he writes: 'This is the contradiction of racism, colonialism, and all forms of tyranny: in order to *treat a man like a dog*, one must first recognize him as a man' (1960, 111). A similar passage appears in his essay on Memmi, that 'in order to give [humans] orders, even the harshest, the most insulting, you have to begin by acknowledging them' (1957a, 61). Note that for Ranciere the equality of speaking beings is constitutive of politics, while for Sartre scarcity is.

10 Disidentification, as we will see in Chapter 4, also plays an important role in the micropolitics of aesthetics (see Rancière, 2009a, 73).

11 As Flynn notes, 'Passive activity is not originative; it is an ontological deformation of praxis because of practico-inert mediation' (1984, 105).

12 By distinguishing between a fundamental form of scarcity and its historical forms, Sartre observes Marx's distinction, established in the *Economic and Philosophic Manuscripts*, between objectification (*Vergegenständlichung*) and alienation or externalization *(Entfremdung* or *Entäußerung).*

13 As Sartre later summarizes the concept of seriality: 'A group is said to be a serial group when each of its members, though he may be in the same circumstances as all the others, remains alone and defines himself according to his neighbor insofar as his neighbor thinks like the others' (1972, 166).

14 This phrasing is deliberately chosen in contrast to the communist motto 'From each according to his abilities, to each according to his needs.'

15 Admittedly, I read Sartre's analysis as a method of undermining substantial ontological commitments. Like Samuel Chambers, I consider Ranciere's opposition to ontological accounts of politics to be a definitive feature of his thought (see Chambers, 2013, 18–21).

16 Note that while Sartre cautions against equating consciousness with the for-itself and the world with the in-itself, he sometimes is loose with his terminology. I will move, like Sartre, between discussing consciousness and the for-itself.

17 Sartre names Hegel and Spinoza, and we will remain at the level of his account without evaluating his accuracy as a reader of history of philosophy.

18 Though we should note here Beauvoir's correction to Sartre's thought: the 'notion of ambiguity must not be confused with that of absurdity. To declare that existence is absurd is to deny that it can ever be given a meaning; to say that it is ambiguous is to assert that its meaning is never fixed, that it must be constantly won' (1947, 129). Then: 'Only the freedom of others keeps each one of us from hardening in the absurdity of facticity' (1947, 71).

19 See Sartre's later self-critique in 'The Itinerary of a Thought' (1969, 33–34): 'I

re-read a prefatory note of mine to a collection of these plays – *Les Mouches*, *Huis Clos* and others – and was truly scandalized. I had written "Whatever the circumstances, and wherever the site, a man is always free to choose to be a traitor or not...." When I read this, I said to myself: it's incredible, I actually believed that!'

20 This claim is important because it acknowledges the intersubjective character of facticity without the pessimism that accompanies many of Sartre's comments on the relation between the for-itself and others. As Thomas Flynn points out, Sartre defines intersubjective relations as ontologically – rather than historically – conflictual (Flynn, 1984, 20). If Sartre followed through with the claim that there is 'equal dignity' between being-for-others and being-for-myself, he would have to search out the historical conditions of interpersonal or social conflict.

21 For an extensive argument against renewing the project of authenticity see Sherman, 2007, 135ff.

22 Ranciere's discussion, in *The Philosopher and His Poor*, of aesthetic misinterpretation anticipates this discussion of homonymy (1983, 200), which we will discuss in Part II, especially Section 3.5. The concept of homonymy plays an important role in *The Names of History* insofar as Rancière notes ironically that an 'unfortunate homonymy in the French language designates lived experience, its faithful narrative, its lying fiction, and its knowledgeable explanation all by the same name. Exact in their pursuit of the traps of this homonymy, the English distinguish *story* and *history*' (Rancière, 1992, 3).

23 Compare the French to Rose's translation, which blunts the existential terminology of the passage: the phrase '*la liberté du* démos *n'est aucune propriété déterminable mais une pure facticité*' becomes in translation 'the freedom of the demos is not a determinable property but a pure invention.'

24 In 'Who is the Subject of the Rights of Man?' Rancière criticizes Agamben for capturing theoretically all political struggles in the 'biopolitical trap' of the destiny of being: 'Any kind of claim to rights or any struggle enacting rights is thus trapped from the very outset in the mere polarity of bare life and the state of exception, a polarity that appears as a sort of ontological destiny: we are all, every single one of us, in the same situation as the refugee in a camp' (Rancière, 2004c, 66).

25 Metapolitics, then, is for Rancière a politics of mistrust: the 'point of view of mistrust [is that] behind things is where their reasons lie.' By constrast, trust is egalitarian: 'trust affirms that no one can see for those who do not see and turn others' ignorance into knowledge' (Rancière, 1990, 122; 123).

26 Lynn Hunt makes a similar point when she argues that human rights become self-evident due to the emergence of new convictions and practices concerning equality, empathy, and autonomy – convictions and practices that have literary

and cultural as much as juridical origins, and whose ramifications extend beyond traditional rights frameworks. Nonetheless she concludes by endorsing the distributive structures of passive equality: 'The human rights framework, with its international bodies, international courts, and international conventions, might be exasperating in its slowness to respond or repeated inability to achieve its ultimate goals, but there is no better structure available for confronting these issues' (2007, 213). She makes no mention of the possibility of transforming 'available structures' through a radical or revolutionary politics of equality.

27 Micheline Ishay (2008) claims that a 'new realism of human rights' should criticize the human rights abuses of imperialism but should nevertheless 'seize opportunities to advance its cause whenever Western powers confront repressive governments' (290), or be prepared to offer 'a substantive agenda linking human rights and international security' (289). Through this model, she argues, globalization can be made to advance the cause of 'the wretched of the earth' (293). One of the central planks of Fanon's philosophy is that the self-determination of the oppressed cannot be advanced by imperialist intervention. To intervene and implement rights from above repeats the civilizing gesture of the old imperialism. Any reference to rights must take place through local conflict and struggle, from the organization of the masses from below. In addition, when Ishay appeals to presenting a 'substantive agenda' of human rights, she is speaking within a Western framework. The framework of rights-security is already Western and imperialist, and often has little accountability to those (the oppressed) to whom Ishay or nongovernmental organizations appeal for their moral legitimacy.

28 Joan Wallach Scott underlines, from a different perspective, how de Gouges's literary activities were, in this sense, political: 'For de Gouges, writing, signing and publishing demonstrated, for her contemporaries and for posterity, what the law erased: the fact that women could be, already were, authors. Under revolutionary legislation women did not have the rights of authors, of individuals who possessed their intellectual property, because they did not have the rights of active citizens' (Scott, 1996, 37).

29 We should nevertheless signal the limits of de Gouges's egalitarianism. Madeleine Dobie argues that 'while [de] Gouges was clearly sympathetic to the predicament of the enslaved, she also tended to project a liberal socioeconomic philosophy inflected with feminist ideas onto the colonial context, without giving much consideration to the tensions and contradictions that this projection entailed' (Dobie, 2010, 270). For example, in the wake of the upheaval in Saint-Domingue, 'rather than speaking to enslaved men and women in the language of rights and freedom,' de Gouges prefaced the publication of her play *Black Slavery* by 'condemning the crimes they had committed in freedom's name. Instead

of attacking slavery as a moral offense, [de] Gouges embarks on a prolonged denunciation of violence, extremism, and disorder…[reproaching] the slaves for their failure to differentiate between good and bad masters in their blind pursuit of revenge' (278).

30   Jim House and Neil MacMaster examine competing accounts of the police massacre of Algerians. While prefacing their remarks that 'a conclusive or definitive figure as to the number of Algerian deaths will never be arrived at,' they conclude, after noting that official statistics exclude 'the large number of deaths which never reached the morgue and went unrecorded,' that *'during September and October* well over 120 Algerians were murdered by the police in the Paris region, a figure that compares quite closely to the estimates by Linda Amiri in particular (about 130), the FLN (200), and [Jean-Luc] Einaudi (200), but which have been widely and misleadingly attributed to the single night of 17 October' (House and MacMaster, 2006, 166–167). I would like to thank an anonymous reviewer for suggesting this source.

31   In a later discussion of the significance of May 1968, Rancière maintains that the claim 'We are all German Jews' offers 'a model of political subjectivation involving the creation of space through a declaration by subjects,' a space that cannot be identified in advance. 'The creation of the subject does not imply the emergence of an underlying social force, but rather a rupture in the system of class and identity' (Rancière, 2008, 154).

Part II

Aesthetics

Hypothesis

In Part II, I propose and defend the hypothesis that what Rancière calls the politics of aesthetics is composed of micropolitical practices of artistic production, reception, and aesthetic experience that interrupt and transform the practico-inert structures of visibility, intelligibility, and place that orient a given distribution of the sensible. The micropolitics of aesthetics includes practices that he calls fragmentary emancipation, literary misunderstanding, misinterpretation, and aesthetic suspension. In each case, aesthetics works to transform the significations that relate words, things, and affects. By introducing new modes of visibility, intelligibility and place that relate words, things, and affects, the micropolitics of aesthetics interrupts, contests, and revolutionizes the practico-inert structures of everyday life. The hypothesis that the politics of aesthetics is micropolitical casts a stark contrast between Rancière's aesthetics and Greenberg's modernism, Benjamin's messianic modernity, and Badiou's inaesthetics. Rancière contests both the historical teleologies that orient – for different reasons – the work of Greenberg and Benjamin and the evental monumentalism of what I will call the Platonic regime of art, as it is elaborated by the work of Schelling and Badiou. The politics of art is practised without a historical and teleological destiny, and this politics is more pervasive than the proponents of monumentalism proclaim. The micropolitics of aesthetics takes place in those discourses and practices that challenge and interrupt the practico-inert structures of everyday life.

3

Modernity, Modernism and Aesthetic Equality

3.1. Disagreement and misunderstanding

In Part I, I outlined Rancière's account of political subjectivation, in which he argues that the supposition of equality is the starting point for thinking historical forms of political agency. I accented, along the way, the Cartesian and existentialist aspects of his political thought while reconsidering the egalitarian premises of Cartesianism and existentialism. Finally, I concluded that, while Rancière's work opens a new, egalitarian reading of modern and contemporary French philosophy, and while – in contrast to his poststructuralist predecessors – he places emancipation at the forefront of political thought, he must nevertheless concede that politics is, as he defines it, rare.

That politics is rare is a consequence of Rancière's strict distinction – like Sartre's distinction between the free activity of praxis and the alienated and alienating experience of the practico-inert – between politics and policing. Rancière's concession could leave the impression that a given distribution of the sensible within a regime of policing is relatively static, for where politics takes place policing is interrupted, while where policing happens politics does not. In Part II, I will contend that Rancière's account of the politics of aesthetics (and the politics of literature) is a micropolitics that maps the more diffuse and quotidian transformations of what he calls a 'polemical common world' (2010b, 152).

Before the discussion of the micropolitics of aesthetics, and Rancière's treatment of what he calls literary misunderstanding, aesthetic distance or suspension, and the various regimes of art, it is necessary to note a difference in his argumentative strategies regarding politics and aesthetics. As Rancière explains in *The Politics of Aesthetics*, his account of politics aims to demonstrate that egalitarianism cannot be reduced to the political project initiated by the French Revolution, intensified by communist and proletarian struggle, and subsequently extinguished by the collapse of the Soviet Union. Instead, politics exists when a 'supernumerary subject' interrupts the 'calculated number of groups, places, and functions in a society' (Rancière, 2004b, 51), and there exists a relation between politics and philosophy when philosophy confronts the supposition of equality. Hence Rancière's readings of the paradigmatic figures of archipolitics and parapolitics – Plato and Aristotle – which show how their respective political philosophies sought to foreclose on the radical potential the equality of the *demos*. Moreover, in Chapter 1, I aimed to reinforce Rancière's claims concerning the relation of politics and philosophy by showing how equality emerges as an important philosophical problem at the beginnings of what we often call early modern philosophy. Thus equality is not merely a problem and project related to a historical sequence that begins with the French Revolution and ends with the fall of state communism, but rather – given the attention paid to it by Plato, Aristotle, Descartes, and Beauvoir, among others – it is one of the preeminent problems of philosophy.

With his aesthetics, Rancière employs a different argumentative strategy. Broadly speaking, he argues that what we call art – and this claim holds for literature as well – is not a transhistorical constant, but rather the name of a set of practices that emerges in the late eighteenth century (2004a, 68; 2004b, 51; 2006b, 4).[1] His account of this emergence of the aesthetic regime of art delineates the historical conditions of possibility that transform what had previously been considered the fine arts into the singular experience of *art*. Rancière likens his strategy to Foucault's archaeology: 'aesthetics can be understood in a Kantian sense – re-examined perhaps by Foucault – as the system of *a priori* forms determining what presents itself to sense experience' (2004b, 13). As Joseph Tanke notes, Foucault's 'archaeology is a form of historical analysis designed to place in sharp relief two periods of discursive and visual practice' (Tanke, 2011, 76). Though Rancière likens his archaeology of aesthetics to Foucault's method, there are two differences that separate them. First, Rancière's aesthetics is not concerned with the discursive forms that make a particular episteme possible and stable, but rather the conditions that make change and transformation possible within a distribution of the sensible. Second, he appropriates only one sense of Foucault's concept of historical discontinuity – Rancière seeks to outline the emergence of the aesthetic regime of art without declaring the dissolution or historical atavism of other regimes of the identification of art or the arts.

In the final sections of *The Order of Things*, Foucault studies the emergence and dissolution of the figure of man within the modern episteme constituted by the sciences of biology, economics, and philology. According to Foucault, man – who lives, speaks, and produces – is not a historical or epistemological constant, about which the human sciences from the nineteenth century onward finally discovered the truth; rather the figure of man emerges concomitantly with these sciences as the rules governing the discourse of the classical episteme dissolve. While, he claims, we still think in this modern epistemological space – constituted by the domains of biology, economics, philology, and the self-reflexive thinking of finitude established by Kantian critique – psychoanalysis, ethnology, and linguistics have 'dissolved' what was once considered the self-foundational ground of man into the historical relations of norms, rules, and significations by which man is constituted (1966b, 384). Thus, Foucault concludes, it 'is no longer possible to think in our day other than in the void left by man's disappearance' (1966b, 342). In an interview published in the same year as *The Order of Things*, Foucault gives this conclusion its full polemical force: if it is no longer possible to make man the basis of historical reason, then Sartre's philosophical anthropology – along with its model of political praxis – is a historical atavism. Foucault dismisses Sartre as a man of the nineteenth century attempting to think the twentieth (Foucault, 1966a, 569–70). In Rancière's inquiry into the historical *a priori* of aesthetics, it is not possible to declare, with historical finality, that a concept or discourse is for us a thing of the past. He writes: 'I differ from Foucault insofar as his archaeology seems to me to follow a schema of historical necessity according to which, beyond a certain chasm, something is no longer thinkable, can no longer be formulated' (Rancière, 2004b, 50). Thus when Rancière formulates his archaeology of the aesthetic regime of art he maintains that two alternative regimes of art, the representative regime of the arts, and the ethical regime of images, remain possible discursively and practically. On this point, we will examine the relationship between the aesthetic regime of art, the ethical regime of images, and what I call the Platonic regime of art – within the framework of the debate between Rancière and Badiou – in the next chapter.

Given that our account of political subjectivation has emphasized the relationship between Rancière and Sartre, we also ought to address why we will not extend our analyses of this relationship – in a manner similar to our reconsideration of the critique found in *The Philosopher and His Poor* – to the politics of literature and aesthetics. In the case of literature, such a rapprochement might be possible. Christina Howells notes that, despite Rancière's criticisms of *What is Literature?*, 'Rancière conspicuously fails to … look beyond *Qu'est-ce que la littérature* to *L'Idiot de la famille*, where, twenty-five years later, Sartre, like Rancière himself, carries out an exceptionally fine and nuanced discussion of Flaubert's style, and comes to many of the same conclusions as Rancière' (Howells, 2011, 91). Whether or not Rancière is, as Howells claims, a 'careless, prejudiced and insensitive reader of Sartre' concerning Flaubert (Howells, 2011, 93), there is a pronounced difference between their respective accounts – conceptually and historically – of what Rancière thematizes as 'literary misunderstanding'.

According to Rancière, disagreement and misunderstanding are two modalities of introducing the miscount of dissensus into the policing of a distribution of the sensible:

> Disagreement invents names, utterances, arguments and demonstrations that set up new collectives where anyone can get themselves counted in the count of the uncounted. Misunderstanding works on … the count from another angle, by suspending the forms of individuality through which consensual logic binds bodies to meanings. *Politics works on the whole, literature works on the units.* (Rancière, 2006b, 41, my emphasis)

As we have seen in Part I, disagreement is a dynamic of political subjectivation, through which a collective *we* or *us* emerges as a political agent. Literature – and, as Rancière notes, aesthetics – introduces a miscount into the relations between words and things, images and affects, and the divisions of spaces; it introduces through an affective shock a challenge to, or interruption of, sedimented or practico-inert regimes of sense. Literary misunderstanding 'diverges' from political disagreement insofar as it 'dissolves the subjects of utterance [that is, political subjectivity] in the fabric of the percepts and affects of anonymous life' (Rancière, 2006b, 43). While politics affects the whole by introducing a miscount into a given set of social relations, literature and aesthetics are politically transformative when the micropolitics of misunderstanding interrupts those percepts and affects that bind the units – words, images, bodies, and meanings – of a given distribution of the sensible.[2]

Rancière contends that, for Sartre, by contrast, misunderstanding 'does not refer to any structural specificity by means of which a work might elude comprehension' (Rancière, 2006b, 34). Instead, it refers to a historical conflict between a writer – such as Flaubert – and his or her public. Though he does not identify the intra-textual specificity of misunderstanding, Sartre claims that the writer – working between the revolutionary upheavals of 1848 and the absolute negation of literature by the surrealists (in Sartre's chronology, between 1848 and 1918) – refuses to serve any end that the public assigns to literature, whether that public is the bourgeoisie or the proletariat.[3] Both Sartre and Rancière characterize this divergence between politics and literature in similar terms. The autonomy of literature, as Sartre characterizes it, 'amounted to saying that it claimed it had no privileged subject and could treat any matter whatever' (Sartre, 1948b, 111). For Rancière, the 'radical equality' of literature inscribes the micro-events of percepts and affects in the 'impersonal flow of haecceities. Literature tells the truth and offers it to us to feel by freeing these haecceities from the shackles of individualization and objectification' (Rancière, 2006b, 62tm).[4] For Rancière, the politics of literature produces a miscount of the units – affects, words, bodies, meanings – into a distribution of the sensible. For Sartre, however, the divergence between literature and politics is historically temporary. Divorced from his public, contemptuous of democracy, Flaubert – on Sartre's account – petrifies the 'democratic nature of prosaic language' (Rancière, 2006b, 7). According to Sartre, 'Flaubert writes to disentangle himself from men and things. His sentence surrounds the object, seizes it, immobilizes it and breaks its back, changes into stone and petrifies the object as well' (Sartre, 1948b, 118). The autonomy of literature, as it was conceived and practised from 1848 to 1918, is characterized by Sartre as a historical moment of abstract negativity that must be synthesized in the dialectic of freedom. The 'essence' of literature, he contends, is the realization of freedom: 'at the heart of the aesthetic imperative we discern the moral imperative' through which the reader recognizes, in the freedom of writing, the demand for the historical realization of the human freedom of all (Sartre, 1948b, 67).[5] A crucial difference between Sartre and Rancière revolves around the politics of literature.

Ultimately, for Sartre, the intransitive aspects of literature must be mediated by the prosaic politics of freedom, which he links to the dialectics of historical materialism. Not only does his insistence on the necessity of mediation inflect his interpretation of Flaubert, it also limits his appreciation of Negritude. In 'Black Orpheus', Sartre characterizes Negritude as a moment of separation or negativity, an 'anti-racist racism' that must overcome its particularity in the universality of class struggle heralded by the European proletariat (Sartre, 1948a, 319–20). And yet another interpretation of Negritude, drawing on Sartre, is possible. When Sartre writes that the negritude poet 'degallicizes' French words, that 'he will pound them, break down their customary associations, join them together violently', his claims are very similar to Rancière's claims about what literature does (Sartre, 1948a, 281). However, while Sartre recognizes the tension between this poetic parataxis and political struggle, he seeks to subsume the revolutionary potential of Negritude under Western proletarian struggle, reinforcing the Eurocentric standpoint that he set out to critique in

'Black Orpheus'. Though we cannot pursue it here, an interpretation guided by Rancière's concept of literature, which marks the difference between egalitarian politics and the micropolitics of literature, could provide a new account of how Negritude self-reflexively thought its emancipatory potential.[6]

The politics of aesthetics goes beyond reorienting around the praxis of emancipation the debates between existentialism and poststructuralism. In this chapter, I will argue that Rancière's aesthetics – namely, the archaeology of the aesthetic regime of art – provides an important egalitarian framework for conceptualizing a radical relation of politics and aesthetics that avoids numerous problematic claims and confusions found in prominent accounts of – or critiques of – modernity and modernism. Rancière avers that the label *modernity* 'diligently works at masking the specificity' of the aesthetic regime of art (Rancière, 2004b, 24). The concept of modernity, at the hands of its critics,

> arbitrarily sweeps together such figures as Hölderlin, Cézanne, Mallarmé, Malevich, or Duchamp into a vast whirlwind where Cartesian science gets mixed up with revolutionary parricide, the age of the masses with Romantic irrationalism, the ban on representation with the techniques of mechanized reproduction, the Kantian sublime with the Freudian primal scene, the flight of the gods with the extermination of the Jews in Europe. (2004b, 11)

A reader versed in twentieth-century Continental philosophy will recognize in this passage the type of generalizations present in Heidegger's critique of Western metaphysics and technicity as well as claims found in the work of the later Lyotard.[7] Rancière is not alone in pointing out how these generalizations conflate the aims and consequences of historically distinct artistic and philosophical engagements, in order to foreclose on the possibility of engagement – political or artistic – itself. A similar critique can be found in the fourth chapter of Badiou's *Manifesto for Philosophy*, 'Heidegger Viewed as Commonplace'. Given that Rancière is committed to a politics that affirms subjective, egalitarian praxis, it is not difficult to see the tone of casual dismissal of the conflations collected under the rubric of a critique of modernity.

Nonetheless, Rancière maintains that his aesthetics, too, offers a 'counter-history of "artistic modernity"' (Rancière, 2011a, xiii). With his counter-history of aesthetics, Rancière aims to resituate those artistic practices subsumed historically and conceptually under the label 'modern art'. First, he argues that what we consider to be modern art and what we consider to be the experience of modernity, often formulated by reference to the works of Baudelaire and Manet, are made possible by the emergence of the aesthetic regime of art in the late eighteenth century. Thus Rancière's account is more historically extensive than many received accounts of modernity and modernism.

Then, on this historical basis, Rancière contends that previous accounts of the relationship between the politics and aesthetics of modern art, which often take Baudelaire or Manet as the historical and conceptual starting points of either the historical avant-gardes or the modernist avant-garde, are too narrow. In broad terms, the historical avant-gardes such as Surrealism, Futurism and Constructivism demanded that the ultimate task of art was, after the necessary destruction of genres, forms and subject matters, to abolish the distance between art and life, since a historically actual art would not be an art but fully imbricated in social life, while the proponents of modernism – such as Clement Greenberg – argue that the socio-historical task of art is to practise what Rancière calls a 'politics of resistant form': 'form asserts its politicity by distinguishing itself from every form of intervention into the mundane world' (Rancière, 2004b, 39–40); through the self-critique of the medium of an art, modernism resists being appropriated by commodification and kitsch.[8] Rancière does not argue that these two critical demands – that art becomes life, or that life becomes art – are false. Instead, as we will see in Section 3.2, he argues that they both become possible through the emergence of the aesthetic regime and the collapse of what he calls the representative regime of the arts. We will see that, for Rancière, aesthetics marks the collapse of the alignment between the valuation of social hierarchies and artistic hierarchies, not the end of the use of representation or figuration in art.

After outlining Rancière's aesthetics, I will address his readings of Greenberg's modernism and Benjamin's account of the politics of aesthetics and critique of modernity. Both Greenberg and Benjamin are, from Rancière's standpoint, pivotal and influential figures for thinking artistic modernity. However, for differing reasons, neither fully accounts for the egalitarian aspect of aesthetics. On the one hand, Rancière claims that Greenberg's theorization of modernism 'is in fact a liquidation of the dominant tendency of the aesthetic regime, which is to abolish the boundaries between "mediums", between high art and popular art, and ultimately between art and life' (Rancière and Davis, 2013, 205). On the other hand, Rancière claims, in 'The Archaeomodern Turn' (1996a), that Benjamin disrupts the conceptual structure that links emancipation to modernity as a moment of historical awakening, though without dispensing with this historical model. Therefore to show how Rancière breaks with the conceptual frameworks of modernity and modernism, I will address, in Section

3.3, how Rancière provides the resources to critique the anti-egalitarianism that orients Greenberg's Marxist sociology, and, in Section 3.4, how Rancière underlines the egalitarian potential of the micropolitics of aesthetics against Benjamin's messianism. In Section 3.5, I will reiterate, using his interpretation of Kant's concept of aesthetic judgement, Rancière's philosophical commitment to intellectual and aesthetic equality. Rather than search out, like Greenberg, a form of art that resists the commodification of kitsch, or, like Benjamin, a practice of artistic production that politicizes art without aestheticizing politics, Rancière holds that art is political because it opens the possibility for egalitarian social transformation.

3.2. From mimesis to aesthetics

Rancière's account of the aesthetic regime of art is formulated in terms that allow us to reconsider the discourses and practices that are typically understood to be part of artistic modernity, including the historical avant-gardes such as Dadaism, Futurism or Surrealism, and modernist art. As he writes in *The Future of the Image*, the aesthetic regime of art is similar to what is usually called modernity, except that he wants to 'avoid the teleologies inherent in temporal markers' (Rancière, 2003, 38). Tanke has observed that absent from Rancière's work 'is the idea that the history of art culminates in a single form or style'; instead, he 'attempts to describe how different practices transformed the fabric in which we experience art' (Tanke, 2013, 126). Hence Rancière approaches moments of the aesthetic regime of art as a number of singular events he calls 'scenes'. These scenes place in relation works and texts to show how a 'given artistic appearance requires changes in the paradigms of art', where something that was once not art becomes art, how a work takes on a novel significance, how a text makes possible new constellations of words, things, places, and meanings (Rancière, 2011a, xi).

While Rancière rejects the supposition of a historical teleology that guides aesthetics, the aesthetic regime of art nevertheless has a history. The aesthetic regime of art emerges in the late eighteenth century as the norms and rules that govern the representative regime of the arts begin to collapse. Before the emergence of the aesthetic regime, Rancière claims, an artwork was considered as belonging to one of the fine arts, each of which was governed by a series of artistic hierarchies analogous to social hierarchies; superior arts required the correct subject matter, proper technical ability, and the proper representation of subjects and actions. Aesthetics undermines the representative regime of the arts by dispensing with the normative rules of classifying and valorizing the various arts, genres, and subjects. This does not occur because aesthetics gradually dispenses with representation or figuration, rather aesthetics undermines the hierarchies between the various fine arts, genres, and subjects; the aesthetic revolution breaks with the representative regime of the arts through 'the abolition of the parallelism that aligned artistic hierarchies with social hierarchies' (Rancière, 2003, 106).

In this sense, Rancière's aesthetics is anarchic: the aesthetic regime, he writes, 'strictly identifies art in the singular and frees it from any specific rule, from any hierarchy of the arts, subject matter, and genres' (Rancière, 2004b, 23). Such a definition, as Rancière notes, confirms that aesthetics designates a confusion, not only of the arts, subject matter, and genres, but also between the proper domains of a science of sensation and a philosophy of art. At the beginning of his *Aesthetics*, Hegel begrudgingly acknowledges that, for a science of the beautiful in art, the term 'taken literally, is not wholly satisfactory, since "Aesthetics" means, more precisely, the science of sensation, of feeling' (Hegel, 1835, 1). And yet, for Schiller, the imprecise use of the term affirms the total singularity of aesthetics: the aesthetic character of an object is different from physical, logical, or moral determinations because it relates 'to the totality of our various functions without being a definite object for any single one of them' (Schiller, 1795, 141–3n). Schiller's aesthetics, as we will see in the next chapter, 'suspends' or challenges the philosophical distinctions between appearance and reality, form and matter, activity and passivity, and understanding and sensibility (Rancière, 2004a, 30).

Rancière, then, appropriates Schiller's use the term to name a specific sensory experience of art. While within the representative regime of the arts, mimesis governs the relation between *poiesis* and *aisthesis*, within aesthetics, *poiesis* and *aisthesis* stand 'in immediate relation to each other' (Rancière, 2004a, 8). To interpret this claim, we must recall that Rancière is undertaking an archaeology that seeks to show how the experience of art in the aesthetic regime of art becomes possible. He does not mean that there is an immediate identity between the two terms, that with aesthetics we have uncovered the true, authentic *aisthesis* of *poiesis*. Instead, he argues that the aesthetic regime of art is distinct from the representative regime because *aisthesis* and *poiesis* are no longer regulated by the mimetic norms that align social hierarchies with artistic hierarchies. To refine the point further, immediacy does not designate identity, as identification is, for Rancière, a technique of policing rather than emancipation. On this point, his politics and aesthetics are consistent. While politics is defined by disagreement, aesthetics is defined by relations of misunderstanding and aesthetic suspension or aesthetic distance. Aesthetics, on his account, is an experience of relations between artwork and text, between art and non-art, between art and politics, and these are relations of tensions and differences, practices that are staged between art and text, art and non-art, and art and politics. Moreover, like literary misunderstanding, aesthetics involves a suspension of the practico-inert forms of a distribution of the sensible: the 'politics' of art 'consists in suspending the normal coordinates of sensory experience' (2004a, 25). Aesthetics, Ranciere contends, opens new possibilities – in, as we should stress, a micropolitical sense – for transformative and egalitarian practices.

3.2.1. Breaking with mimetic norms

The aesthetic regime names, according to Rancière, a singular experience of art. Aesthetics is not confined to the experience of *an* art, such as literature, painting or film. It instead names the experience of an *aisthesis* of 'whatever falls within the domain of art' (Rancière, 2004b, 22), as the boundaries of the domain of art are often shifting. 'Art exists', he writes, 'as a separate world since anything whatsoever can belong to it' (Rancière, 2011a, x). Aesthetics involves a paradoxical relation between autonomy and heteronomy: art is a singular and autonomous practice and experience that disrupts the everyday sense of the practico-inert, and yet there is no self-identical or insular domain of art separate from the totality of social relations. Since his aesthetics is concerned with the way that art suspends or interrupts our practico-inert experience of a given distribution of the sensible, Rancière does not necessarily privilege a particular artform – even though he has dedicated a significant number of books to literature and practices of writing: the politics of writing is arguably one of the major themes of his works on history such as *Proletarian Nights* (1981) and *The Names of History: On the Poetics of Knowledge* (1992), while *Mallarmé: The Politics of the Siren* (1996b), *The Flesh of Words: The Politics of Writing* (1998b), *Mute Speech* (1998d), *The Aesthetic Unconscious* (2001) and *The Politics of Literature* (2006b) take up more typically literary themes.[9]

In what follows, I will examine Rancière's treatment of literature as a specific set of practices within the aesthetic regime of art. There are several reasons to do so. First, he contends that the break between the representative regime and aesthetic regime took place first in literature (Rancière, 2004b, 32). While Balzac, Hugo and Flaubert are the canonical, as it were, figures of Rancière's account of literature, he elsewhere shows that they are preceded by the criticism of Vico, Winckelmann and Schiller, who – in their respective interpretations of Homer, the *Belvedere Torso* and the *Juno Ludovici* – sought to articulate an aesthetics that would no longer rely on the norms of mimesis.[10] Given that Rancière holds that 'a theoretical discourse is always simultaneously an aesthetic form, a sensible reconfiguration of the facts it is arguing about' (Rancière, 2004b, 65), we should not expect a strict distinction between literature and criticism. Indeed, the aesthetic 'scenes' in his recent *Aisthesis* are staged between artworks and critical texts. Second, and perhaps because the break between the representative regime and aesthetics takes place first with literature, Rancière's account of literary production provides the most extensive discussion of the differences between the norms of mimesis and aesthetics. Finally, this discussion of literature will serve as the basis from whence we can distinguish Rancière's aesthetics from Greenberg's and Benjamin's.

The defining feature, Rancière contends, of the representative regime of the arts – whether we are discussing the criticism of Voltaire and his eighteenth-century peers or the paradigmatic text of the representative regime, Aristotle's *Poetics* – is the parallel it establishes between social hierarchies and artistic hierarchies. Rancière outlines four principles that guide the norms of mimesis: the principle of fiction, the principle of genre, the principle of decorum, and the principle of presence (Rancière, 1998d, 44–50). First, mimesis is defined by the principle of fiction. According to Aristotle, the arts of poetry and history are not distinguished because one uses verse and the other prose, but rather poetry is of 'more philosophic and graver import' than history because it is a universal and organic representation of action and plot that legislates what ought to happen, whereas history describes singular cases of what has been (1451b5–6). On Rancière's reading, the principle of fiction separates the poetics of action – what he describes as 'the causal rationality of action' – from the prosaic world of maintaining and reproducing quotidian life (Rancière, 2006b, 9).

Second, the fiction of mimesis is regulated by genre. Genre is not determined by formal principles; instead, it is defined by what it represents. Though Aristotle's claim that tragedy (and epic poetry) represents 'serious subjects in a grand kind of verse' in order to arouse the affects of catharsis, while comedy treats those who are ridiculous, appears to be a formal distinction between genres, the hierarchy of genres parallels social hierarchies (1449b10). He adds that comedy imitates those who are worse than ordinary people, while tragedy imitates those who are more noble (1448a18; 1454b9). Moreover, tragedy only affects pity, fear, and catharsis if the subject or character is one of 'great reputation and prosperity'

– such as Oedipus – whose misfortune is the result of ignorance or an error of judgement (1453a10). Tragedy would have no cathartic effects if one represented the good characters falling into misery, bad characters attaining happiness, or bad personages falling from happiness to misery. As Rancière summarizes, the generic principle separates two forms of humanity and two forms of imitation: the epic poet or tragedian must represent noble actions and deeds with the highest degree of perfection, while the comedian represents lowly or vicious people with ridiculous or satiric affects (Rancière, 1998d, 45).

Third, the principle of decorum requires that the speech and actions of the subjects be appropriate to their nature. An imitation is pleasing if it follows the criteria of decorum: imitations must conform to 'the nature of human passions in general', to the manners and mores of historical characters or figures, to the codes of decency and taste held by the audience, and to 'the logic of actions and characters proper to a particular genre' (1998d, 46). Aristotle concedes – a concession relative to the misogyny that permeates his work (see Chapter 1) – that a female character may be good or moral, though 'it is not appropriate' to make her 'manly, or clever' (1454a23–4). Rancière provides numerous instances of similar claims from Voltaire's *Commentaires sur Corneille*, where Voltaire objects to warriors or princesses speaking and acting like shepherds and servants, since such vulgar speech is not appropriate to a person of such noble standing. Voltaire's adherence to the principles of decorum extend beyond his criticism; Schiller will later note that, unlike Greek tragedy,

> We can scarcely believe that a hero of a French tragedy *suffers*, since he expresses how he feels in the manner of the calmest men and the constant concern for the impression being made on others never lets him indulge the natural freedom within him. The kings, princesses, and heroes of a Corneille and Voltaire never forget their *position* even in the most passionate suffering and would far sooner doff their *humanity* than surrender their *dignity*. They are like the kings and emperors in the old picture books, who take their crowns with them to bed. (Schiller, 1793, 46)

Schiller, as this passage shows, satirizes the hyperbolic observance of the norms governing the representative regime of the arts. He argues, as we will see in Chapter 4, that the sensibility of art involves an entirely different aesthetic experience.

The final principle governing the representative regime of the arts is the principle of presence (*actualité*; read: relevant to the present moment), which uses efficacious speech, or 'speech in action', as the model for mimesis. There is, Rancière states, a double economy of the system of representation by which fictitious speech refers back to political oratory or rhetoric: it is a 'relationship of address regulated between speech acts and defined audiences on whom these speech acts were supposed to produce the effects of mobilizing thoughts, emotions and energies' (Rancière, 2006b, 12).[11] The parallel between artistic hierarchies and social hierarchies extends to the relation of the arts and their audiences. Whether it is a public of 'princes, generals, magistrates and preachers' or of republican orators, speech is the model for the arts because they address a public that acts through speech.

3.2.2. Mute speech and literary equality

Examining what Rancière calls mute speech and literary equality will make the differences between the aesthetic regime of art and the representative regime of the arts more concrete. He argues that the practice of literature involves a 'strict and term-for-term reversal' of the four principles that guide the practices of the representative regime (Rancière, 1998d, 50). More importantly, literature introduces a series of practices and a hermeneutics that replace the norms governing the arts and relation between artistic and social hierarchies with an aesthetics of tensions, conflicts, and contradictions. While the representative regime can be characterized as a mode of artistic policing, literature and aesthetics are by definition political. The terms with which Rancière characterizes this new regime of writing and its politics – mute speech, literary equality, literary democracy – have multiple and conflicting meanings endemic to the practice of literature itself. As he writes, 'there is no *one* politics of literature'; instead, there are several – at least three – conflicting practices of literary production (Rancière, 2006b, 21).

Literature is political, first, insofar as it undermines the norms of mimesis. For the moment, we will outline how literary misunderstanding or literary equality reverses the mimetic priority of the principles of fiction, genre, decorum, and presence. As we have seen, Aristotle means to establish the fiction of a 'causal rationality of action', the superiority of the acts and deeds of great men, that is superior to history and everyday life. Literature replaces this causal fiction with a new hermeneutics of 'mute speech' that is at once 'more mute and more talkative' (2006b, 14). Mimesis, Rancière argues, is a fiction that links significance to a 'will to signify,' in which speech and deeds are a mode of address from will to will – hence the model of speech in action. Whereas the representative regime of the arts is a system that lends visibility to the words and deeds of great men, literature, Rancière argues, both verbalizes the prosaic world of those who live and labour outside of the courts and assemblies of great men and deciphers the signs written on the mute things that support the actions of the characters – in short, the poetics of the stage on which the story takes place, of 'the laws of a world on the body of mundane things and in words of no importance' (2006b, 21). Literature relates signs to signs; it seeks to decipher the mute meanings of objects and of language itself. Whereas the representative regime presents a poetics of great men and deeds, literature shows 'the world of prosaic reality as an immense fabric of signs that bear, as written, the history of a time, a civilization or a society' (2006b, 15). The immersion of human deeds in the mute yet garrulous signs of the multitude of things, of the prosaic world, also undermines the hierarchies of genre and decorum. Rancière argues literary equality introduces an indifference toward subject matter and characters. Recall that for Aristotle, the superior genres are to portray noble characters and noble deeds, while lowbrow, as it were, genres portray lesser men. While dismantling the link between social distinction and the distinction of genres, literature also dispenses with the principle of decorum. Style is no longer governed by the speech the audience ought to expect from a character such as a prince or general; it is not the style of a character or subject. Instead, whether through a process of absolutization or indifference, style is established through the work.

Finally, while the representative regime privileges the ideal of speech in action as the norm for mimesis, literature – and hence aesthetics – makes writing its model. This claim that literature is modelled on writing seems redundant.[12] Writing, however, stages another form of mute speech – a form of speech available to anybody and everybody. To delineate what he means by this reference to mute speech, Rancière returns to one of the foundational texts on the art of writing, Plato's *Phaedrus*. Using Plato as a philosophical signpost for elaborating on mute speech is a problematic move, given that Rancière holds that literature is not a transhistorical constant, that it only emerges in the late eighteenth century. However, I think his reading of the *Phaedrus* presents an implicit critique of Derrida's interpretation found in 'Plato's Pharmacy'. In 'Plato's Pharmacy', one of the emblematic texts of deconstruction, Derrida shows that the opposition between living speech and writing is itself supplemented by the opposition between two types of writing: one which is an inscription on the soul, internal, living, intelligible, and accessible by *anamnesis* (memory), the other an imitation of the inscription of the soul, and as an imitation, external, moribund, ignorant, and merely a technique of reminding or rote memorization. This opposition of good writing and bad writing will, according to Derrida, come to 'dominate all of Western philosophy' (Derrida, 1972, 149).

Rancière, though he dismisses the framework of the critique of metaphysics that guides Derrida's analysis, takes up the latter's suggestion that writing is democratic. As Derrida notes, Plato derides democracy for treating everyone equally regardless of competence, and written discourse – unlike the writing of the soul – is an orphaned and 'errant democrat' (Derrida, 1972, 145) that

> roams about everywhere, reaching indiscriminately those with understanding no less than those who have no business with it, and it doesn't know to whom it should speak and to whom it should not. And when it is faulted and attacked unfairly, it always needs its father's support; alone, it can neither defend itself nor come to its own support. (Plato, 275e)

By contrast, philosophy is a discourse written in the soul, which possesses the mastery to defend itself, and which knows when it should speak (and to whom) and when it should stay silent (276a). While Derrida reads this passage as a decisive moment in the history of Western metaphysics, Rancière emphasizes that the opposition between these two types of writing is grounded in a 'sociology' and an 'aesthetics' that distinguishes between two types of speech acts (Rancière, 1983, 47).[13] Philosophy asserts its truth as a speech that directs the soul to the good; it knows which kind of speech is appropriate to each kind of soul – for example, it knows to engage in dialectics with other philosophers, and to narrate the myth of the metals of the soul for the many. Indeed, it is 'speech in action' that separates two categories of beings within the community, a duty to speech that distinguishes between the workers who are lulled to sleep mid-day by the songs of cicadas and those whose speech bestows upon them the divine gift of the philosophical life (Rancière, 1998d, 94). Even the respite of the countryside and the chorus of the cicadas serves as a reminder of Plato's archipolitics: for those who work this leisure is a time to rest, while those who do philosophy must speak lest the cicadas mistake them for the multitude, slaves, or sheep.[14] As Rancière writes, the 'chorus of cicadas traces the circle that isolates free dialectic from the occupations of those whose vigilance merely follows the curves of fatigue and heat' (1983, 49).

The mute speech of writing upsets the sociology and aesthetics of Plato's archipolitics. The philosopher knows when to speak and when to keep silent, and, despite the buffoonery of some of Socrates's interlocutors, he or she knows how to establish the competency of those to whom he or she speaks. Writing, that 'errant democrat', however, is a type of speech that is simultaneously mute and too loquacious (Rancière, 1983, 40/1998d, 93–4). It is too mute, for even if writing says something as though it has knowledge, when interrogated it can only repeat what it has already said (275d); it can neither defend itself nor support itself. Yet at the same time, writing is too loquacious, speaking to anybody and everybody regardless of competency, roaming the streets addressing those in the know and those who aren't. For Plato, this errant speech is nothing more than a democratic anarchy that undermines social hierarchies. For Rancière, this mute loquacity of the written word carries an emancipatory potential that, when literature takes up writing as its metaphorical model, subverts the primacy of speech in action – the principle of presence – that governed the representative regime of the arts.

One politics of literature, then, dismantles the parallelism that binds social hierarchies and artistic hierarchies within the representative regime of the arts; this politics opposes literary equality to the hierarchies that governed the norms of mimesis. There are at least, on Rancière's account, two other politics of literature: one a form of political and literary symptomology or metapolitics (2006b, 21), and the other a form of 'molecular democracy' (2006b, 26). He does not mean that literature sets out a political programme. Instead, literature is political 'by being literature', by interrupting and transforming a given distribution of the sensible. When Rancière discusses literary democracy he invokes conflicting practices of literature that entangle – in different ways – political subjectivity in the mute loquaciousness of words, things, and affects. These two other types of the politics of literature involve new relations between words and things, new relations between *poiesis* and *aisthesis,* and new modes of conceptualizing these relations that do not prioritize mimesis as a basis of artistic norms.

The first form is a poetic and metapolitical symptomology. As discussed in the Introduction, in *Disagreement* Rancière classifies Marxist political theory as a form of metapolitics as well. Metapolitics, politically speaking, looks behind the staging of the conflict of egalitarian politics and regimes of policing in order to identify the economic motor of historical struggle; in terms of literature, it submerges the men of speech and action who once oriented the causal rationality of the representative regime within the world of the banal objects of everyday life that seem trivial, or insignificant; it is a hermeneutics that deciphers the mute signs of everyday and commonplace objects, giving back to them – as Rancière says, echoing Benjamin's appropriation of Marx's analysis of commodity fetishism – 'their suprasensible, fantasmagorical aspect for us to see the secret writing of the functioning of society' (Rancière, 2006b, 22). In his work on literature and aesthetics, Rancière claims that this poetics structures the conceptual apparatus of metapolitics, as the distribution of the sensible that makes symptomal reading possible. Balzac, for example, presents a model of social forces that distinguishes social consciousness from the social unconscious: in *Lost Illusions*, the protagonist Lucien discovers, behind the stage of human actions and the efforts of talent and genius, the social mechanisms that drive social relations.[15] Thus Rancière reverses the priority between Marxist or Freudian criticism (especially in their structuralist forms) and literature: when they 'believed they were demystifying literary naiveté and formulating its unconscious discourse' they did not realize that the 'explanatory models they used to tell the truth about the literary text are the models forged by literature itself' (Rancière, 2006b, 22). This point, as we will see below, bears on Rancière's interpretation of Benjamin.

Yet there is another politics of literature that remains in tension with this literary symptomology. 'Molecular democracy', on Rancière's account, frees mute speech from symptomal hermeneutics by making the 'mute word ... the sheer intensity of things without rhyme or reason' (2006b, 25). This practice of literature, he states in terms borrowed from Deleuze, seeks out molecular intensities in the interstices of the 'molar equality' of political subjects as well as the molar phantasmagoria of symptomal hermeneutics. Rancière illustrates this point with one of Flaubert's jokes, that he, Flaubert, is 'less interested in the poor man dressed in rags than in the lice devouring him' (2006b, 25). Rancière uses this concept of molecular democracy to interpret Flaubert, and the concept could also be an important tool for rereading those works that are so often classified as modernist literature, but this is beyond the scope of this book. For our purposes, it is important to underline that it is the tension between three types of the politics of literature that delimits how the micropolitics of literature transform the sensible fabric of the social world. This tension and play between sense and nonsense, between the mute and garrulous speech of things that set the stage of collective life and micro-events that dissolve meanings into the intensities of percepts and affects define, for Rancière, the autonomy of literature. Though 'autonomy' is not a central category of his aesthetics, Rancière's use of the term contrasts sharply with its usage by modernist critics, for whom 'literary modernity has been styled as the implementation of an intransitive use of language as opposed to its communicative use' (Rancière, 2006b, 5). For modernist critics, such as Greenberg, the autonomy of an art consists in the interrogation of the opacity of its unique medium, but for Rancière, the autonomy of aesthetics is premised upon the rupture with the representative regime of art, the autonomy of literature upon misunderstanding and literary equality.

3.3. Artistic autonomy and sociology in Greenberg

Rancière's treatment of artistic autonomy places him at odds with the most prominent advocate of modernism, Clement Greenberg. Indeed, Rancière has more in common with social historians of art such as T. J. Clark or Linda Nochlin, who look at the social conditions that make the experience of, or discourse about, art possible. Clark, for instance, argues that if 'flatness was compelling and tractable for art' in the works of Manet and his contemporaries – Manet being for Greenberg one of the first painters to affirm the flatness and two-dimensionality of the medium of painting – it took on values 'which necessarily derived from elsewhere than art' (Clark, 1999, 13). On Clark's account, Manet's *Olympia* (1863, exhibited 1865) upsets the assumptions of spectator's gaze by evoking, in part through the flatness and stark modelling of Olympia's flesh, bourgeois anxieties concerning class and the commodification of sex (Clark, 1999, 138–9). Far from being Baudelaire's flâneur who sees and enjoys but who is not seen, the spectator is met by the gaze of Olympia, who, as Clark notes, 'looks out at the viewer in a way which obliges him to imagine a whole fabric of sociality in which this look might make sense and include him'; in recognizing markers of acceptable and unacceptable relations between classes and genders, 'the viewer might have access to Olympia; but clearly it would no longer be access to a nude' (Clark, 1999, 133).[16] While I think their research is largely compatible with Rancière's despite their differences over the analytic value of the term 'modern art,' Rancière claims that social historians such as Clark are anti-aesthetic insofar as they focus too narrowly on the 'reality of economic, political, and ideological constraints laying out the conditions for artistic practice', while he wants to stress how art disrupts, in a micropolitically emancipatory way, those limiting constraints (Rancière, 2004a, 2).[17]

This brief summation, however, strikes me as an overgeneralization, for some of the political and aesthetic concerns of the social history of art foreshadow Rancière's own. Let us look, for an example, at Nochlin's interpretation of Courbet's *A Burial at Ornans* (1850). She notes that far too much emphasis is often given to Courbet's choice of subject matter at the expense of interpreting the significance of the pictorial innovations of *A Burial at Ornans*. For Greenberg, at least at one point, Courbet is the 'first real avant-garde painter' for both rejecting bourgeois artistic ideals in favour of 'prosaic contemporary life' and introducing a 'new flatness' in painting that pays equal attention to all parts of the canvas (Greenberg, 1940, 29).[18] On Nochlin's account, by contrast, the 'flatness', as it were, of the serpentine movement of the provincial figures attending the funeral is pictorially innovative for treating the 'concreteness and the randomness of ordinary life' on a scale previously reserved for historical painting – with the grand scale of the historical genre reserved for that type of history that is the 'elevated realm of kings, nobles and heroes' (Nochlin, 1965, 28).

She demonstrates that Courbet shatters the link between social hierarchies and artistic hierarchies by comparing *A Burial at Ornans* to both Thomas Couture's *The Romans of the Decadence* (1847) and the lesser-known *A Village Burial* by Augustin Roger (shown in the Salon of 1822). *The Romans of the Decadence* contraposes the vices of the present against a 'fading classical grandeur' represented by antique statuary and architecture shrouded in mist through a spatial depth that lends psychological and metaphysical depth to Couture's allegorical commentary on the corruption of Louis-Philippe's regime. By contrast, Courbet portrays, on the grand scale of historical painting, the specific individuals of Ornans in a winding and seemingly haphazard procession back and forth across the canvas, occluding the possibility of a central point of focus. However, Nochlin notes, Courbet's break with the conventions of historical paintings lies not in painting ordinary people in the midst of everyday life; similar subject matter is portrayed in Roger's *A Village Burial*. Courbet's innovation concerns the composition of *A Burial at Ornans*. While Roger's painting emphasizes the vertical contrast of the 'dominating church' to the overgrown foliage and the anguish of the figures, as well as the light from out of the dark sky which illuminates the burial and allegorizes the religious overtones of the passage from life to death, the narrow and horizontal composition of the landscape of *A Burial at Ornans* emphasizes the specificity of *this* funeral and the social bonds it evokes rather than transcendent and religious significance of funerals in general (Nochlin, 1965, 27). There are two features of Nochlin's interpretation that suggest – that foreshadow or prepare for the reception of – Rancière's account of the rupture between the representative regime of the arts and aesthetics. First, she shows that Courbet's *A Burial at Ornans* disrupts the parallel between a concept of history that recounts great deeds and the grand style of historical painting. And second, her description of the way that Courbet's composition precludes the allegorical and historical meanings that – as in the case of Roger – orient portrayals of ordinary life anticipates Rancière's definition of aesthetic autonomy; discussing Hegel's interest in Murillo's paintings of the poor, Rancière writes: the 'autonomy of painting is first and foremost the autonomy of its figures in relation to histories and allegories in which they had their place and their function' (Rancière, 2011a, 31).

Rancière seeks, like Clark or Nochlin, to rethink the significance of artistic practices outside of the narrow conceptual limits of modernism. I will delineate, using Rancière's work, a two-pronged critique of Greenberg. First, I will argue that Greenberg's modernism presents only one side of what Rancière describes as the aesthetic revolution, which sets in motion not only an impetus toward aesthetic equality, but also the critical demands that art should become life or life should become art. Modernism, as a practice of resistant form, can only account for the latter demand. This is not to say that there was not a historical practice of artistic abstraction, or that Greenberg's account of modern art is false. Rather Greenberg's criticism is a productive discourse, amplifying specific features and works of modern art, but one which, as we will see, leaves many aspects – if we are not satisfied with his opposition between avant-garde and kitsch – of modern art partially described or unexplained. After outlining this account of modernism, I will then address Rancière's more recent criticism, developed primarily in *Aisthesis*, of the sociology that guides Greenberg's politics of modernism. More specifically, we will examine the opposition that Rancière has recently drawn between aesthetics and modernism:

> the dominant modernist paradigm (the Greenbergian theorization of the avant-garde) is in fact a liquidation of the dominant tendency of the aesthetic regime, which is to abolish the boundaries between 'mediums,' between high art and popular art, and ultimately between art and life. (Rancière and Davis, 2013, 204–5)

As we will see, Greenberg's version of the politics of resistant form is, despite its socialist rhetoric, a discourse of what Rancière calls intellectual stultification rather than aesthetic emancipation.

In 'Towards a Newer Laocoon' (1940), Greenberg offers a 'historical apology for abstract art' that begins in terms seemingly compatible with Rancière. As we have seen, for Rancière, literature and aesthetics emerge with the collapse of the norms of the representative regime of the arts. Greenberg traces the impetus for the modernist aesthetic to a historical rupture between Romanticism and the conventions of the literary arts of the seventeenth and eighteenth centuries: Romanticism was a revolution in subject matter, 'abandoning the oratorical and frivolous literature of 18th century painting' while introducing 'a greater boldness in pictorial means' (Greenberg, 1940, 26–7). Nevertheless, Greenberg draws from this revolution conclusions diametrically opposed to Rancière. While Rancière sees in aesthetics a productive confusion – a confusion that sets the course for an 'indeterminate singularity' of art as the domain and practice of challenging boundaries between mediums, between highbrow and lowbrow art, between discourses about art, and between art and life (Rancière, 2004a, 6) – for Greenberg the confusion of the arts arises when the dominance of one art causes the others to be 'perverted and distorted'. And while Rancière holds that literature initiates the break with the norms of mimesis, Greenberg treats literature – and by this term he means narrative techniques – as the paradigmatic artform of the confusion of the arts, a confusion in which each art other than literature must suppress its medium to imitate the effects of another (Greenberg, 1940, 26).[19] The modernist aesthetic revolution takes place, according to Greenberg, when the various arts take the absolute and abstract – non-imitative – character of music as a paradigmatic artistic method of approaching the unique medium of an art rather than seeking a kind of aesthetic effect (1940, 31).

Though Greenberg frames the origins of modernism in historical terms in 'Towards a Newer Laocoon', in other essays he argues that modernism is made possible by the confluence of the intellectual revolutions that followed from Kant's *Critique of Pure Reason* (see 'Modernist Painting', 1965) and Marx's historical materialism, the industrial revolution, and urbanization (see 'Avant-Garde and Kitsch', 1939). For Greenberg argues that the philosophies of Kant and Marx ground the general intellectual milieu for modernist self-criticism, which was nevertheless carried out in 'a spontaneous and subliminal way', and only subsequently available for theorization through art criticism (Greenberg, 1965, 9). Kant and Marx provide the intellectual resources for the modernist avant-garde to formulate, again in an unconscious way, a mode of artistic and cultural production that was neither bourgeois nor kitsch. According to Greenberg, the modernist avant-garde derives, however diffusely, its motivation from historical materialism, and its method – the self-critique of an art through the interrogation of its unique medium – by analogy to Kantian critique. Though many of the members of bohemia and the avant-gardes were 'demonstratively uninterested in politics', the circulation of revolutionary ideas emboldened avant-garde artists to reject the mores and norms of the bourgeoisie and the markets of capitalism (Greenberg, 1939, 5).

While Greenberg's claim that the Kantian and Marxist revolutions influenced the modernist avant-garde is open to dispute, I am more interested in the interpretative choices Greenberg makes when discussing Kant and Marx. According to Greenberg, Marx makes 'the only real beginning in the discussion of the problem of culture' (Greenberg, 1953, 26), but his reading of Marx is loosely economistic.[20] This is evident when Greenberg writes, in passages that seem to echo parts of the 'Preface to *A Critique of Political Economy*', that 'Marx assumed that scientific technology – industrialism – would eventually do away with class divisions' (1953, 26) – with no mention of the role of mass political struggle. While Greenberg places stress on class divisions in the formation of the modernist avant-gardes, he treats industrialization as the agent of historical change. On his account, the modernist avant-garde emigrates from bourgeois society, much like the intellectuals described in *The Communist Manifesto*, but it does not join the revolutionary proletariat, for the proletariat and petty bourgeoisie 'set up a pressure on society to provide them with a kind of culture fit for their own consumption', the commodification of culture through kitsch (Greenberg, 1939, 10). For Greenberg, the bourgeoisie and proletariat are both culturally reactionary. Hence the modernist avant-garde must seek out a form of cultural production that resists being assimilated by bourgeois taste (even if it continues to rely on bourgeois patronage) or kitsch.

While he relies on Marx to formulate the motivation for the modernist avant-garde, Greenberg outlines its method of self-critique through an analogy to Kant's *Critique of Pure Reason*. Kant introduces an immanent critique of reason to overcome the impasses of Hume's scepticism and Wolff's dogmatism in order to demonstrate how synthetic judgements *a priori* are possible. Delimiting boundaries of reason makes it possible for philosophy to 'secure its rightful claims while dismissing all its groundless pretensions', to secure against the sceptics the possibility of *a priori* cognitions without uncritical reliance on dogmatic principles (Kant, 1781/1787, A, xi). The self-critique of reason makes it possible to establish the autonomy and 'competency' (as Greenberg has it) of philosophy.

Greenberg argues that the modernist self-critique employs, like Kant, 'the characteristic methods of a discipline to criticize the discipline itself' in order to reinforce the autonomy of each art (Greenberg, 1965, 5). Modernist art adopts a 'politics of resistant form': an art is self-justificatory insofar as it produces an experience that cannot be derived from any other activity; its value as a domain of experience cannot be reduced to exchange value or its value as entertainment. To establish its autonomy or competency, each art must exhibit and make explicit 'that which was unique and irreducible not only in art in general, but also in each particular art' (1965, 5). In the case of painting, flatness is the sole condition that is unique to its medium.[21] Representation or figuration then becomes secondary. Hence for Greenberg, Manet's paintings 'became the first Modernist ones by virtue of the frankness with which they declared the surfaces on which they were painted' (Greenberg, 1965, 6). The modernist self-critique of painting requires divesting the medium of the characteristics of the other arts, especially the 'tactile associations' of sculpture and the narrative support of literature. Manet's work, on this account, is modern insofar as it displays what Greenberg calls a 'syncopated kind of shading-modeling' that dispenses with the sculptural modelling of European painting since the Renaissance (Greenberg, 1967, 242). This syncopated modelling produces the effect of flatness through the use of abrupt juxtaposition of light and dark values. Divested of sculptural and literary (i.e. narrative) techniques, modernist painting then orients itself to interrogating the flatness and two-dimensionality of pictorial space. By challenging 'all theories about art for their relevance to the actual practice and experience of art,' by dispensing with all aspects of an art except that which is unique to its medium, modernism becomes, according to Greenberg, subversive (Greenberg, 1965, 9).

As a social experience, then, modernist art refuses both the accolades of bourgeois taste – it must, in fact, resist appropriation by the ideology of the ruling class – and the commercialization of kitsch. Modernist art is justified according to its capacity to exhibit a critical experience of art. The motivation for the avant-garde is, on this account, the preservation of living culture. By contrast, kitsch, according to Greenberg, is defined by two necessary conditions: an object is kitsch if it is (1) mechanically reproducible as a commodity, and (2) formulaic or non-critical – that is, its aesthetic effect is already included or 'predigested' in the object, or in Sartre's terms, already practico-inert; it imitates the effects of art rather than being the cause or occasion for critical aesthetic reflection.[22] The consumer of kitsch (for example, a kitsch painting) 'recognizes and sees things in a way in which he recognizes and sees things outside of pictures – there is no discontinuity between art and life' (Greenberg, 1939, 14). Kitsch relies on banal experience, and when Greenberg sarcastically notes that it 'tells a story', this reflects his belief that modernist painting must divest itself of literary techniques. By contrast, the viewer of a modernist painting is required to reflect upon the plastic qualities of the work; the plastic values are not immediately present in the work, 'but must be projected into it by the spectator sensitive enough to react sufficiently to plastic qualities' (1939, 15). The modernist avant-garde, Greenberg claims, is political insofar as it resists being appropriated by capitalist mechanisms, and insofar as it maintains a self-critical culture, it remains a threat to capitalism.

Greenberg's modernism, therefore, is diametrically opposed to the critical imperative that drove the historical avant-gardes – that art becomes life. As Rancière contends in *Aisthesis*, the demand that art is to become imbricated within social life has a history that begins over a century before the historical avant-gardes, from Winckelmann, Kant, and Schiller, through Emerson and Whitman, to the 'committed Whitmanian culture [Rancière is commenting here on James Agee and Walker Evans's book *Let Us Now Praise Famous Men*] that drove painters, photographers and writers to cross poor city neighbourhoods and poor country roads to exalt the work of men, gather testimonies of social misery, or photograph the picturesque calendars that decorated the walls of peasant houses' (Rancière, 2011a, 260). When he claims that Greenberg's modernism liquidates this 'cultural democracy stemming from Whitman' this judgement is not merely aesthetic, but trenchantly political.

In terms established in Rancière's *The Ignorant Schoolmaster*, Greenberg's discourse is one of intellectual stultification rather than intellectual emancipation: while kitsch is a product of industrialization, it is ultimately a threat to culture due to the desires of the petty bourgeoisie and that class which is ostensibly revolutionary – the proletariat. Instead, the proletariat is, on Greenberg's account, culturally reactionary, necessitating the modernist avant-garde. Though the industrial revolution establishes a universal literacy that makes formal culture accessible to more members of society, it does not provide to the masses the leisure, time, and knowledge necessary to cultivate an appreciation of high culture. Therefore the masses, 'insensible to the values of genuine culture' and suffering from boredom, settle for the 'vicarious experience and faked sensations' of kitsch (Greenberg, 1939, 10). Just as kitsch imitates the effects of art, the proletarian culture imitates bourgeois culture. As Rancière summarizes Greenberg's conclusions, 'roughly speaking: the death of culture and of high art happens when the sons and daughters of peasants', who form the proletariat and the petty bourgeoisie, 'take up leisure activities and want culture' (Rancière and Davis, 2013, 205).

We could formulate Rancière's claim here in terms found in *The Philosopher and His Poor*. This requires briefly considering his polemic against Pierre Bourdieu, which later situates the opening passages of *Aesthetics and Its Discontents* (2004a, 1).[23] Bourdieu argues that Kant's concept of disinterested aesthetic judgement functions as a 'denegation of the social' that masks the social division between the dominating classes and the dominated classes, between those who have the leisure to engage in disinterested aesthetic judgement and those are confined to the popular pleasures of their habitus. In short, for Bourdieu, Kant universalizes a bourgeois concept of taste, and this process of universalization masks social divisions and conflicts. Now, Greenberg is not Bourdieu, but both effect a similar sociologization of the problem of aesthetic judgement. First, Rancière contends that Bourdieu's attempt to unmask the class assumptions behind the concept of disinterestedness reaffirms the class distinctions that Bourdieu denounces. As Jeremy F. Lane summarizes it, Bourdieu's sociology 'works from the assumption that workers or the "dominated classes" possess a set of limited intellectual and political capacities that are defined, *a priori*, by the social roles they play', meaning that political agents are not capable of 'being anything other than the sum of the material circumstances incorporated into their habitus and ethos' (Lane, 2013, 34; 37). On Rancière's reading, Bourdieu's sociology moves from the claim that 'Kant universalizes a bourgeois concept of taste' to 'the proletariat is not capable of exercising, due to its material circumstances, disinterested aesthetic judgments'. In effect, classes must stay in their respective places, not only in politics, but also in aesthetics.

In a similar fashion, Greenberg sociologizes the politics of modernism. While certain a new culture will 'inevitably' emerge with socialism, he claims that, until such a time when the development of productive forces sounds the death knell of capitalism, the modernist avant-garde is necessary to preserve living culture. On his account, the modernist avant-garde plays a role analogous to the communist intellectuals described in *The Communist Manifesto*. However, for Rancière, this always prepares a stark division of labour between intellectuals and the masses in political struggle. The task of intellectuals is to know and to command, and the task of the masses is to act on that knowledge. As Rancière writes, the 'ongoing political education' of the proletarian masses 'is bound up with the dissolution of the ruling class, which constantly sends them masses of combatants trained in its school and philosophers to lead their fight' (Rancière, 1983, 92). With Greenberg, their ongoing aesthetic education is also dependent on the dissolution of the bourgeoisie. Possessing universal literacy, but unable to command the leisure and knowledge necessary for an appreciation of modern art, the proletariat needs the modernist avant-garde to preserve what is living in culture.

3.4. Benjamin's 'archaeomodernism'

Greenberg attempts to isolate a form of artistic production and aesthetic spectatorship that resists becoming reified as kitsch or commodity, but this sociologization of art – insofar as it liquidates the 'cultural democracy' of the aesthetic regime – is both anti-egalitarian and anti-aesthetic. By contrast, Walter Benjamin aims in his analyses to recover the emancipatory potential of history, art and politics. In his reflections on Dadaism, Surrealism, and

Baudelaire, Benjamin seeks to establish links between artistic novelty and social transformation, to demonstrate the increasing imbrication of art in everyday life. It would seem, then, that there would be an important affinity between the work of Benjamin and Rancière. Rancière himself suggests such an affinity when he states that in tracing the emancipatory potential offered by politics and aesthetics, he aims to describe 'something like an archaeology more open to the event than that of Foucault but without Benjaminian messianism' (Rancière, 2006a, 476).

Before establishing Rancière's critique of Benjamin's messianism, let us look at two examples of their similarities. First, without imputing Rancière's concept of literature to Benjamin, there are numerous passages in the latter's work that indicate common aesthetic and literary concerns. In a short piece from 1934 entitled 'The Newspaper', Benjamin writes that 'the literarization of the conditions of living masters the otherwise insoluble antinomies' between 'science and belles lettres, criticism and literary production, [and] culture and politics' (Benjamin, 1934b, 742; 741). Furthermore, as he points out in 'The Author as Producer', this literarization of social conditions describes an authorial competency that replaces specialization with a polytechnical education that recasts 'conventional distinctions between genres, between writer and poet, between scholar and populizer ... even the distinction between author and reader' (Benjamin, 1934a, 772). These passages bear a strong similarity to both Rancière's account of literary misunderstanding and those of the *The Philosopher and His Poor* or *Proletarian Nights*, where he analyses the emancipatory practices of the 'worker-militants [who] began by taking themselves for poets or knights, priests or dandies', if not philosophers or authors (Rancière, 1983, 200).

Moreover, let us look at Benjamin's treatment of Baudelaire, who is often cited for his formulation of the task of the painter of modern life. Art must, Baudelaire claims, 'distil the eternal from ... the transient, the fleeting, the contingent' character of modern life (1863, 402–3). Since the fashion, gestures, and pace of modernity must be met by 'an equal speed of execution' in art, he praises the work of Constantin Guys and Honoré Daumier, who work in those media often associated with either popular or mechanical (reproducible) arts rather than fine arts: watercolours, pastel, etching, and lithography (1863, 394). Thus, according to Baudelaire, the painter of modern life immerses himself, like the flâneur, among the crowd, the streets, the shop windows, and the circulation of commodities to distil through the work a moment of intoxication derived from the fleeting moment.[24] The dandy or flâneur, that 'last flicker of heroism in decadent ages', possesses a passion for originality that refuses both the decadence and decline of the aristocracy and the levelling tendencies of democracy (1863, 421).

And yet, despite these formulations, Benjamin makes the case that Baudelaire's poetics refuses the quasi-aristocratic airs of the dandy. Instead, the work of the ragpicker functions as an 'extended metaphor' for Baudelaire's poetic practice; the ragpicker functions as a double of the poet or flâneur: 'poets find the refuse of society on their streets and derive their heroic subject from this very refuse' (Benjamin, 1938, 48).[25] The following passages from Benjamin's 'The Paris of the Second Empire in Baudelaire' bear a strong similarity to Rancière's account of the rupture between the representative regime and the aesthetic regime: while the 'segregation of words into those that seemed suitable for elevated speech and those that were to be excluded from it influenced poetic production generally', Baudelaire 'is on the lookout for banal incidents in order to liken them to poetic events'; furthermore, '*Les Fleurs du mal* is the first book of poetry to use not only words of ordinary provenance but words of urban origin as well' (Benjamin, 1938, 61–2). Thus, on Benjamin's account, Baudelaire practises an aesthetics that refuses the parallelism between social hierarchies and artistic hierarchies.

Despite these similarities, we will conclude this chapter by examining why Rancière distinguishes his work from Benjamin's. To summarize, Rancière aims to describe a politics of aesthetics that accounts for the shifting relationship between art, politics, and a 'polemical common world' (Rancière, 2010b, 152) while avoiding the metapolitics – the messianism – that underlies Benjamin's dialectical criticism of modernity.[26] This requires addressing two central points of contention:[27]

1. The status of the relation of a regime of artistic production to technology.
2. What Rancière critiques as Benjamin's 'archaeomodernism', which I will argue is a type of metapolitics.

3.4.1. The politics of art and technology

First, let us address Rancière's critique of Benjamin's concept of an 'age of mechanical reproduction'. Many of Benjamin's works of the 1930s and after suggest that technological change, including the expanding distribution and reproducibility of the mechanical arts, produces new forms of visibility for and of the masses. For Benjamin, technological change contributes to dismantling the barriers between the artworld and the social experience of the proletariat, opening new avenues for the dispossessed to produce literature and art. In a similar vein, Rancière claims that, by overturning the principle of presence that structured the relation between author and audience in the representative regime of art, literature and aesthetics become available to anybody and everybody. Despite this similarity in their respective conclusions, Rancière argues that neither technological change nor technological properties of an art – such as photography – are sufficient to explain the new relations between artistic production and the social world of everyday life (Rancière, 2004b, 31).[28]

We will focus this critique on Benjamin's 'Little History of Photography', which outlines the social changes that follow in the wake of the invention of photography. He distinguishes between what he calls photography-as-art and art-as-photography. In the case of photography-as-art, Benjamin describes an optical unconscious that is revealed through photographs, details imperceptible to the eye that are presented by photographic means: not only the 'forms of ancient columns in horse willow, a bishop's crosier in the ostrich fern, totem poles in tenfold enlargements of chestnut and maple shoots, and gothic tracery in the fuller's thistle', but also the singular visibility of the anonymous lives of the masses, whose photographs instil an 'unruly desire' for their subjects' lives to be rediscovered (Benjamin, 1931, 512; 510). In such passages, Benjamin finds, in photography, the power of what Rancière calls molecular democracy. Yet the ramifications of this molecular democracy pale by comparison, he claims, to those of photography-as-art, that is, the photographic reproduction of works of art. The understanding and appreciation of great works of art, Benjamin argues, underwent a significant shift at the same time as the development of techniques of mechanical reproduction. With the photographic reproduction of great works of art, such works 'can no longer be regarded as the products of individuals; they have become a collective creation, a corpus so vast it can be assimilated only through miniaturization' (Benjamin, 1931, 523). Thus artworks become the property of collective social life.

However, Rancière argues that neither photography nor new techniques of artistic reproduction are sufficient to explain how new forms of aesthetic equality or new properties of collective social life become visible. Instead, he contends, photography and the other reproducible arts count as art because the aesthetic regime of art – by breaking with the norms of the representative regime of the arts – makes new forms of aesthetic equality and a new *aisthesis* of collective life possible. These aesthetic revolutions first took place in literature. On the one hand, as we have already seen, molecular democracy, for Rancière, is the equality of micro-events and intensities that evade molar significations; it is encapsulated by one of Flaubert's jokes, that he, Flaubert, is 'less interested in the poor man dressed in rags than in the lice devouring him' (Rancière, 2006b, 25). On the other hand, the idea that the artwork is the endowment of a people rather than the product of an individual already guides the idea of a new mythology found in both the 'Älteste Systemprogramm des deutschen Idealismus' (dated between spring 1796 and early 1797) and, later, Schelling's philosophy of art (see Chapter 4). A new mythology, according to Schelling, 'shall be the creation, not of some individual author, but of a new race, personifying, as it were, one single poet' (1800: 233/3: 629). In his lectures from 1802–5 that form the basis of the posthumously published *The Philosophy of Art*, Schelling argues that it is a necessary law of modern poesy 'that the individual form that part of the world revealed to him into a whole, and from the subject matter of his own age, its history and its science create his own mythology' (1802–5: 240tm/V, 154; see also 73/V, 444). An individual artist – Schelling cites Dante, Cervantes, and Goethe as examples – cannot provide a new mythology alone, but rather supplies fragments of a future mythology of a people. With the idea of these fragmentary mythologies, Schelling evokes the collective endowment of art that emerges in a form that he did not foresee, a polemical common world around which art is, on Benjamin's account, politicized.

While I think that Rancière's general claim that technological innovation is not sufficient to explain the micropolitics of aesthetics obtains, it is important to note that Benjamin's claims about the relationship between technology and artistic production during the age of mechanical reproduction are not always as straightforward as the 'Little History of Photography' suggests. By the end of that text, even, Benjamin proposes that photography captures a glimpse of the 'literarization of the conditions of life' that is already underway (Benjamin, 1931, 527). Later, in 'The Work of Art in the Age of Its Technological Reproducibility' he makes the case that in 'critical periods' of art, particular forms such as painting or literature strain 'after effects which can easily be achieved only with a changed technical standard – that is to say, in a new art form' (Benjamin, 1936, 118). Dadaism, for instance, pursued new forms of montage that, he claims, anticipate techniques in film. Finally, in *The Arcades Project*, Benjamin states explicitly the dialectical formula for the decline of the aura discussed in the various versions of 'The Work of Art in the Age of Its Technological Reproducibility': 'Mass production is the principal economic cause – and class warfare the principal social cause – of the decline of the aura' (Benjamin, J64a, 1). In each case, Benjamin underlines how technological transformation is imbricated in – though not the sufficient cause of – social practices within, and transformations of, a given distribution of the sensible.

3.4.2. Archaeomodernism and metapolitics

If there is some degree of rapprochement between Benjamin and Rancière concerning the relationship between artistic production and technology, Benjamin's 'archaeomodernism' – that is, the way he conceptualizes his critique of modernity – remains a central point of contention between the two thinkers. Rancière aims to affirm the relation between politics and aesthetics, and to affirm the imbrication of art in social life, without orienting these commitments within the framework of the project of modernity. This phrase, project of modernity, has a specific meaning for Rancière; it names a discursive constellation for thinking a particular experience of social transformation which sometimes elides between a number of analytically distinct dynamics. As David Craven notes, following the work of Perry Anderson and Marshall Berman, there are important differences between the terms modernity, modernism, and modernization: 'just as the various tendencies of modernism were ambivalent and varied responses to the social experience of modernity, so the latter was a complexly mediated manifestation of the economic project of capitalist modernization and its allied programme of western imperialism' (Craven, 1996, 33). When Rancière critiques the concept of modernity, he does not deny modernism, modernity, or modernization. Instead, he argues that the seemingly emancipatory 'project of modernity' is guided by a metapolitics and poetics of 'awakening' that neglects the transformative micropolitics of aesthetics.

Benjamin, Rancière argues, remains at the threshold of this metapolitics of modernity, this 'archaeomodernism' that is both fulfilled and disrupted by his messianic concept of historical materialism. Before defending these claims, I would like to note a difficulty with presenting Rancière's criticisms of Benjamin. His most sustained critique is found in 'The Archaeomodern Turn' (1996a), but Rancière also engages with Benjamin's work in other texts such as *The Politics of Literature*. The first difficulty is that 'The Archaeomodern Turn' deals not so much with Benjamin's aesthetics as his concept of history, though Rancière's critique focuses on the problem of interpreting a particular kind of *aesthesis* present in working-class political praxis, which he characterizes – in his discussion of Kant's idea of an aesthetic *sensus communis* – as 'misinterpretation', a precursor to his discussions of literary misunderstanding and political disagreement. Furthermore, Ranciere introduces terms, such as the 'archaeomodern turn', that he does not reiterate elsewhere, while the terminology of his other critiques of Benjamin – such as noting that the critique of the phantasmagoria of commodity fetishism is grounded in a literary metapolitics

– does not appear in this text. However, I think they pursue the same type of criticism: that the politicization of art that Benjamin is attempting to work out in *The Arcades Project*, 'On the Concept of History', and related texts, the way he seeks to blast art out of its separation from everyday life in order to make it available to proletarian struggle through the concept of the dialectical image, is nonetheless inscribed within a messianic metapolitics instead of a micropolitics of social change. Despite this criticism, Rancière nevertheless acknowledges that Benjamin's interest in the archives suggests an alternative way to politicize aesthetics. The upshot is that Rancière provides an entry point into Benjamin studies that bypasses the debate – which has been revitalized in the wake of Agamben's work on Benjamin's messianism – of whether he is dialectical materialist who evokes theological concepts while maintaining their secularized content (Tiedemann, 1983, 188) or a theologian and metaphysician who utilized Marxist concepts as a 'heuristic principle' (Scholem, 1975, 214; see also Scholem 1972, 51–3). At stake, in Rancière's reading, is disentangling two possible poetics: Benjamin, the archivist, and Benjamin, the symptomologist, whether by that one means historical materialist or theologian.

Rancière contends that the concept of modernity is structured by an 'archaeomodern turn'. Modernity, on Rancière's account, interprets itself as a break from myth, superstition, and dogmatism, but it itself is structured according to a myth of the dispersion or 'unfulfilment' of meaning – that despite this break with the past of myth or dogmatism, modern consciousness remains incomplete or unfulfilled. The archaeomodern turn is a procedure whereby 'in order to ground the good emancipation of meaning, the prose of science and philosophy, one has to lock up the dispersive power [of meaning], to make of it a sleeping meaning, waiting for its liberation but also anticipating it' (Rancière, 1996a, 27). The archaeomodern turn thinks emancipation as a process of awakening historical consciousness. From this standpoint, modernity always comes too soon and too late: on the one hand, consciousness of modernity always comes after the transformations of modernization, but, on the other hand, it always comes too soon to fulfil the promise of emancipation. In other words, consciousness is both always dreaming and anticipating. Rancière alludes – as does Benjamin in an epigram to Convolute N in *The Arcades Project* – to Marx's letter to Arnold Ruge, dated September 1843, where Marx writes: 'The reform of consciousness consists solely in letting the world perceive its own consciousness by awakening it from dreaming about itself, in explaining to it its own actions' (Marx, 1977, 38). This, Rancière acknowledges, is cited from the 'early' Marx, but he adds that for the 'later' Marx 'the political scene' remains enthralled to false consciousness, necessitating the attempt to ground revolutionary struggle in the contradictions of the social forces of production.

This metaphor of the 'dreaming cogito', as Rancière refers to it, is not peculiar to Marx. Benjamin's *Arcades Project* collects instance after instance of writers in the nineeenth and early twentieth centuries formulating the relation of waking and dreaming within the phantasmagoria of modernity. Let us cite an example that forms a key point of reference for Rancière's description of literary symptomology, from Balzac's *La Peau de chagrin*. Early in the novel, the protagonist Raphael enters an antique shop and is overwhelmed in reverie: 'For him this ocean of furnishings, inventions, fashions, works of art and relics made up an endless poem'; climbing the staircase from the ground floor, pursued 'by the strangest of forms, by fabulous creations poised on the confines between life and death, he walked along as in the enchantment of a dream' (Balzac, 1831, 37; 38). Benjamin describes the effect of the 'chaotic medley' (as Balzac phrases it) of commodities from all countries and civilizations on earth as the 'pathological element in the notion of "culture"' (Benjamin, N19, 3). Rancière argues that this symptomal poetics makes possible Benjamin's analyses of the phantasmagoria of the commodity and the arcades, and Benjamin's extension of these analyses into all aspects of social life (Rancière, 2006b, 22). While Marx did not extend this phantasmagoric character to the social forces of production, Rancière argues that Benjamin was 'faithful to the more fundamental framework – or plot – in which the theory of fetishism took place: the plot of unfulfillment, the plot of enthralled reason' (Rancière, 1996a, 36). As a consequence, Benjamin also recognized that awakening from the nineteenth century, from the phantasmagoria of capital, from the dreams of the homogeneous progress of historical time, means awakening from the dialectic of dreaming and awakening. Benjamin suggests as much when he asks if awakening is 'perhaps the synthesis of dream consciousness (as thesis) and waking consciousness (as antithesis). Then the moment of awakening would be identical with the "now of recognizability" in which things put on their true – surrealist – face' (N3a, 3). This synthesis seeks to undermine the difference between the phantasmagoria and social reality, the real and the surreal, to recognize that the social imaginary and social praxis are not necessarily opposed as a form of misrecognition or false consciousness.

The pivotal problem, in thinking through Benjamin's work, is how the 'now of recognizability' is to 'blast open the continuum of history', to seize in the moment of now-time (*Jetztzeit*) the emancipatory potential of the past in the present (Benjamin, 1940, 396). Rancière argues that it is on this point that Benjamin's work poses a dilemma. It is possible to think the emancipation of historical praxis in two ways: first, under the rubric of a messianic historical materialism, or, second, as a micropolitics of 'fragmentary emancipation'. Benjamin, he argues, ultimately settles on messianism.

Rancière does not dispute Benjamin's contention that emancipatory history must liberate the history of the oppressed from the 'patrimonial catastrophe' (Rancière, 1996a, 38) that is history conceptualized by the victors, for whom, today, all the barbarism of oppression is subsumed under the concept of historical progress. However, he argues that Benjamin's messianic historical materialism repeats the gesture of the archaeomodern turn. Benjamin attempts to safeguard the significance of the past – its dialectical images – by casting historical redemption as the testimony to a unique and, as Rancière claims, 'unsharable' witnessing of a historical singularity or monad: 'the past can be seized only as an image that flashes up at the moment of its recognizability, and is never seen again' (Benjamin, 1940, 390). The struggle of the oppressed, then, is situated between the ruins and catastrophe of progress and the moment of full redemption. Until that moment of redemption, the task of the historian, for Benjamin, is to decipher, within the appearances of phantasmagoria of modernity, the dispersed potential of 'the fullness of the past' that has a claim on the present (Benjamin, 1940, 390). We may in fact be awake within the phantasmagoria of capitalism, but we still act in a time stretching between melancholy and an anticipation of redemption. Messianism, in other words, is a form of metapolitics, despite being enlisted by Benjamin for the purposes of class struggle – the 'weak messianic power' of contemporary struggle, and its capacity to redeem humanity, draws its significance from the memory of an irretrievable loss.[29]

3.5. Fragmentary emancipation, common sense, and aesthetic equality

Yet Benjamin also suggests an alternative to messianism, what Rancière calls 'fragmentary emancipation'. Rancière acknowledges that Benjamin anticipates this micropolitics of fragmentary emancipation, establishing 'the pattern of a history of social practices which can be simultaneously a history of the social imaginary', dispensing with 'the old painstaking explanations of the ideological reflection of economic processes and social relations' – although it must also reflect upon its own fictive 'conditions of construction' (Rancière, 1996a, 39–40). Such a social history remains incomplete in the work of Benjamin:

> When we look at the collection of citations which constitutes the Arcades book, we cannot help being struck by a strong disparity: in light of Benjamin's deep theoretical concern with the archaeology of the arcade, conceived as the embodiment of the bourgeois dream, the sections devoted to the working-class movement, the barricades, social thought, and so on are essentially made of plain notes and citations from secondhand books with few comments. They form something like a heap of scraps or wreckage which makes no real sense, only an impression. (Rancière, 1996a, 33)

This part of the archive, copied but rarely commented upon by Benjamin, Rancière argues, forms the 'absolute' and 'unforgettable' reference of the irretrievable meaning that for Benjamin lays claim to messianic redemption.

Instead of searching out in literature and art those dialectical images that might light the flame of the proletarian revolution that finally brings relations of domination to a standstill and illuminate a redeemed humanity, or relegating the aesthetics of everyday life to the vagaries of commodification, kitsch, and vulgar taste, Rancière seeks in the aesthetic regime of art those moments of fragmentary – partial, transitory, incomplete – emancipation that take place in the interstices of those relations of domination; moments where those whose social task it is to work, consume, and be serious, instead come to formulate the terms of, and participate in, their freedom. Rancière does not claim that his aesthetics is true whereas the concepts and histories of modernity and of modernism are false. Instead, he proposes his archaeology of the aesthetic regime of art as a framework for thinking and recovering the egalitarian and emancipatory potential of aesthetics. Having criticized Benjamin's archaeomodernism and Greenberg's modernism, we will conclude by looking at the way that Rancière revisits Kant's account of the common sense of aesthetic judgement as a philosophical expression of aesthetic equality.

When, in *Aisthesis*, Rancière contends that Kant's claim that there can 'be no rule in accordance with which someone could be compelled to acknowledge something as beautiful' signals a rupture with the representational regime of the arts, this interpretation harkens back to the final chapter of *The Philosopher and His Poor*, where he holds that aesthetic judgement is potentially a moment of intellectual emancipation (Kant, 1790, 5: 215–16; Rancière, 2011a, 11; see also 2009a, 64). When Kant rejects the necessity of learned criteria – what Rancière will later call the norms of mimesis – or refined senses as a basis of good taste as opposed to the lack of taste or bad taste, in favour of the universality of aesthetic judgement, an aesthetic *sensus communis*, Rancière claims that Kant is 'seeking the anticipation of the perceptible equality to come' (Rancière, 1983, 198).

For our purposes, we are interested in how Rancière affirms the egalitarian character of aesthetic judgement without concluding that this aesthetic common sense operates according to consensus, for Kant argues that taste is a subjectively universal judgement that 'ascribes assent to everyone' (Kant, 1790, 5: 237). Terry Eagleton, for instance, reads common sense as a process of ideological interpellation. Though he notes that aesthetic judgement offers the Kantian subject a spontaneous and immediate feeling of community that is not available through either pure reason or the rational strictures of the moral law, Eagleton concludes – despite hedging these claims with phrases such as 'one might argue' and 'from one viewpoint' – that the aesthetic is the 'very paradigm of the ideological', even that the 'aesthetic *is* the ideological' (Eagleton, 1990, 93–4, 99). Kant's distinction between cognition and aesthetics is, on Eagleton's account, the same as Althusser's between science and ideology. Aesthetic judgements have the form of epistemological claims – that is, we take them to be necessary – though, by lacking a concept, their validity does not rest on truth or falsity, or even a sense of duty or obligation, but rather subjective feeling. And this subjective feeling is 'always already', as Althusser would say, established by prior social consensus, a *sensus communis* whereby 'we are always already in agreement, *fashioned* to concur; and the aesthetic is this experience of pure contentless consensus where we find ourselves spontaneously at one without necessarily even knowing what, referentially speaking, we are agreeing over' (Eagleton, 1990, 96). Thus Eagleton describes Kant's account of taste as a 'parody of conceptual understanding' and a 'caricature of rational law' (Eagleton, 1990, 85, 88).

For Eagleton, then, the role of *sensus communis*, common sense, is to 'hail' or interpellate the subject as a member the community of consensus, to give an individual a feeling of social solidarity. By contrast, for Rancière, Kant's aesthetic *sensus communis* makes possible social change through what he calls, but does not expressly thematize as, misinterpretation. We can consider their differences by reference to Kant's own treatment of common sense – not to adjudicate who is right and who is wrong, but rather to underline the respective interpretative decisions of Rancière and Eagleton. As Paul Guyer points out, Kant characterizes common sense in three different ways: as a subjective principle of judgement, as a feeling, and as a faculty of (or capacity for) taste.[30] Eagleton emphasizes the emotive aspect of common sense. Given that he maintains a strict distinction, like Althusser, between science and ideology, between cognition and the 'pseudo-knowledge' of aesthetic judgement, this is not surprising; and, given that he claims that aesthetic judgements are performative statements 'masquerading as constatives', Eagleton treats the claim that there is a *principle* of common sense as a misnomer for a *feeling* (Eagleton, 1990, 93).

By contrast, judging from his readings of Kant's *Critique of the Power of Judgment* in *The Philosopher and His Poor* and *Aesthetics and Its Discontents*, Rancière interprets aesthetic common sense as a faculty or capacity equally shared by anyone and everyone. In this regard, Rancière's reading of Kant's aesthetic *sensus communis* is similar to his treatment of Descartes – common sense is the aesthetic counterpart to Descartes's supposition of the intellectual equality of good sense. Indeed, in Section 1.5, we have already considered a passage in *The Philosopher and His Poor* where Rancière opposes an egalitarian 'good sense' *or* 'common sense' to the Platonic distribution of virtue and moderation along the lines of the division of labour in the city. Moreover, Rancière's other references to Kant's *sensus communis* emphasize both its emancipatory potential and the repeated failure of various philosophers to fully consider the universal and democratic character of aesthetic equality (see Rancière, 1983, 161, 163, 208).

Rancière does not support these claims through an exegesis of Kant's 'Analytic of the Beautiful'. Instead, he adduces two seeming 'commentaries' on the *Critique of the Power of Judgment*. First, he cites a passage from the writings of Gabriel Gauny, whose work plays a pivotal role in Rancière's *Proletarian Nights*:

> Gauny seems to be commenting on the [*Critique of the Power of Judgment*] when, from the room in which he lays a parquet floor, he offers the gaze of an aesthete on the décor of his servitude: 'Thinking himself at home, as long as he has not finished the room in which he nails down the boards, he likes the layout of the place; if the window opens onto a garden or over a picturesque horizon, he stops moving his hands for an instant and shifts his thoughts toward that spacious view in order to enjoy it better than the owners of the neighboring homes.' (Rancière, 1983, 199)

Then, he offers a 'fictive commentary' – as Rancière puts it – from Baudelaire: 'What is more trivial than wealth as seen by poverty? But here, the feeling is complicated by poetic pride, by partly glimpsed pleasures of which one feels worthy ... We too, we understand the beauty of palaces and parks. We too, we know the art of happiness' (quoted in Rancière, 1983, 200).

These passages from Gauny and Baudelaire illustrate what Rancière describes as an 'aesthetic and militant passion for reappropriation' already anticipated by Kant. For Eagleton, this 'poetic pride' elucidated by Baudelaire would be a kind of aesthetic illusion or misrecognition of social relations of oppression. Rancière argues that the model of ideology that orients Althusser's or Eagleton's work 'naturalizes words by attributing them to the vocabulary of a class' such as the bourgeoisie (Rancière, 2012b, 209). Any borrowing of this vocabulary, according to this ideological model, merely reflects the 'ideological capture' of the oppressed classes who attempt to speak with it. By contrast, for Rancière, aesthetic judgement is the first step of emancipation, a moment when it is possible to suspend the interests and practico-inert tasks that orient much of our activity. This aesthetic suspension is a moment of novelty or what Rancière calls 'misinterpretation', which foreshadows his later discussions of homonymy and literary misunderstanding. From a dominant discourse (or discourse of domination), workers borrow and appropriate terms to verbalize a 'heretical' discourse of egalitarian struggle. In the 'Banquet des Travailleurs socialistes' of 1848, these militant workers praise the bourgeois values of property, order, and family. But Rancière does not read this document as the manifestation of the interpellation of workers by ideas and values that mask the reality of oppression. Instead, the activation of dissensus 'opposes word to word and deed to deed' (see Rancière, 1998a, 87; 2007, 47). In the case of this 'Banquet des Travailleurs socialistes', these workers oppose one type of inequality within the social order to another. The inequality of the coming socialist society, of 'true society', will not produce the forms of exclusion and privilege, of 'organized arbitrariness', that structure bourgeois society (reproduced in Faure and Rancière, 1976, 291). Instead, the inequality of socialist order is similar to the Cartesian good sense that is directed along different paths: 'Inequality, or rather the necessary diversity of expression [*L'inégalité, or plutôt la diversité nécessaire des manifestations*], does not result in social inequality and disorder. If everyone is born with diverse aptitudes, it is to play a particular part in the great social concert' (reproduced in Faure and Rancière, 1976, 289). For Rancière, malapropisms and misinterpretations become the watchwords of social change. It is this play of misinterpretation that introduces new ways of, and spaces for, being, seeing, and acting into a given distribution of the sensible.

We see, then, that Rancière's politics and aesthetics both rest upon the supposition of equality, even if there is a fundamental difference between the politics of equality and the micropolitics of aesthetics. For Rancière, the politics of equality is an invariable feature of politics as such, whether – as we have seen – he is discussing plebian revolts in ancient Rome or nineteenth-century revolutionary activity in France. Yet the micropolitics of aesthetics is a distinctly modern practice. So when Rancière qualifies both as moments of equality, it gives the impression that we have arrived, that equality is here at this historical moment, when clearly this is not the case. Equality, in Rancière's terms, is neither a state nor a milieu, but a practice. We have nevertheless distinguished the practices of the egalitarian politics and the micropolitics of aesthetics. This disjunction allows us to acknowledge the real transformations of aesthetics – its producers, its objects, and its audiences – over the last two hundred years, while recognizing the difficult and seemingly transitory character of the insurrectionary politics of egalitarianism.

Notes

1 As Oliver Davis (2010, 102) notes, the idea of a literary revolution at the end of the eighteenth century is not unique to Rancière. It had already been discussed by Raymond Williams and Pierre Macherey within the framework of Marxist literary criticism, and from a post-Heideggerian standpoint by Philippe Lacoue-Labarthe and Jean-Luc Nancy's *The Literary Absolute* (1978).
2 Raji Vallury also notes that Rancière's distinction between political disagreement and literary misunderstanding echoes Deleuze and Guattari's distinction between macropolitical and micropolitical assemblages, though Vallury seeks to subvert such a distinction (Vallury, 2009, 237). I think there is value – both analytic and political – in distinguishing between disagreement and misunderstanding, lest we mistake writing about political subjectivation with political subjectivation.
3 Though it seems that Sartre is equivocating between Dadaism and Surrealism here – Tristan Tzara's 'Dada Manifesto' was published in 1918 and André Breton's first *Surrealist Manifesto* in 1924 – the journal *Littérature* began publishing automatic writing in 1919. Note that Sartre claims also that there is a form of misunderstanding between Surrealism and the oppressed classes: 'the surrealist is very little concerned with the dictatorship of the proletariat and sees in the Revolution, as pure violence, the absolute end, whereas the end that communism proposes to itself is the taking of power, and by means of that end it justifies the blood it will shed' (Sartre, 1948b, 159).
4 Rancière draws on Deleuze and Guattari's concept of haecceity: 'There is a mode of individuation very different from that of a person, subject, thing, or substance. We reserve the name *haecceity* for it. A season, a winter, a summer, an hour, a date have a perfect individuality lacking nothing, even though this individuality is different from that of a thing or a subject. They are haecceities in the sense that they consist entirely of relations of movement and rest between molecules or particles, capacities to affect and be affected' (Deleuze and Guattari, 1980, 261).

5   The reader might be sceptical of Sartre making essentializing claims, but Sartre writes that 'the essence of the literary work is freedom totally disclosing and willing itself as an appeal to the freedom of other men' (1948b, 133).
6   I have sought to address some of these concerns in a review of Souleymane Bachir Diagne's *African Art as Philosophy: Senghor, Bergson and the Idea of Negritude* (2007; see Shaw, 2013). We should also note here that Rancière's aesthetics draws mostly on the modern history of Western art, and while his work offers innovative ways to rethink this history outside of the boundaries of canonical and marginal works as well as highbrow and lowbrow art, his 'counter-history' of artistic modernity does not address how modernity relates to colonialism or postcolonialism. Nevertheless, Vallury writes: 'If Rancière's formulations of the node constituted by aesthetics and politics are concerned primarily with the artistic practices of the western European tradition, they nonetheless offer an extremely rich vantage point from which to explore the politics of colonial and postcolonial literature. Inversely, the postcolonial novel provides an interesting margin from which Rancière's theses can be tested and challenged' (Vallury, 2009, 238). See also Craven's critique, which takes Greenberg as its point of departure, 'The Latin American Origins of "Alternative Modernism"' (1996).
7   John Phillips suggests this passage also makes reference to Bachelard, Foucault, Adorno, Horkheimer, Baudrillard, Benjamin, and Lacan (2010, 152).
8   A few terminological clarifications: I will treat *modern art* and *artistic modernity* as synonyms that include both the historical avant-gardes and modernist art. Since the latter two are not synonymous, I will refer to the avant-gardes in Greenberg's account as the *modernist avant-garde* in order to distinguish this form of avant-gardism from the more cohesive and self-consciously vanguardist movements such as Futurism and Surrealism, which I will refer to as the *historical avant-gardes*.
9   More recently film has come to play an important role in his aesthetics, though this topic is beyond the scope of the present study.
10 On Vico, see Rancière, 1998d 57–9; on Winckelmann, Rancière, 2011a, 1–20. Concerning Schiller, see Chapter 4.
11 Rancière discusses the relationship between art and audience as also governed by the principle of decorum, but thematically – especially when, as we will see, the norm of 'speech in action' is overturned by the politics of literature and the emergence of mute speech – it fits better with the principle of presence.
12 *Seems*: only if we remain within a Western historico-philosophical domain. While we cannot address them here, see Ngũgĩ wa Thiong'o's remarks on world literature, literature (though he does not mean the same thing as Rancière by this term), and orature in his recent *Globalectics* (2012).

13 In *The Philosopher and His Poor* Rancière uses scare quotes to signal the deliberate anachronism of applying these terms to Plato.
14 Rancière quotes the following passage from the *Phaedrus*, where Socrates reminds Phaedrus that if the cicadas were 'to see us two behaving like the multitude at midday, not conversing but dozing lazy-minded under their spell, they would rightly laugh at us, taking us for a pair of slaves who had invaded their retreat like sheep, to have their midday sleep beside the spring' (1983, 48–9; 259a).
15 Balzac writes: 'The poet [Lucien] had seen the kitchen of fame, the wires that can be pulled in the publishing trade; he had gone *behind* the scenes in the theatre, and he had seen, what was more, the seamy side of consciences, the *machinery* at work *behind* Parisian life, the *mechanism* of it all' (Balzac, 1837–43, 299; my emphases).
16 Despite her differences with Clark, Lisa Moore underlines how the presumed pleasures of the spectator's gaze – as a form of a male viewer's agency – upon a nude are frustrated directly by Olympia's gaze and indirectly by the absence, from a Eurocentric and heteronormative standpoint, of a male viewer or a stand-in figure with which he can identify within the frame (Moore, 1989, 226).
17 These differences can also be illustrated from Clark's perspective. In Chapter 4 of *The Painting of Modern Life*, Clark interprets Manet's *Un Bar aux Folies Bergère* (1882) in the context of the production of 'the popular' and popular entertainment at *café-concerts*. In a note to this chapter, he acknowledges his debts to Rancière's 'Good times, or, pleasure at the barrière' (1978), but then notes his disagreement with Rancière's treatment of the *café-concert* as a 'site of real subversion' (Clark, 1999, 304 n.11).
18 Note that, however, Greenberg will later write of Courbet that 'From Giotto to Courbet, the painter's first task had been to hollow out an illusion of three-dimensional space on a flat surface' (1954, 136).
19 Later, Greenberg will write: 'Modernist painting asks that a literary theme be translated into strictly optical, two-dimensional terms before becoming the subject of pictorial art – which means its being translated in such a way that it entirely loses its literary character' (1965, 8).
20 Though Greenberg interprets the history of class struggle as the development of modes of production, he does not treat modernism as *merely* an expression of disaffected artists who nevertheless adhere to bourgeois ideology, as a stronger economistic reading would suggest.
21 This self-critique begins with Manet and continues through Cézanne, Picasso, Braque, Mondrian (among others) to what we often call abstract expressionism, and what he calls 'American-Type' painting, including Pollock, de Kooning, Barnett Newman, Rothko and Clyfford Still. The inclusion of Still is, for our

purposes, an interesting case. In *Aisthesis*, Rancière argues that Greenberg's modernism repudiates the 'cultural democracy [of art] stemming from Whitman', although he does not cite an explicit case where Greenberg castigates Whitman for being, at least in part, kitsch (Rancière, 2011a, 262). In '"American-Type" Painting', Greenberg praises Still's work, with the caveat that 'Still's uncompromising art has its own affinity with popular or bad taste. It is the first body of painting I know of that asks to be called Whitmanesque in the worst as well as the best sense, indulging as it does in loose and sweeping gestures, and defying certain conventions ... in the same *gauche* way that Whitman defied meter. And just as Whitman's verse assimilated to itself qualities of stale journalistic and oratorical prose, Still's painting assimilates to itself some of the stalest and most prosaic painting of our time ... the kind of open-air painting in autumnal colors ... which has spread among half-trained painters only since Impressionism became popular' (Greenberg, 1958, 223).

22   Kitsch includes 'popular, commercial art and literature with their chromeotypes, magazine covers, illustrations, ads, slick and pulp fiction, comics, Tin Pan Alley music, tap dancing, Hollywood movies, etc., etc.' (Greenberg, 1939, 9).

23   Whether or not Rancière's reading of Bourdieu is correct or persuasive is not at issue here; instead, we are concerned with a particular logic of considering class distinctions. For more on Bourdieu, see Lane 2013.

24   I have used the masculine pronoun here because, as Griselda Pollock notes, 'there is no female equivalent of the quintessential masculine figure, the flâneur; there is not and could not be a female flâneuse' (Pollock, 1992, 50).

25   What the dandy, the flâneur, the poet, and the ragpicker all have in common is relative anonymity in the crowd. Note that Irving Wohlfarth argues that the ragpicker's activity functions as an extended metaphor for Benjamin's approach in *Arcades Project*, which 'seeks to abandon the traditional prerogatives of authorship for a marginal, anonymous and subterranean position from which, ideally, to let the historical materials speak for themselves' (Wohlfarth, 2006, 13–14).

26   Newmark (2011) defends Benjamin against Rancière's criticisms, but does so by equivocating between Rancière's concepts of political equality and aesthetic equality.

27   In numerous works, Rancière reminds the reader that the social practices he designates as the politics of aesthetics and the aesthetics of politics 'have nothing to do with Benjamin's discussion of the "aestheticization of politics" specific to the "age of the masses"' (Rancière, 2004b, 13; see also 2004a, 25). When, however, he claims that there '*never has been* any "aestheticization" of politics in the modern age because politics is aesthetic in principle' (1995, 58/88), it seems like Rancière is conflating two problems: the description of the relation between politics, aesthetics, and a given distribution of the sensible; and Benjamin's attempt to

conceptualize the pernicious features of F. T. Marinetti's elision between aesthetic judgements and political and moral judgements (see Benjamin, 1936, 120–2).

28 Rancière is also weary of the reception of Benjamin's theses on art, which sometimes connects 'the categories of Marxist materialist explanation and those of Heideggerian ontology, which ascribe the age of modernity to the unfurling of the essence of technology' (Rancière, 2004b, 31). Simay (2005) and Hanssen (2005) criticize the equation of Benjamin's and Heidegger's theses on history and art.

29 Messianism, when appropriated by Agamben – who both mocks what he considers the 'common and tedious paradigm of the history of the subaltern' (2008, 98) and affirms Schmitt's thesis that 'the most meaningful concepts of the modern doctrine of the state are secularized theological concepts' (2000, 118) – is used to obstruct the emancipatory potential of political struggle.

30 Guyer writes that, as a principle, as it is first described in §20, 'common sense would presumably be a belief or presupposition, such as the belief in the universal similarity of the operations of the higher cognitive faculties, which would allow one to impute a pleasure attributed to these faculties to others' (Guyer, 1997, 249). In the second paragraph of §20, Kant also refers to common sense as a feeling of pleasure as an 'effect of the free play of our cognitive powers' (Kant, 1790, 5: 238). Finally, in §40, as Guyer notes, Kant identifies taste with common sense. In this case, common sense is treated as a faculty that makes it possible to judge 'apart from the subjective private conditions of judgment', that is, according to the standpoint of others (Kant, 1790, 5: 295).

4

Aesthetics, Inaesthetics and the Platonic Regime of Art

4.1. The return from exile

In Chapter 3, we examined Rancière's concept of the aesthetic regime of art and the reasons he opposes this aesthetics to Benjamin's messianic modernity and Greenberg's modernist sociologization of art. Moreover, we saw that Rancière opposes the aesthetic regime of art to the representative regime of the arts; indeed, he maintains that the aesthetic regime emerges with the collapse of the mimetic norms governing the representative regime. Nonetheless, this account of his aesthetics remains incomplete until we consider the distinction he draws between aesthetics and what he calls, in *Aesthetics and Its Discontents* and *The Politics of Aesthetics*, the ethical regime of images (Rancière, 2004a, 26–8, 64–5; 2004b, 20–1).

The paradigm for the ethical regime of images is established in Book X of Plato's *Republic*. Rancière argues that for Plato – as for this ethical regime – there is no specific domain of art, only the arts of doing or making. These arts are evaluated according to how they affect the community. Plato evaluates the craft of poets as he evaluates the function of every other part of the community. Recall, from the Introduction, Rancière's discussion of Plato's archipolitics. In Plato's republic, the 'image of justice is the division of labor' (Rancière, 1983, 25). Having a part in the city is defined by practising one's occupation and no other: 'it is right for someone who is by nature a cobbler to practice cobblery and nothing else, for the carpenter to practice carpentry, and the same for the others is a sort of image of justice' (443c). This division governs not only artisans, but the separation between artisans, warriors, and philosophers. Conversely, injustice is defined as 'a meddling and doing of another's work, a rebellion by some part against the whole soul [or, analogously, the whole city] in order to rule it inappropriately' (444b).

Plato's justice valorizes ways of doing or making that reinforce the hierarchical structure of the division of labour and the order of the city. He admits 'hymns to the gods and eulogies to good people', but he banishes the poets of 'the pleasure-giving Muse' for waging a double rebellion against the city (607a). There are two arguments to banish, if we may use an anachronism for a moment, artists. First, the poet or painter is an artisan who does not observe the division of labour. Every other part of the community has an occupation with a specific goal: philosophers who deliberate, warriors who defend the city, and artisans who produce objects by imitating models or forms. By contrast, the artist produces appearances or imitations that are 'simulacra of arts' (Rancière, 2004a, 64). As Jean-Philippe Deranty notes, Plato judges images according to their 'ontological veracity … the truthfulness with which they accurately represent an ideal model' (Deranty, 2010b, 120). The images produced by artists do not imitate the ideal form of a thing; instead they imitate a craft which itself is modelled on the knowledge of forms. Thus artists produce imitations of imitations, doubly removed from knowledge. Like a carpenter, a painter can produce furniture, but the painter can also make all plants, all animals, the earth, the heavens, the gods, and Hades (596c); using meter, rhythm, and harmony, the poets deceive their audience into believing that they 'know all crafts, all human affairs concerned with virtue and vice, and all about the gods as well' (598d). The poet, in this sense, is the double of the philosopher who deliberates upon all human occupations and affairs, virtue and vice, and the nature of the gods. However, for Plato, the philosopher legislates and deliberates using reason and knowledge. By contrast, the poet, whose speech is doubly removed from knowledge, persuades people with images that appeal to their desires; he 'arouses, nourishes, and strengthens [the] part of the soul [that is inferior to reason] and so destroys the rational one, in just the way that someone destroys the better sort of citizens when he strengthens the vicious ones and surrenders the city to them' (605b). Hence the craft of the painter or poet, that is, the craft of the imitator, Rancière avers, 'implicates all members of a society by putting in question their very simplicity, i.e. their adherence to their respective functions' (Rancière, 1983, 17). This is the second reason to banish artists. The poet's activity, by imitating various other occupations, suggests that all members of the community could do something other than their respective occupations. The poet is, by producing merely the appearances of truth and by appealing to the basest impulses of the people, which are the passions of tyranny and democracy (568b–d), the artisan of injustice.

Plato's adherence to the ethical regime of images closes the archipolitical circle of the ideal city. Plato's republic, on Rancière's account, proscribes both politics and art (Rancière, 2004a, 26). Yet Plato suggests that poetry could 'return from exile' when its 'defenders, who aren't poets themselves but lovers of poetry ... speak in prose on its behalf ... to show that it not only gives pleasure but is beneficial both to constitutions and to human life' (607d). The focus of this chapter is a particular form of art's 'return from exile' that I will call the Platonic regime of art. I will use the phrase 'Platonic regime of art' to designate a specific discourse about art that binds novel practices of artistic production (and the production of novelty) to philosophy, truth, and politics that, like the aesthetic regime of art, emerges with the collapse of the representative regime of the arts, but which differs from both the ethical regime of images and the aesthetic regime of art. The Platonic regime of art is different from the ethical regime of images for two reasons. First, whereas Plato evaluates images according to how they affect the community and the city, the philosophers in question – we will look at F. W. J. Schelling and Alain Badiou – consider art to be a specific and autonomous domain that demands fundamental philosophical attention.[1] Like Rancière, these thinkers hold that art is both autonomous – activating a domain of practices that cannot be subsumed under other forms of social relations – and heteronomous, meaning that the domain of art always *relates to* practices outside of its domain. Thus it is a regime of art rather than a regime of images. Second, it would be a misnomer to call this regime an *ethical* regime of art because (a) these theorists are not necessarily committed to an archipolitics; and (b) when Rancière critiques the 'ethical turn' in aesthetics, of which Lyotard's work is emblematic, he is attacking theories of artistic production that are antipolitical, that is, that preempt the possibility of thinking the relation of art and politics by linking art to an ethics of alterity (2004a, 88–132).

Before distinguishing the Platonic regime of art from the aesthetic regime of art, it should also be noted that the partisans of this Platonic regime are distinct from the contemporary, ostensibly anti-Platonic theorists who nevertheless share Plato's assumptions regarding what Rancière calls, in an analysis of theatre in *The Emancipated Spectator*, 'the paradox of the spectator' (Rancière, 2009a, 2). This paradox occurs because art requires an audience. As Rancière states, 'There is no art without eyes that see it as art' (Rancière, 2003, 72). For Rancière, aesthetics is defined by a necessary distance between artistic production and artistic reception. Far from being an abyss into which all artistic intentionality irretrievably falls, this distance is the basis of interpretation. Interpretation, for Rancière, does not involve formulating propositions about intention that are true or false. Instead, the significance of art is always mediated in the relations between the artwork, artists, and audiences. The spectator, on his account, engages in a 'poetic labour of translation ... of putting her experience into words and her words to the test; of translating her intellectual adventures for others and counter-translating the translations of their own adventures which they present to her' (Rancière, 2009a, 10–11). This does not mean that every interpretation is valid. It means that the social and political significance of the work arises in, and derives its context from, the way it is related to other social practices. As Gabriel Rockhill writes, 'it is not the work *in and of itself* that produces political consequences, but the life of the work, with its various strategies and propositions, as it is received, interpreted, circulated, mobilized for various ends, etc.' (Rockhill, 2011, 49).[2] By virtue of this task of translation, counter-translation, and – if we recall a key term of Rancière's *The Ignorant Schoolmaster* – verification, the work of interpretation undermines the 'fixity and hierarchy' of the boundaries of knowledge and ignorance.

Plato begins with the presupposition that activity is knowing and passivity is ignorance. The spectator occupies the wrong side of these dichotomies. She views rather than knows and, as part of an audience, she remains passive rather than intellectually active. These suppositions produce the paradox of the spectator: there is no art without a spectator, but a spectator is always separated from the 'capacity to know and the power to act' (Rancière, 2009a, 2). For Plato, theatre is dangerous because the passivity of the audience makes it possible to persuade with pleasure instead of reason. Rancière's critique of the paradox of the spectator extends beyond Plato's ethical regime of images. There are ostensibly revolutionary and anti-Platonist theorists who accept the presupposition that activity is knowing and passivity is ignorance. Instead of banishing art from political praxis, theorists such as Bertolt Brecht and Guy Debord attempt to make passive spectators into militants.[3] However, in the terms of Rancière's *Ignorant Schoolmaster*, their approach to art – and their respective attempts to abolish the passivity of the audience by activating their engagement through the work – is closer to the Master than the emancipator; as Rancière writes, the master *interrogates* the student (that is, 'demands speech, that is to say, the manifestation of an intelligence that wasn't aware of itself'), while the ignorant schoolmaster *verifies* the student's attentiveness to thinking critically and interpretatively (Rancière, 1987, 29). Thus Brecht or Debord interrogate their audience, who they presume are caught in the false consciousness of the spectacle, rather than verify their attention.

The Platonic regime of art is premised on a form of egalitarianism that avoids the paradox of the spectator. The fragment now entitled the 'Älteste Systemprogramm des deutschen Idealismus' (hereafter, 'System Program') – written sometime between spring 1796 and early 1797 and by turns attributed to Hölderlin, Hegel, and Schelling (see Shaw, 2010, 56) – articulates two key theses of this Platonic regime of art. First, the author proclaims that the Idea of beauty – with the term *Idea* 'taken in its higher, Platonic sense' – will unify the divisions of philosophy through a 'supreme act of reason' that is also an aesthetic act (quoted in Krell, 2005, 24). With this announced system of philosophy the poets return from exile. However, their return subverts the archipolitics that organizes Plato's republic. This anonymous Platonist then contends, in a second thesis, that by bringing philosophy and poetry into relation, philosophy can cultivate an aesthetic sense while poetry can elaborate a new mythology 'in service to the ideas'. This new mythology, which emerges from a 'monotheism of reason and of the heart [and the] polytheism of the imagination and art', abolishes the hierarchies that not only structure the oppressive, mechanistic apparatus of the state and the superstitions of a hypocritical priesthood but also those reified boundaries that divide the sciences and that separate the truths of philosophy from the common world of the people (quoted in Krell, 2005, 25). With the instantiation of a new mythology,

> eternal unity will prevail among us ... Only then can we expect the *equal* formation of *all* powers [*Kräfte*], in particular persons as well as in all individuals. No longer will any power [*Kraft*] be suppressed; universal freedom and equality of spirits [*Geister*] will then prevail! (quoted in Krell, 2005, 26tm)

With a new mythology comes universal freedom and the equality of spirits. We should keep in mind, moreover, the Kantian resonances – recall Section 3.5 – of the terms *Kraft* (power, force, capacity) and the double significance of the German term *Geist* (spirit, mind). The new mythology will realize, according to this passage, the equal formation of all capacities and all minds, that is to say, the equality of intelligences. The author affirms here the legacy of Cartesian good sense and Kantian aesthetic common sense. But we cannot conclude that equality is only the *product* of the realization of a new mythology. Poetry could not be, as the author writes, the 'instructress of humanity' (rather than the instructress of the ignorant) if intellectual and aesthetic equality is not presupposed (quoted in Krell, 2005, 25). In effect, equality must already be supposed for a new mythology to embody those capacities that are already shared.

By analysing this fragment, it is possible to elaborate the basic theses of the Platonic regime of art.[4] First, the Platonic regime proposes a universal concept of art. In its initial formulation, in the 'System Program', it affirms the supposition of equality as its form of universality. However, other formulations found in the work of Schelling and Badiou affirm the universal intelligibility of art while opposing the Idea of art to the levelling forces of culture and consensus. While it is possible to articulate the Platonic regime in egalitarian terms shared by the aesthetic regime, there are two features that are particular to the Platonic regime that Rancière contests in his critique of Badiou. First, and like the ethical regime of images, the Platonic regime of art tests, as Deranty puts it, the 'ontological veracity' of art – in other words, art is judged according to its relation to the Idea. However, the Idea does not describe an ideal model of a thing, as it does in the ethical regime of images. In the Platonic regime the Idea of art designates, as Benjamin Noys phrases it, the formalization of a 'relation of rupture' (Noys, 2009, 385) that separates the work (or works) of art from a given state of a situation. When Schelling suggests that the novel, by transforming the fragments of modern life into a unified totality, lays the groundwork for a new mythology, he sets monumental art against fragmentary and mechanistic relations that organize modern society, while for Badiou an artistic event is subtracted from the networks of commodification and consensus that structure what he calls 'democratic materialism' (Badiou, 2006b, 1). In sum, the Platonic regime formulates the politics of art in an evental and monumental form.[5]

At this point, it is worth considering why I think it is worthwhile to complicate Rancière's outline of the three regimes of art and the arts. On Rancière's account, this Platonic regime would be one of the metapolitical limits of the politics of aesthetics. When, for instance, in *Aesthetics and Its Discontents*, he analyses the 'System Program', he concludes that its project of aesthetic education via new mythology embraces a form of aesthetic metapolitics: it 'proposes to carry out, in truth and in the sensible order, a task that politics can only ever accomplish in the order of appearance and form' (Rancière, 2004a, 37). The author of the 'System Program' articulates one of the two critical demands that delimit the aesthetic regime of art, that a historically actual art must become life. It is only one type of metapolitics – the other being a politics of resistant form that demands that life must become art.

I think distinguishing the aesthetic regime from the Platonic regime has the following advantages. First, it allows us to think various practices politics of art without overextending the use of the term metapolitics, which for Rancière always betrays a negative connotation. Second, this distinction detotalizes the concept of the aesthetic regime of art. This recasts the politics of art as a space of conflict between various regimes of art, where one does not have a descriptive advantage – instead, the politics of art remains an open and contemporary question.[6]

Finally, reformulating the politics of art as a field of conflict amplifies the prescriptive aspect of Rancière's work. By the aesthetic regime of art, he means to describe the historical modes of artistic production that emerge with the collapse of the representative regime of the arts, but there is also a prescriptive and productive dimension to his analyses of art – the archaeology of a number of immanent aesthetic scenes also serves to conceptualize and practise other possible forms of aesthetic emancipation. The prescriptive and the descriptive, he says,

> constantly intertwine to constitute the landscape of the possible (the one that describes reconfigures the possibilities of a world, the one that prescribes presupposes a certain state of the world which is itself made of sedimented prescriptions), and the configuration of these landscapes is always, in the last instance, a poem: an expression in the common language of the common resources of thought. (Rancière, 2006a, 477)

While the descriptive and prescriptive elements may intertwine in Rancière's work, the weight he gives to their respective importance shifts. Though his avowed purpose in *Aesthetics and Its Discontents* is to 'clarify' rather than 'defend' what aesthetics means (Rancière, 2004a, 14), in *Aisthesis* he affirms, against accounts of modernity that see modern art as a separation 'both from the art of the past and the "aesthetic" forms of prosaic life', that:

> the movement belonging to the aesthetic regime, which supported the dream of artistic novelty and fusion between art and life subsumed under the idea of modernity, tends to erase the specificities of the arts and to blur the boundaries that separate them from each other and from ordinary experience. (Rancière, 2011: xii)

After setting out the stakes of *Aisthesis*, Rancière traces a counter-history of modernity that illustrated by a number of aesthetic scenes that demonstrate the imbrication of art in politics and social transformation. But this form of the imbrication of art and life is fundamentally different from the monumental form celebrated in the 'System Program'. As we have seen, Rancière means by the aesthetic regime of art a form of micropolitics of aesthetics that uses misunderstanding and disidentification as forms of introducing social transformation into a given distribution of the sensible. We will, following a suggestion by

Rancière, categorize aesthetics as heterotopian (Rancière, 2004b 41; 2010a). And with this categorization in mind, it is possible to glimpse an important distinction between the aesthetic regime and the Platonic regime: beginning from the supposition of aesthetic equality, proponents of the aesthetic regime think the politics of art as heterotopian, while Platonists think the politics of art monumentally. We might even say that practices of the politics of art play out between heterotopia and monumentality, that aesthetic equality and the practices of artistic praxis are delimited by these two possibilities as articulated in the conflict between the Platonic regime and the aesthetic regime of art.

At this point, I should stipulate that it is not my purpose here to undertake an archaeology of the Platonic regime of art.[7] I have introduced this concept of the Platonic regime in order to reconsider Rancière's critique of Badiou's inaesthetics outside of its contemporary context. To my knowledge, the accounts of the debate between Rancière and Badiou, at least concerning aesthetics, establish (while possibly defending one against the other's criticisms) how two intellectuals with much in common – both philosophically and biographically – end up talking past each other (see, for example, Shaw 2007, Tanke 2009, Phillips 2010, Rockhill 2010). In this chapter, I would like to show that the central points of contention between Rancière's aesthetics and Badiou's inaesthetics also describe the fundamental differences between Schiller, whose *On the Aesthetic Education of Man* (1795; hereafter, *Ästhetische Briefe*) is 'one of the first formulations of the politics inherent to the aesthetic regime' (Rancière, 2004a, 27) and Schelling, whose philosophy of art systematized an avowed though idiosyncratic Platonism. The conflict between the aesthetic regime and the Platonic regime, in both cases, concerns whether the politics of art is monumental or heterotopian, that is, whether it is evental or micropolitical. In this chapter, I will contend that, after the collapse of the representative regime, the Platonic regime of art and the aesthetic regime of art emerge as two possible ways of thinking the relations of philosophy, politics, and art. This does not mean that the last two hundred years of philosophy are marked teleologically by this conflict of aesthetics and Platonism; there is no historical destiny of art, only historically situated practices and discourses, which include, among others, some that are Platonic and others that are aesthetic. Instead, I will suggest that thinking the politics of art after the Platonic regime and after the aesthetic regime requires formulating a paradoxical praxis that maintains the possibility of both a monumental and micropolitical art.

4.2. Between aesthetics and inaesthetics

Badiou and Rancière share a common philosophical horizon. In pedagogical terms, both began as students of Althusser, only to find, after the events of May 1968, Althusser's work stultifying.[8] In philosophical terms, both maintain that a contemporary, radical account of politics requires: (1) a theory of political subjectivation, a practice which is (2), opposed to, and operates beyond the confines of, the allocation of rights and the functions of parliamentarianism within, for Badiou, the order of the state or, for Rancière, policing; which is to say that (3), political subjectivation is eventful, breaking with and disrupting apparatuses of oppression and exploitation, rather than ethical – as both view the Lévinasian ethics of the other, which has influenced Derrida, Jean-Luc Nancy and Lyotard, as antipolitical.

Despite these similarities, Badiou and Rancière disagree about what the tasks of politics and artistic praxis are.[9] Though Badiou has criticized Rancière's politics, and Rancière Badiou's inaesthetics, there has been little substantive debate between the two.[10] While Badiou dedicates two chapters of his *Metapolitics* to differentiating between their respective accounts of political subjectivation, he makes only passing references to Rancière's aesthetics; in *The Century* he contends – echoing Foucault's remarks about Sartre being a man of the nineteenth century trying to think the twentieth – that Rancière's politics of aesthetics remains 'steeped in the nineteenth century' (Badiou, 2005, 214 n.48). Rancière's rejoinder rightly ignores Badiou's accusation that his politics remains *too* democratic – that is, compatible with the logic of parliamentarianism (Badiou, 1998c, 120) or, in Rancière's terms, no different than policing – and focuses instead on Badiou's inaesthetics, which Rancière claims is a contemporary and stultifying form of Platonic modernism.[11]

In this section, I will defend the distinction I have made between the aesthetic regime of art and the Platonic regime of art by outlining Rancière's critique of Badiou's *Handbook of Inaesthetics*. By questioning Rancière's characterization of Badiou's inaesthetics as Platonic modernism, I will show that the key points of disagreement between Rancière and Badiou correspond to the tenets that define the differences between aesthetics and Platonism. Badiou's interpretations of artworks are structured by relating their significance to their ontological veracity or verification, meaning that art is a work of truth or the Idea; and second, that Badiou ultimately thinks the politics of art in eventful or monumental terms – that art's relation to a given state of a situation is a 'relation of rupture' (Noys, 2009, 385). When Badiou claims that art is a work of truth, he means that the artistic event is a double form of subtraction: (1) Badiou defines an event as the subtraction of truth from knowledge of a given situation, but (2) the inaesthetic value of art, its ontological veracity – as evidenced in *The Century* – is determined insofar as art thinks subtraction. The second definitive feature of the Platonic regime is perhaps more controversial in the case of Badiou, who asserts that the truths of art are 'irreducible' to the other conditions of philosophy: politics, science and love (1998b, 9; 2005, 152). However, to say that an artistic event is irreducible to politics does not necessarily mean – and again, *The Century* confirms this point – that artistic events do not have an immanent political import. The account that follows is not concerned with establishing who, between Badiou and Rancière, is telling *the* truth about art. Instead, we will establish how the opposition between the aesthetic regime of art and the Platonic regime formulates a number of dilemmas concerning art, politics, and aesthetics.

Before evaluating Badiou's inaesthetics, we will outline his ontology, which he calls a 'Platonism of the multiple' (Badiou, 1989, 103). In *Being and Event* (1988), Badiou defends three claims that have important implications for his inaesthetics: first, that mathematics is ontology; second, that philosophy establishes the concepts – such as the event and the subject – with which it identifies truths; and third, that there are four conditions of philosophy, which themselves are not dependent upon philosophy, that produce truths: politics, science, art, and love. Badiou argues that each event of truth breaks with the state of a situation and reconfigures the co-ordinates of the symbolic order. However, an event takes no object: 'every truth is *without an object*' (Badiou, 1989, 91). Instead, an event induces effects of subjectivation. For each event or truth (as truths are multiple), a subject must make a wager. After deciding in favour of an event, that it has taken place, this subject proceeds in fidelity to this truth, to make sense of it. Finally, while philosophy can think the possibility of the event, there are not philosophical events. Thus, for Badiou, philosophy thinks under the events of its four conditions. While each condition is thought proceeding from an event and from the subject, each is elucidated according to its own logic: the 'process of a truth', he claims, 'thus entirely escapes ontology' (Badiou, 1988, 355). To be more precise: Badiou means that the wager of the event is heterogeneous to *being*, though the meaning of the process of truth is bound, in his inaesthetics, to its ontological veracity – that is, the way that art thinks the Idea.

Though Badiou maintains that art thinks the Idea, the truth of art is not *immediately* ontological. Art is a truth, but not *the* truth. He specifically opposes his ontology to the 'poetic ontology' of Heidegger, which remains committed to 'the figure of being as endowment and gift, as presence and opening' evoked by the poem (Badiou, 1988, 9). By contrast, Badiou argues that mathematics – specifically the Zermelo-Fraenkel system of set theory with the axiom of choice (ZFC) – is ontology. Badiou does not claim that being itself is mathematical, but he considers set theory the only demonstrative and fully transmissible discourse on ontology not reliant on some privileged location of unconcealment. Set theory founds the being of the pure multiple through a lack in being and the rupture of the matheme – on the void, with the axiom of the void (or empty set) being his name for the only axiom of ZFC that asserts the existence of a multiple: there exists a set such that there does not exist any element which belongs to it. From the existence of an empty set (the void) it is possible to generate an infinite multiple with no predicates other than being multiple from the other axioms of set theory. But the void is not the presence of an absolute One; instead it is the unpresented suture of the multiple to being.

Badiou maintains that set theory, through philosophical intervention, provides an ontology of the pure multiple. To account for the appearance of unity within presentation, he introduces two concepts: 'the situation' and 'the state of the situation'. A situation is the presentation of the multiple (multiples belong to a situation) in its infinite inconsistency, while a state of the situation is the representation of the multiple (multiples are included in a state of the situation) as consistent. So, for example, an infinite multiple in a political situation can be represented as, among other things, individuals, voters, industrial workers, students, or intellectuals. However, while multiples are always both presented and represented, there is no complete correspondence between the situation and the state of the situation, which makes possible the novelty of the event. An event is supernumerary *vis-à-vis* the situation and its state; it is *subtracted* from the knowledge that circulates within the state of the situation. The event can only be named and discerned retroactively within a situation, and this is a task of the subject. A subject, for Badiou, is not an everyday occurrence, but the subject of an event. The subject must wager that an event has taken place, as there is no objective truth of an event. Then, in deciding that an event has taken place, the subject must pursue the consequences of the novelty introduced: this is the process of a truth and giving the event a supernumerary name. So, to return to the political example, a radical movement could emerge after an event such as May 1968 in France, dedicated to pursuing the latter's consequences, which has a universal address and could include the various representations of political actors such as workers, students, intellectuals, immigrants, etc. Yet this movement itself would not be represented within the state of the situation; it can only continue through subjective political engagement.

It may appear, at this point, that there is little place for art in Badiou's work: his set-theoretical ontology – explicitly opposed to 'poetic ontology' – provides the fundamental concepts of his philosophy. But he also holds that production of truths is not internal to philosophy, but takes place within the four conditions. The demarcation between philosophy and its conditions can already be found in his treatment of set theory: the ontological character of mathematics is not internal to working mathematics, but constructed through a philosophical intervention regarding the ontological capacity of mathematics. In terms of art, severing poetry from its apparent ontological task allows for an appraisal of artistic truths immanent to artistic processes themselves. This appraisal of artistic truths is the task of inaesthetics. Badiou defines inaesthetics as:

> a relation of philosophy to art that, maintaining that art is itself a producer of truths, makes no claim to turn art into an object for philosophy. Against aesthetic speculation, inaesthetics describes the strictly intraphilosophical effects produced by the independent existence of some works of art. (Badiou, 1998b, xiv)

Badiou situates inaesthetics against three schemata that tie together art, philosophy, and the theme of education: didacticism, romanticism, and classicism. Though these are seemingly transhistorical frameworks for considering the relation between art and philosophy, they each have, according to Badiou, a historical and contemporary manifestation.

Plato's *Republic* is the first formulation of didacticism. Badiou argues that Plato banishes (nearly all) the arts from the city on the basis of the thesis that 'art is incapable of truth, or that all truth is external to art' (1998b, 2). For Plato, art is deceptive not because it imitates things, but because it imitates the effect of truth. By appearing to present the truth immediately, art 'diverts us from the detour' of philosophy (1998b, 2). On Badiou's account, Plato constitutes philosophy as the detour that distances thought from empirical immediacy through dialectical labour. Badiou's own Platonism of the multiple is premised on the subtraction of thought from the immediacy of the poem – though he maintains, against Plato's didacticism, that art is a process of truth. Thus while Badiou commends the interruption of the poem by the matheme in *Being and Event*, he finds Plato's conceptualization of art wanting. Plato's didacticism reduces art to 'the charm of a semblance of truth' (Badiou, 1998b, 2). From this position, art is either condemned or instrumentalized pedagogically, the latter option leaving art at the mercy of external prescriptions, namely the political norm legislated by philosophy. The effects of art are evaluated only from the basis of the social Good. In *Handbook of Inaesthetics*, Badiou argues that Brecht is the exemplar of the twentieth-century didacticism that is Marxism. For Brecht, he claims, militant theatre is constructed from the scientific truth of dialectical materialism. If one understands Stalinism as the jurisdiction of dialectical materialist philosophy over politics, then Brecht practised a 'Stalinized Platonism': art is separate from the truth of dialectical materialism, but it educates; in the end, art is the pedagogical tool for the courage of truth, 'against cowardice *in the face of truth*' (1998b, 6).

The didactic relation between philosophy and art is inverted by romanticism, which maintains that 'art *alone* is capable of truth', that art alone embodies the absolute (1998b, 3). Art presents a truth to which philosophy can only point. Badiou's critique of the romantic schema can be seen as a response to Lacoue-Labarthe and Nancy's thesis that 'romanticism is the inauguration of the literary absolute', through which questions of thinking, writing, and sense are modelled on the production of theory as literature or *poiesis* (Lacoue-Labarthe and Nancy, 1978, 12). Literature as criticism and criticism as literature circulate as a deconstruction – albeit incomplete – of the subject, the absolute, and the work as the basis of significance. Lacoue-Labarthe and Nancy's archaeology of the literary absolute recovers the work of the romantics in light of the deconstruction of western metaphysics carried out by Heidegger, who is ultimately Badiou's polemical target.

In *Manifesto for Philosophy*, Badiou criticizes Heidegger for suturing philosophy to poetry, delegating the task of thinking the compossibility of truths to one of philosophy's conditions, 'handing over the whole of thought to *one* generic procedure' (Badiou, 1989, 61). For Heidegger, the thinker, in seeking the originary link between *poiesis* and Being that was severed by the Platonic intervention of the matheme, can only reiterate the announcement of the destiny of the poetic gods, and shepherd thought towards the saving power of the poem (Badiou, 1998a, 21–32). Badiou argues that Heidegger's account owes its persuasive power to the way that it ties the poetic destitution of objectivity – carried out during the 'Age of Poets' that proceeds from Hölderlin to Celan – to the critique of metaphysics. However, he adds, 'the fundamental criticism of Heidegger can only be the following one: the Age of Poets is completed, it is also necessary to de-suture philosophy from its poetic condition' (Badiou, 1989, 74). The Age of Poets can be 'completed' because this 'age' was not immanent to the poets, but a philosophical category engendered by the poetic suture (Badiou, 1992a).

Between 'didactic banishment' and 'romantic glorification' is a 'peace treaty of sorts' that Badiou calls the classical schema (1998b, 3). It is first established by Aristotle, who, according to Badiou, bases the classical schema on two theses: first, art is mimetic, its regime is that of semblance; and second, the purpose of art is neither truth, nor pedagogy, but therapy. The classical schema holds that art's mimetic effects provide the possibility of catharsis, which Badiou defines – in terms meant to evoke those of psychoanalysis – as 'the deposition of the passions in a transference onto semblance' (1998b, 4). Art, constrained to the imaginary relation of transference, is evacuated of the weight of the traumatic encounter with the Real. The price of this 'relative peace' between philosophy and art is that the latter becomes what Badiou calls a 'public service', a kind of escape mechanism for social pressures.[12] Insofar as art serves this purpose, it can be managed and legitimated – or funded – by the state. The contemporary manifestation of the classical schema is psychoanalysis, insofar as it interprets art as the manifestation of desire (whether it is the desire of the artist or spectator). The work of art makes it possible to inscribe the object of desire, the *objet petit a*, in the Symbolic, thus breaking the impasse of the Real. Though contemporary Lacanians would object to this generalization of psychoanalytic theory, Slavoj Žižek himself has attacked Jacques-Alain Miller's turn to a 'psychoanalysis in the city' that seeks social legitimation through state sanction (Žižek, 2004, 103; cf. Miller, 2003). In such a case, art renders service to psychoanalysis, and the latter likewise renders service to the state.

Having accounted for Marxism, Heideggerian hermeneutics, and psychoanalysis in *Handbook of Inaesthetics*, Badiou argues that no new schema was introduced in the twentieth century. The avant-gardes, from Dada to the Situationists, were a hybrid and unstable entanglement of didacticism and romanticism, vacillating between the attempt to exhaust art of its alienated or alienating separation from social life and the attempt to realize the absolute legibility of the autonomous and separate place of art. The former attempt is didactic, while the latter is romantic; yet above all, these 'partisans of the absoluteness of creative destruction' were anticlassical (Badiou, 1998b, 8). Nevertheless, the 'aesthetic voluntarism' of the avant-gardes could not escape what Badiou calls the recent 'saturation' of the attempt to think art and philosophy.

To break with this interpretative saturation, Badiou proposes inaesthetics as a new modality of the relation between art and philosophy. He contrasts inaesthetics with the three previous schemata by reference to the categories of singularity and immanence (see Table 4.1). A relation of art to truth is singular if it cannot be given elsewhere than art and cannot 'circulate among other registers of work-producing thought' (Badiou, 1998b, 9). A relation is immanent if truth is 'internal' or 'coextensive' to art's effects – in other words, if art is not the instrument of an external truth. For didacticism, the relation between art and truth is singular but not immanent: art has a singular pedagogical role but truth remains external to it. For romanticism, the relation is immanent but not singular – in this case, the truth of philosophy and art is the same: as mentioned above, in crossing the philosophical critique of objectivity (that is, the critique of truth as adequation; see Heidegger, 1961) and the poetic destitution of objectivity, Heidegger sutured philosophy to the truth procedure of art. For the classical schema, there is no relation between art and truth; art is relegated to the imaginary effects of verisimilitude, catharsis, and transference. Furthermore, it is possible to extrapolate from Badiou's account that the avant-gardes vacillated between the disjunction of absolute immanence and a singular task for art, sometimes resulting in schisms and sectarianism. From this standpoint, Raoul Vaneigem's condemnation of later Surrealism's turn to mythology as intolerable and counter to the goals of a revolution of everyday life in his *A Cavalier History of Surrealism* (1977) would be a fine example of the didactic Marxist/Situationist critique of Surrealist romanticism.

Table 4.1 The relation of art to truth

Relation:	Immanent	~Immanent
Singular	Inaesthetics	Didactic
~Singular	Romantic	Classical

Badiou formulates the method of singular and immanent interpretation of – he would say affirmation of – the relation of art to truth by contrasting inaesthetics to didacticism and romanticism. He affirms, like didacticism, that 'only art can exhibit truth in the form of semblance' (1998b, 9), but he maintains, like romanticism, that truth is immanent to art – that is, art thinks the Idea. Nevertheless, he jettisons two features of romanticism: first, its reliance on the thematic of productive genius; and second, its conception of the truth of art as incarnation, in which *an* artwork descends to the sensible incarnation of the Idea

(1998b, 11). Instead, Badiou proposes that discerning the truth of an artistic event requires the concepts of the artistic configuration and the subject-point. An artistic configuration is a sequence of works that proceed from an event; the novelty of the event is registered by configurations which *will have taken place* insofar as they are unprecedented within previous configurations. A truth is singularized within a configuration, and for each event there are multiple works, or differential subject-points, which delineate the 'subject', or 'theme', of fidelity to the event. He writes: 'a truth is an artistic configuration initiated by an event … and unfolded through chance in the form of works that serve as its subject points' (1998b, 12). Badiou's account keeps a work from being understood as an absolute object while at the same time it prevents a subject from being understood as a subject of genius. Instead of locating the truth of art in subjects or objects, truth is localized in artistic procedures, which circulate between configurations and differential subject-points, constrained by a post-evental rupture with the state of the situation.

In what follows, I will challenge Badiou's claim that inaesthetics is the first novel account of the relation between philosophy and art since romanticism. First, I will look at Rancière's criticisms of what he considers to be Badiou's Platonic modernism. Then, after locating the impasses of Rancière's critique, I will argue that Badiou's inaesthetics is a contemporary form of the Platonic regime of art. As the reader has probably surmised, there are numerous similarities between Badiou's schemata and Rancière's regimes of art and the arts. Both Badiou and Rancière are critical of Plato's *Republic* (the model of both didacticism and the ethical regime of images) and Aristotle's *Poetics* (which delineates the norms of the representative regime of the arts and the classicism that remain influential in psychoanalysis).[13] However, in Badiou's schemata, there is no place for what Rancière has characterized as the aesthetic regime of art.[14]

Let us be clear about what is at stake in Rancière's critique of Badiou. Rancière contends that inaesthetics is a form of 'Platonic modernism' (Rancière, 2004a, 71), a hybrid of the ethical regime of images and Greenberg's modernism – but above all, inaesthetics is anti-romantic, a claim borne out by the introductory paragraphs of Badiou's 'Third Sketch of a Manifesto of Affirmationist Art' (2004; hereafter, 'Manifesto of Affirmationist Art'). However, this is not a quarrel about who is telling *the* truth about art. Instead, Rancière's argument – as it is with Greenberg – is that Badiou's theoretical decision to separate inaesthetics from 'aesthetic speculation' depoliticizes art. In the case of Badiou – to paraphrase a claim of André Breton – art must be monumental or it will not be at all. Hence the final claim of Badiou's 'Manifesto of Affirmationist Art': 'It is better to do nothing than to work formally toward making visible what the West declares to exist' (Badiou, 2004, 148). From Rancière's perspective, then, Badiou precludes the possibility of the micropolitics of aesthetics.

For Rancière, the significance of the micropolitics of art is tied to the collapse of the mimetic norms that governed the representative regime of the arts. These norms not only distinguished what was proper to an art, and policed the lines between the fine arts, but also established parallels between artistic hierarchies and social hierarchies. As we have seen, the aesthetic regime of art, which emerges from the collapse of these mimetic norms, names a double movement of the constant negotiation and identification of: (1) the boundaries between art and non-art, the negotiation of which ruins the hierarchies that stabilized the representative regime; and (2) the exorbitant promises of an aesthetic revolution of the forms of art and forms of life (Rancière, 2004a, 14). The aesthetic regime of art, as formulated by Schiller and others, defines art according to a paradoxical relation of autonomy and heteronomy: 'all the new, *aesthetic* definitions of art that affirm its autonomy in one way or another say the same thing, affirm the same paradox: that art is henceforth recognizable by its lack of any distinguishing characteristics – by its indistinction' (Rancière, 2004a, 66).

Rancière identifies three processes 'by which Badiou's modern Platonism confronts the equivocations of art's homonymy' (Rancière, 2004a, 86). First, he contends that Badiou, by attempting to purify inaesthetics of 'aesthetic speculation', attempts to isolate the specificity and univocity of art at the cost of subtracting artistic truths from 'the indistiction of the metaphoric universe in which the aesthetic regime ties together forms of art, forms of life and the forms of thinking about art' (Rancière, 2004a, 86). According to Rancière, it is not possible to formalize the 'specificity of art'. In his defence, at this point, Badiou could contend that he and Rancière are much closer than Rancière admits. Rancière maintains that art is aesthetic insofar as it disrupts policing by introducing types of – and relations between – speech, visibility, and place. For Badiou, art is also submitted to the principle of novelty, subtracted from the ordinary circulation of meaning. However, whereas Rancière's micropolitics of aesthetics revolves around the porous boundary of what appears as art and the implications of these demarcations, Badiou emphasizes the monumental character of the artistic event. As Benjamin Noys points out, Badiou's approach to art after *Handbook of Inaesthetics* reflects 'on how the "independent affirmation" of the artwork requires an engagement and rupture with existing conditions ... Badiou has increasingly tried to specify how the subtraction from relation might be formed as a relation of rupture' (Noys, 2009, 384–5).

Therefore, Rancière must be able to identify the way that Badiou's conceptualization of this paradoxical 'relation of rupture' forecloses on the micropolitics of art. For Rancière, it is Badiou's Platonic modernism that does so, which affirms the autonomy of art while denying its heteronomy. As Rancière writes,

> inaesthetics designates the twisted necessity according to which the lines of division that cause the Platonism of truth to conceal itself from aesthetic Platonism [that Rancière locates within romanticism] are made to coincide with those by which modernism seeks to secure 'art's specificity' from slipping into aesthetics' indistinction. (Rancière, 2004a, 86)

Badiou, as Rancière points out, uncritically accepts the modernist concept of mimesis. As we have seen, for Rancière, the aesthetic regime interrupts and undermines the mimetic norms of the representative regime, but it is not against representation or figuration. The modernist concept of mimesis maintains that art is to be purified, as Badiou acknowledges in *The Century*, of 'resemblance, representation, narrative or the natural' (Badiou, 2005, 132). Badiou's modernism is also present in the *Handbook of Inaesthetics*. For example, there he argues that the 'modern poem', as it is inscribed in the period between Hölderlin and Celan, is 'the opposite of a mimesis. In its operation, it exhibits an Idea of which both the object and objectivity represent nothing but pale copies' (Badiou, 1998b, 21). Poetry thinks the disobjectification that subtracts language from the conventions of its representative functions; it manifests both the 'difference within language' and thinks the very 'flesh of language' itself (Badiou, 1998b, 32, 20). This flesh of language is difference rather than incarnation; the poem does not bring the Real of language to fruition, but attests to the gap between presence and absence that makes the poetic event possible.

And yet, according to Rancière, Badiou's modernist assumptions are undermined by his commitment to Platonism. While Badiou adopts both the modernist critique of mimesis, and (as least in *Handbook of Inaesthetics*) the tenet that the specificity of art is the specificity of *an* art, he rejects the claim that the irreducible character of a medium defines this specificity. Instead, he holds that the relation of an art to truth or the Idea defines the singularity of an art. Then the inaesthetic autonomy of art – thought in its singularity and immanence – becomes a form of heteronomy. Rancière distinguishes between two concepts of heteronomy. One is aesthetic heteronomy, which erodes the distinction between poetry and prose, literature and life. Mallarmé's poetics, on this account, deprives the opposition between the essay in prose and the poem in verse of all discriminatory relevance: *Crise de vers* is not a text by Mallarmé *on* poetry; it *is* a piece of Mallarmean poetry, neither more nor less so than the *Sonnet en X*, which, for its part, is indissolubly a poem and a statement *about* poetry. (Rancière, 2004a, 74)

The heteronomy of Badiou's Platonism amounts, via a 'rigorously Althusserian logic', to the subordination of aesthetic sensibility to philosophical truth (Rancière, 2004a, 79). By distinguishing absolutely between art and philosophy, Badiou effects a separation by which 'it is philosophy that acts as the condition of the poem's intelligibility' (Rancière, 2006b, 197). A poem, for example, is not a self-sufficient thinking; it is divided between being an immanent orientation for thought and exhibiting a truth of which it is the task of philosophy to subtract. More generally, Rancière contends that Badiou's formalizations of art become formulatic, granting a univocal purpose to each art, related to the passage of the Idea in the event. Poetry becomes a source for general maxims of thought; Mallarmé's *Un coup de dés*, for example, supplies the maxim that nothing takes place but the place and the undecidable dice-throw or wager of the subject in the wake of the event (see, for example, Badiou, 1988, 191–8; 1992b, 87, 122, 202). Furthermore, dance is treated as the askesis (in Foucault's sense of the term) – though not as an *art* – through which the body becomes the virtual movement of thought (Badiou, 1998b, 69); theatre interrupts democratic consensus – in his later terms, 'democratic materialism' – by making visible and mobilizing the 'excluded and invisible people who, all of a sudden, by the effect of the theater-idea, embody upon the stage intelligence and force, desire and mastery' (1998b, 76);[15] while, by virtue of the montage of 'ambient imagery, from the detritus of other arts' and the indistinction of art and non-art, cinema purifies the impurity of ideas: it turns – 'for the duration of a passage – the impurity of every idea into an idea in its own right' (Badiou, 1999, 111; 1998b, 83).

Though Rancière attacks the 'Althusserian logic' of Badiou's inaesthetics, he stops short of critiquing it, as he does Greenberg's modernism, as a form of anti-egalitarianism. Whereas Greenberg casts the modernist avant-garde as the standard bearer of preserving, from bourgeois philistinism and proletarian kitsch, that which remains of living European culture, Badiou contends that evental, monumental art is an art of 'proletarian aristocratism': of universal address and subtracted from consensus, resemblance or imitation (Badiou, 2004, 147). But before we address the political stakes of the disagreement between Badiou and Rancière, it is important to note that Jean-Jacques Lecercle disputes the claim that inaesthetics amounts to an 'Althusserian logic' of mastery. While

Rancière argues that Badiou's inaesthetics retrenches the modernist distinctions between genres and disciplines, Lecercle interprets the separation of philosophy and poetry as an affirmation of poetry as *logos* or thought. On Lecercle's account, Badiou's inaesthetics sidesteps 'the aporia of the contrast between *pathos* and *logos*, between auratic or lyrical vaticination and the exclusion of thought from poetry or poetry from thought' (Lecercle, 2004, 215). Instead, Badiou holds that thinking takes place in the 'irreducible' form of art. The paradox, for Lecercle, is that Badiou's separation of philosophy and art, which places truth on the side of art as thought, undermines philosophical appeals to interpretative mastery:

> The general irony of Badiou's readings of poetry is of course that they are such strong and decisive readings that they leave a lot of space for other readings, as the poem spectacularly exceeds the truth that Badiou's reading extracts from it. (Lecercle, 2004, 215)

But let us focus on this claim that Badiou posits a 'poetry of *logos*' that thinks through its 'irreducible' form as art. Rancière characterizes Schelling's work in similar terms: for Schelling, it is the 'identity of *logos* and *pathos*,' of 'conscious procedure and unconscious production' that 'attests to the existence of art' (Rancière, 2001, 28). While this summary of Schelling's philosophy of art is accurate, it does not necessarily mean that his thought is *aesthetic*. If it is the case that the Platonic regime of art also attests to the indistinction or indifference of the Idea and art, thought and affect, by which Rancière characterizes the aesthetic regime, then it is politics that divides these regimes. But first, I will challenge Rancière's characterization of inaesthetics as a form of Platonic *modernism* and Badiou's claim that inaesthetics is an entirely new schema of relating philosophy and art by revisiting a moment when Schiller and Schelling proposed competing views of the relationship between philosophy, politics, and art. This moment has been obscured by Hegel's account of the historical development of aesthetics.

4.3. Between aesthetic education and the absolute

In his lectures on aesthetics, Hegel presents a historical development of a concept of art that, he contends, overcomes the opposition between spirit and nature that forces human beings to 'live in two worlds which contradict one another': the world of spiritual life and that of sensuous nature, in which humans are torn between the command of practical reason – the categorical imperative and 'duty for duty's sake' – and their sensuous disposition (Hegel, 1835: 54). It is to the 'great credit' of Schiller to have broken through 'Kantian subjectivity and abstraction of thinking' by venturing that the artistic production of beauty realizes the totality and reconciliation of spirit and nature:

> This *unity* of universal and particular, freedom and necessity, spirit and nature, which Schiller grasped scientifically as the principle and essence of art and which he laboured unremittingly to call into actual life by art and aesthetic education, has now, as the *Idea itself,* been made the principle of knowledge and existence, and the Idea has become recognized as that which alone is true and actual. Thereby philosophy has attained, with Schelling, its absolute standpoint; and while art had already begun to assert its proper nature and dignity in relation to the highest interests of mankind, it was now that the *concept* of art, and the place of art in philosophy was discovered, and art has been accepted, even if in one aspect in a distorted way (which this is not the place to discuss), still in its high and genuine vocation. (Hegel, 1835, 61, 62–3)

Hegel's summary is deceptively straightforward. He claims that Schiller and Schelling overcome Kant's abstractions by making the principle and vocation of art the realization of the unity of freedom and nature. However, he adds that this movement of thought anticipates – already at the juncture between 1795 and 1807 – the realization of the 'Idea itself' in philosophy as the truly highest vocation. This 'distortion', that places art and philosophy in reciprocal relation, has been, on Hegel's account, now surpassed by philosophy.

From Rancière's perspective, Hegel liquidates the emancipatory potential of both literature and the aesthetic regime of art – which encompasses both Schiller's aesthetics and Schelling's philosophy of art – by relegating it to the past.[16] But we should also be skeptical toward the historical continuity of Hegel's account, whereby Schiller surpasses Kant, Schelling Schiller, and Hegel Schelling. Instead of placing them in a continuum between Kant and Hegel, I will contend that Schiller and Schelling chart two distinct paths in the aftermath of Kant's account of aesthetic judgement. Therefore, my position challenges Rancière's categorization of Schelling's philosophy of art as part of the aesthetic regime (see, for instance, 1998d, 76; 2001, 6, 28; 2004a, 9, 37). This, in turn, undermines both Rancière's distinction between Schelling's romantic Platonism and Badiou's Platonic modernism (2004a, 71–3), and Badiou's claim that inaesthetics is a new philosophical engagement with art. Though Badiou does not address the work of Schelling, I think he would treat Schelling's Platonism as romanticism, meaning that Schelling maintains the thesis that art is the *immediate* sensible presentation of the Idea.[17] This would require Badiou to equivocate between immanence and immediacy, since Schelling holds that the Idea of art is immanent but not immediate.

As we have seen (in Section 3.5), in *The Philosopher and His Poor*, Rancière argues that Kant's aesthetic *sensus communis* is premised on the capacity for intellectual and sensible equality. The disinterestedness of aesthetic judgement, according to Rancière, is what makes it possible for an individual to suspend her interests and disidentify with her practico-inert exigencies in order to consider how the social relations that govern her everyday life could be otherwise. Aesthetic judgement, in other words, opens the possibility for what Rancière calls misinterpretation, whereby the oppressed borrow terms and practices from dominant discursive forms and redirect them toward emancipatory ends. However, that Rancière supports his claims with Gauny's and Baudelaire's 'commentaries' on *The Critique of the Power of Judgment* indicates an implicit acknowledgement of the limits of Kant's own interest in the political or emancipatory significance of aesthetics. But this implicit acknowledgement does not undermine Rancière's interpretation. His aim, in *The Philosopher and His Poor*, is to demonstrate, against Bourdieu, that Kant's aesthetics carries an emancipatory potential.[18]

When Rancière revisits the *Critique of the Power of Judgment* in *Aesthetics and Its Discontents*, he explicitly addresses the limits of the politics of Kant's aesthetics. He contends that Kant's conception of beauty allegorizes the politics of aesthetics. Beauty, for Kant, is subordinated to *neither* the epistemological structures of the understanding *nor* the categorical duties of practical reason. Since it concerns the form of an object that is neither cognitive nor practical, aesthetic judgement is a moment of aesthetic 'autonomy': this '*neither... nor...*, the unavailability of this form for the faculties of both understanding and desire, enabled the subject, through the free play of those faculties, to experience a new form of autonomy' (Rancière, 2004a, 91). In political terms, aesthetic judgement, this 'neither...nor...', for Rancière, 'suspends' the established cognitive or practical significations of a given distribution of the sensible, making possible novelty and social transformation. The keywords of Rancière's aesthetics (literary misunderstanding, misinterpretation), and even political disagreement, play on this moment of aesthetic suspension by indicating a novel use of words and practices (and new relations between words, practices, and things) unforeseen by established canons of knowledge and practico-inert fields of experience.

But while a concept of 'fragmentary emancipation' becomes available with

Kant's aesthetics when common sense is treated as an egalitarian supposition, Rancière stipulates in *Aesthetics and Its Discontents* that Kant's concept of common sense – at least within Kant's system – can also function as a principle of consensus or social mediation, by which it may be possible to 'unite the elite's sense of refinement with ordinary people's natural simplicity' (Rancière, 2004a, 98).[19] Rancière then proceeds to argue that Schiller radicalizes Kant's account of common sense by emphasizing the dissensual basis of aesthetics.[20]

4.3.1. Aesthetic emancipation and policing

Rancière's reading of Schiller highlights how aesthetics becomes a way to think emancipation. But, in delineating an archaeology of the aesthetic regime, Rancière outlines *how* art becomes a practice of dissensus, but he does not seek to address *why* the meaning of art becomes a significant problem for philosophy. I think both Schiller and Schelling are motivated by a similar dissatisfaction with Kant's account of practical reason. More specifically, both find that the formal rigidity of Kant's categorical imperative results in an excessively narrow and rule-bound concept of freedom. Freedom, from their respective standpoints, ought to be the activity by which a human being cultivates the totality of her faculties, and yet Kant's view of practical reason as an infinite task of approximating the moral law is but a fragment of this activity. To think artistic production and aesthetic experience, for both Schiller and Schelling, requires a broader concept of freedom: Schiller's account proposes a concept of aesthetic freedom, while Schelling proposes what we might call an account of absolute freedom. Moreover, both maintain that their respective concepts of freedom cannot be expressed fully in statist political forms. In sum, both Schiller and Schelling hold that philosophical engagement of art entails: first, a critique of Kant's concept of freedom; and second, a new way of thinking social and political change – as Rancière notes, the politics of art entails a new concept of revolution.

Highlighting the critique of Kant's concept of freedom reinforces Rancière's distinction between the significance granted to the disjunction of the 'neither... nor...' of aesthetic autonomy by Kant and by Schiller and Schelling. While Kant argues that our judgements concerning the beautiful are neither theoretical (as taste only expresses subjective pleasure or displeasure in relation to the representation of an object, and not the cognition of an object through a concept) nor practical (that is, grounded 'in the idea of freedom as given *a priori* by reason') the applicability of taste is circumscribed to subjective, though universal, validity (1790, 5: 280). Indeed, for Kant, practical reason, rather than aesthetics, is the keystone of the system: he states that 'the concept of freedom, insofar as its reality is proved by an apodictic law of practical reason, constitutes the *keystone* of the whole structure of a system of pure reason, even of speculative reason' from which all other concepts 'get stability and objective reality' (Kant, 1788, 5: 3–4). Kant's successors, however, are interested in how aesthetics makes possible a concept of freedom or autonomy unbound from the formal rigidity of the categorical imperative, a concept of freedom that is based on the totality of human being, what Schiller calls our 'sensible-rational nature' (Schiller, 1795, 69tm). For Schiller, the aesthetic character of an object differs from its physical, logical, or moral determinations because aesthetics relates 'to the totality of our various functions without being a definite object for any single one of them' (Schiller, 1795, 141–3n). And, for Schelling, artistic production – as an aesthetic intuition – realizes creatively through the artwork what philosophy intuits in the ideal, namely, the identity of subject and object, freedom and nature, and conscious and unconscious production. Despite their differences, both Schiller and Schelling turn to artistic production and aesthetic experience to think a concept of freedom that encompasses the totality of the 'sensible-rational nature' of human being.

Both Schiller and Schelling also politicize art. Schiller's aesthetics evinces a moment of what Rancière calls the aesthetic revolution. This aesthetic revolution has a double meaning. On the one hand, it is a revolution through which the aesthetic regime of art and the paradoxical aesthetic experience of free play and free appearance suspends the typical oppositions that guide philosophical inquiry, such as freedom and necessity, subject and object, and activity and passivity. On the other hand, it is an *aesthetic* concept of revolution, which seeks to change the sensible fabric of social relations rather than seizing institutional power. Schiller, Rancière argues, treats philosophical categories and hierarchies that govern them – for example, activity and passivity, form and matter – as political categories.

By suspending the oppositions between form and matter as well as activity and passivity, Schiller's aesthetics challenges, at a micropolitical level, the basic categories that organize the sensible fabric of social relations. Thus, for Rancière, we cannot establish Schiller's politics by reference to traditional political categories. According to Lesley Sharpe (1995), debates over Schiller's politics typically split over whether the *Ästhetische Briefe* is an engagement or retreat from politics. This approach presupposes that there is a consensus concerning what politics is (for instance, some form of engagement – by individuals or by classes – with apparatuses such as the state, civil society, or public sphere), and then asks if or how Schiller's work is politically engaged. The answers, from this approach, vary. De Man glibly concludes that Schiller's popularizing aesthetics is proto-totalitarian (1983, 154–5), Habermas portrays Schiller as a theorist of communicative action (1985, 45–50), Eagleton concludes that he is a discontent bourgeois ideologist (1990, 102–19), for Pugh he is a neo-Platonic pessimist (1996, 363), while Beiser places Schiller within the modern republican tradition of Machiavelli, Montesquieu, Rousseau and Ferguson (2005, 123–34). From Rancière's standpoint, this approach to deciding Schiller's political intentions is equivalent to establishing whether he supports a better or worse form of policing. But he does not proceed to claim that Schiller outlines a form of the politics of equality; instead, Rancière argues that Schiller presents one of the first formulations of the micropolitics 'inherent to the aesthetic regime of art' (Rancière, 2004a, 27): aesthetics is political when it suspends (and subsequently transforms) the philosophical and political categories that organize practico-inert and inegalitarian social relations.

The aesthetic revolution, Rancière contends, is not preoccupied with state power or social domination. Instead, aesthetics offers the possibility of social transformation in the interstices of power and domination. Schiller denounces two interrelated forms of domination: the state and the division of labour, both of which fragment humanity.

Schiller criticizes the state for stifling the full cultivation of the sensible-rational nature of humanity. There are two forms of state power. The natural state, founded on force rather than law, only guarantees the physical subsistence of its subjects. In the natural state, individuals encounter each other as opposing forces that impose mutual limits on each other's activity. The second form is the moral state or ethical state. At the outset of the *Ästhetische Briefe*, Schiller argues that aesthetic education, which would cultivate the harmony of each individual's sensible-rational nature, would prepare humanity for the transition from the natural state – which he initially sees to be 'at present' the cause of social ills (Schiller, 1795, 45) – to the moral state founded upon law. However, in Letter XXVII, Schiller contends that the ethical state, given that it is founded on law and duty, concomitantly oppresses the sensible character of humanity. His criticism shifts from a particular form of the state to the state form itself, though such a critique is foreshadowed in Letter VI.[21] There, he argues that the 'crude and clumsy mechanism' of the state relates to the individuals that comprise it as fragments – identified according to their respective specializations or occupations (Schiller, 1795, 35). We can restate Schiller's critique in Rancière's terms: here Schiller is criticizing the policing apparatus of the state, whereby individuals are classified, and their roles and places partitioned, according to their occupations.

In Letter V, Schiller opposes aesthetic education to the politics of the French Revolution, which, at one point, had seemed to topple the foundations of the natural state in order to inaugurate the 'true freedom' of moral law. However, the ethical state cannot be sustained, if it imposes its laws from above upon a fragmented humanity, as one imposes form on matter. For the 'political artist' or politician, he writes in Letter IV, 'Man is at once the material on which he works and the goal towards which he strives' (Schiller, 1795, 19), but Schiller criticizes, in a political allegory, in Letter XIII, the imposition of form upon sensibility as unconditional subordination of sensibility (Schiller, 1795, 85n.). Moreover, as he states in Letter VI, the policing of identifications through the state and the division of labour is doubly stultifying: a human being 'becomes nothing more than the imprint of his occupation or of his specialized knowledge', dividing humanity between those who work and those who think, while narrowing these capacities to a particular occupation or a particular branch or knowledge (Schiller, 1795, 35). To this subordination, Schiller opposes the reciprocity of play. Rancière summarizes Schiller's opposition of the French Revolution – that is, of political revolution as the seizure of political power – to the regulative ideal of the aesthetic state of free play and appearance as the emergence of a different concept of social transformation:

> The power of 'form' over 'matter' is the power of the class of intelligence over the class of sensation, of men of culture over men of nature. If aesthetic 'play' and 'appearance' found a new community, then this is because they stand for the refutation, within the sensible, of this opposition between intelligent form and sensible matter which, properly speaking, is a difference between two humanities. (Rancière, 2004a, 31)

Similar motifs and metaphors can also be found in the 'System Program' and Schelling's *System of Transcendental Idealism*. This is unsurprising, given Schiller's influence on the young Hegel, Schelling, and especially Hölderlin. The author of the 'System Program' argues that there is no Idea – in the Platonic sense – of the state, since the state is a mechanism that 'treat[s] free human beings like cogwheels' (quoted in Krell, 2005, 23). By contrast, beauty – 'the supreme act of reason' – unifies all Ideas through an act that makes Ideas aesthetic. When Ideas become aesthetic, and when art becomes rational, then there will emerge the true freedom of reconciled community of a new mythology, unfettered by the wretched apparatus of state and superstition. A similar distinction is made in the *System of Transcendental Idealism*, where Schelling opposes the present age, in which the community is governed by 'mechanical conformity to law', to the emergence of universal freedom through a new mythology (Schelling, 1800, 212/3: 604; 233/3: 629).

Though both Schiller and Schelling denounce apparatuses of policing, they politicize art in different ways: one through micropolitics, the other through monumental events. I have introduced this distinction in place of Rancière's characterization of the politics of aesthetics as metapolitics. On his account, the new mythology proposed in the 'System Program' is a form of metapolitics because it envisions the coming of a fully reconciled and organic community. This, he claims, precludes the possibility of dissensus. Given that Schelling comes to privilege the universality of the new mythology over its form of equality, I will readily admit Rancière's critique. However, he also claims that Schiller's aesthetics is a form of metapolitics that he opposes to statist revolutions (Rancière, 2004a, 33, 99). At one point, he argues that Schiller's concept of play 'becomes the principle of politics or, more exactly, of a metapolitics, which, *against the upheavals of state forms*, proposes a revolution of the forms of the lived sensory world' (Rancière, 2004a, 99, my emphasis). By contrast, in *Disagreement*, metapolitics designates a political philosophy that forecloses on the politics of equality by dismissing it as a superstructure that masks the forces – such as the transformations and contradictions of the forces of economic production – that drive social relations. Neither Schiller nor Schelling propose a politics of art that is metapolitical in that sense. Instead, they oppose artistic production and aesthetic experience to forms of policing. While the politics of art is not the politics of equality, neither is it a form of policing.[22] If the politics of equality disrupts and overturns the operations of policing, the politics of art offers modes of introducing new modes of visibility and legibility that are irreducible both to the politics of equality and to the oppressive forms of policing.

4.3.2. Schiller's aesthetic freedom

Having established their respective critiques of policing, we will now consider Schiller's and Schelling's competing accounts of the practices and politics of art. That is, we will consider how both Schiller and Schelling consider artistic practices as part of a critique of Kant's concept of freedom and as a practice of emancipation.

For Rancière, Schiller's *Ästhetische Briefe* is one of the first formulations of the politics of the aesthetic regime of art. Rancière interprets Schiller's remark that the proposition 'man only plays when he is in the fullest sense of the word a human being, and he is only fully a human being when he plays' will 'prove capable of bearing the whole edifice of the art of the beautiful, and of the still more difficult art of living' (1795, 107–9) as an affirmation of the paradoxical specificity of the aesthetic regime (Rancière, 2004a, 28). Play, on Rancière's account, is an activity that suspends the relations of power and domination that organize the policed world of the practico-inert. Schiller's proposition, Rancière contends, recognizes both the autonomy and heteronomy of aesthetic suspension. On the one hand, the 'whole edifice of the art of the beautiful' refers to the way that aesthetic experience is separated from the tasks and interests of the practico-inert world. On the other hand, play is, as a formative practice (*Bildung*) of 'the still more difficult art of living', a form of practical autonomy that expresses the 'sensible-rational nature' of human freedom.

Rancière's interpretation of the *Ästhetische Briefe* does not begin with an examination of Schiller's transcendental deductions of the regulative ideas of beauty and play. Instead, Rancière begins, *in media res*, with Schiller's illustration of the aesthetic experience of viewing the statue *Juno Ludovisi*. This experience, Rancière writes, 'allegorizes' a specific mode of the relation of art to politics. Schiller dispenses with the requirements of technical and normative standards that govern the representative regime of the arts. He states that the appearance of 'idleness and indifferency' in the portrayal of the gods separates art from all forms of utility; Greek artistic production 'freed' the gods, 'those ever-contented beings from the bonds inseparable from every purpose, every duty, every care, and made idleness and indifferency the enviable portion of divinity – merely a more human name for the freest, most sublime state of being' (Schiller, 1795, 109). This aesthetic experience demarcates a specific and autonomous space of art separate from practico-inert tasks and interests, where these interests are, in Rancière's terms, 'suspended'. At the same time that this aesthetic experience demarcates an autonomous space for art, it is also heterotopic, separate from practico-inert social relations. As Rancière notes, Schiller calls this space – of an aesthetic state or condition (*Zustand*) – that of 'appearance' (*Schein*). Though Schiller does not use the term in his description of the *Juno Ludovisi* in Letter XV, this illustration anticipates his definition of the *topos* of '*Schein*' in the later letters of the *Ästhetische Briefe*. There he reiterates the separation of aesthetic appearance from the imperatives of 'reality': the necessities of physical subsistence and the duties of the moral law.[23] Aesthetic semblance must remain autonomous (see 1795, 195), for it is by means of play with aesthetic semblance that we engage in a practice of 'aesthetic freedom' (1795, 143, 145); that is, aesthetic experience gives way to a free disposition that suspends the constraints and categories that divide the sensible world into categories such as intelligible and sensible, or activity and passivity. The aesthetic freedom of play 'takes under its protection no single one of man's faculties to the exclusion of others, it favours each and all of them without distinction'; moreover, while enjoying beauty, 'we are at such a moment master in equal degree of our passive and of our active powers, and we shall with equal ease turn to seriousness or to play, to repose or to movement, to compliance or to resistance, to the discursions of abstract thought or to the direction contemplation of phenomena' (Schiller, 1795, 151, 153).

For Rancière, 'free appearance' designates a specific form of the autonomy of aesthetic experience that is separate from the practico-inert coordinates of the policing of a given distribution of the sensible. Schiller's discussions of 'appearance' are only one half of aesthetic experience. In Letters XI–XV, he proceeds through a transcendental deduction of play as a regulative idea (meaning that the aesthetic state and free appearance are also regulative) that opens the possibility of aesthetic dissensus.

The purpose of Schiller's transcendental inquiry is to explain how the experience of beauty is possible. The idea of beauty – more specifically, the regulative idea of beauty – must, he argues, be deduced from the 'sheer potentialities' of the basic features of the sensible-rational nature of human activity. An idea of beauty, then, will reflect both the basic conflict between the rational drive and the sensible drive of human activity and, because it is a demand of reason (1795, 103), their unity. Technically speaking, Schiller's deduction begins with two principles that make individuality possible, both of which cannot be grounded upon the other: an individual is both her person (which persists outside of time) and her condition (*Zustand*, which is situated in time). But given that Schiller places his thought in the lineage of the critical philosophy of Kant and Fichte, I think his transcendental account gets its impetus from describing human activity rather than being. Even his concept of person, which is described as 'eternal' is meant to explain the status of moral judgements rather than the metaphysical status of the individual. A moral judgement becomes a moral law when the individual treats one moment of life as a regulative idea, '*as if* it were eternity', as if, that is, it were a universal law (1795, 83, my emphasis).[24]

Therefore Schiller's inquiry focuses on how to explain human activity on the basis of – and through the relationship between – two fundamental drives: the sensuous drive, which aims to give content or reality to individuality through sensation (to express individuality through feeling, affect, and physicality); and the formal drive, which aims to give form to the materiality of the individual's condition, to bring harmony to the diversity and multiplicity of appearances.[25] The sensuous-rational nature of humanity makes two demands: as 'the first demand is that we should *materialize form*, i.e. we should externalize and embody it in something particular. The second demand is that we should *formalize matter*, i.e. we should internalize it and make it our own' (Beiser, 2005, 139).

The fundamental problem of Schiller's inquiry is delineating the relationship between the two drives, between reason and feeling. This relationship constitutes a problem, he contends, because reason demands that a complete concept of human nature requires the unity of human faculties, a unity between the formal drive and sensuous drive (1795, 103). In Letter XIII, Schiller develops the basis of his critique of Kant's concept of freedom. He argues that when a philosopher presumes that the rational drive and sensuous drive are diametrically opposed, when Kant or Fichte posit a primary antagonism between rationality and feeling, the only way to maintain the unity of the human faculties is to subordinate the sensuous drive to the rational. The result, however, is that this unity lacks harmony (1795, 85n.). Kant defines freedom by reference only to an 'apodictic law of practical reason' (Kant, 1788, 5: 3–4), while Fichte's account of practical reason demands that the self should strive through freedom to be absolute, 'that everything should conform to the self, that all reality should be posited absolutely through the self', and this demand treats nature and feeling as passive obstacles to be overcome and subsumed by the self's infinite striving (Fichte, 1794–5, 232; see Beiser, 2005, 144–7, 227–9).

Subordinating feeling and sensation to reason, Schiller argues, does not unify human nature. Instead, treating sensation and reason as competing drives (that is, as activities that are two competing ways of treating a common object) leaves the self divided. Human beings, he argues, are neither exclusively matter or sensibility nor exclusively rationality or spirit (Schiller, 1795, 103). Therefore, his aesthetics aims to account for the drives in their unity and opposition. Schiller holds that the two drives are opposed in aims and objects. The sensuous drive aims to give life and materiality to individuality, while the formal drive aims to give harmony and form to the multiplicity of phenomena. These activities then reciprocally limit each other when the individual cultivates – through culture – their capacities to the same degree. On the one hand, cultivating sensibility preserves the 'life of sense against the encroachments of Freedom' (1795, 87). I take this claim to be a critique of both Kant's concept of freedom, which subordinates the individual's sensible activity (that is, feelings, desires, affects) to the rational strictures of the categorical imperative and Fichte's treatment of anything outside of the self's activity as an obstacle. On the other hand, Schiller holds that the cultivation of reason is necessary for critical and reflective free activity.

After establishing how their activities are mutually limiting, Schiller turns, in Letters XIV and XV, to considering their unity. Since the individual is neither exclusively matter nor exclusively spirit, he states, there must be some activity that expresses a complete idea of human nature. The sensuous drive and the formal drive ought to be unified, ideally speaking, through the play drive [*Spieltrieb*]. While the object of the sensuous drive is life in its fullest material sense and the object of the formal drive is the form of things and relating these things to reason, the object of the play is living form or beauty (1795, 101). As we have already seen, play is the free act that suspends the mutually reciprocal constraints that arise from the opposition of form and sense: divisions between activity and passivity, freedom and necessity, reality and appearance, knowledge and sensibility.

Rancière treats Schiller's account of play as a political allegory. Schiller, he argues, undermines the Platonic apparatus of the ethical regime of images. In Plato's republic, 'there exists no appearance without a reality that serves to judge it, no gratuity of play compatible with the seriousness of work' (Rancière, 2004a, 31). By contrast, Schiller's concepts of free play and free appearance open a space of dissensus that suspends relations of domination and power. Through the dynamics of play and appearance, and a paradoxical interplay of autonomy and heteronomy, aesthetics constitutes a momentary space that disrupts the subordination of appearances to reality and the identification of individuals with their occupations and specializations. For Rancière, Schiller's *Ästhetische Briefe* formulates the heterotopian practices of the micropolitics of the aesthetic regime of art.

I will add that, for Schiller, it is the regulative status of play, beauty, and the aesthetic state that makes dissensus over these concepts possible.[26] Though, on Schiller's account, transcendental philosophy can deduce a regulative ideal of beauty, and deduce those *a priori* conditions that make the experience of beauty possible, it does not provide technical rules for judging art as beautiful. Instead, these ideals demand that we make judgments about beauty by making singular cases universal while admitting that these judgments are not the final word on beauty or the significance of play. These ideals demand that these judgments appeal to anyone and everyone while nonetheless remaining subject to dispute and misunderstanding.[27]

4.3.3. Schelling on artistic production and practical reason

While Schiller appropriates the regulative structure of practical reason for aesthetic ends, Schelling's critique of the transcendental idealism of Kant and Fichte subverts the primacy that they accord practical reason by using the regulative structure of the categorical imperative against it. While Schiller adopts the regulative principle for aesthetics in order to make possible dissensus concerning the significance of beauty and play, Schelling contends that practical activity is ultimately limited by the infinite task of approximating the moral law. This infinite task, according to Schelling, is limited to an ideal; all attempts to realize objectively the moral law are forestalled by the very structure of practical reason, which separates willing from objectivity. He then argues that the activity of aesthetic intuition, by contrast, produces in the artwork what philosophy intuits ideally: the identity of subjectivity and objectivity, conscious and unconscious activity, as well as freedom and nature.[28] Furthermore, systematically speaking, it unifies the principles of transcendental idealism and nature-philosophy. Aesthetic intuition, then, shows through the artwork the identity of the self's conscious activity and nature's unconscious productivity. Schelling's philosophy of art, in effect, transgresses the boundaries of Schiller's transcendental philosophy. In the *Ästhetische Briefe*, Schiller writes, were man

> to be at once conscious of his freedom and sensible of his existence, were, at one and the same time, to feel himself matter and come to know himself as mind, then he would in such cases, and in such cases only, have a complete intuition of his human nature, and the object which afforded him this intuition would become for him a symbol of his accomplished destiny and, in consequence ... serve him as a presentation (*Darstellung*) of the infinite. (Schiller, 1795, 95tm)

For Schiller the experience of an absolute artwork that presents the infinite in the finite world is not possible. Instead, this aesthetic experience of beauty is what we would desire, and strive for, ideally in the activity of play. However, for Schelling, aesthetic intuition is that act whereby the infinite idea is produced in sensible form in the artwork.

At this point, we should examine the specific claims set forth in the *System of Transcendental Idealism* in more detail.[29] In this work, Schelling posits the identity of subjectivity and objectivity, and then attempts to explain the genesis of objectivity through the self's repeated attempts to realize its activity consciously and objectively. In the theoretical section of the *System*, he argues that representation and objectivity become possible through the self's striving toward consciousness. So, theoretical philosophy explains, Schelling maintains, the genesis of objectivity and the activity of representation, but not consciousness. The self only becomes conscious through practical reason, as a self who wills but whose will is limited by the wills of others. Through practical reason, the self realizes its activity – as will – consciously though not objectively. Indeed, practical reason is driven by a contradiction between willing (freedom) and the 'compulsion to represent' (necessity) that results in the transcendental illusion of freedom (Schelling, 1800, 176tm/3: 409).

Practical reason demands that the self transforms the world according to its will – 'to transform the object as it is into the object it ought to be' (1800, 177/3: 559) – but the fundamental distinction between ideal and object treats the self's activity as a will fundamentally separated from the necessary laws of the natural world. Thus practical reason sunders the identity of subjectivity and objectivity as well as freedom and necessity; that is, the self becomes conscious of itself as willing but not as productive – the feeling of necessity that accompanies objectivity and the self's real limitations, which can be discovered through transcendental inquiry, remains inaccessible to consciousness and cannot be recovered objectively by the striving of practical activity. In other words, the goal of the system is to show the identity of subjectivity and objectivity, but this identity 'cannot be evidenced in free action itself, since precisely for the sake of free action ... it abolishes itself' (1800, 213/3: 605). Nevertheless, practical reason is a necessary part of the system because it explains the genesis of consciousness, just as theoretical reason explains the genesis of objectivity and the categories of representation. Theoretical reason explains the necessity that accompanies the self's productivity, while practical reason deduces the genesis of consciousness as will, but a system of philosophy that proceeds no further than theoretical and practical reason remains incomplete; for it 'man is forever a broken fragment, for either his action is necessary, and then not free, or free, and then not necessary according to law' (1800, 216/3: 608).

Aesthetic intuition also begins with the contradiction between freedom and necessity, but resolves this contradiction by producing the artwork. Art realizes, as the product of aesthetic intuition, the identity of subjectivity and objectivity, freedom and necessity, and conscious and unconscious activity. To account for the contradiction between freedom and necessity in aesthetic intuition, Schelling provides what we might now call a phenomenological account of artistic production: according to the 'testimony of all artists', artistic activity is driven by both free, conscious intention and by an involuntary and 'irresistible urge of their own nature', and this conflict is resolved by the production of the artwork (1800, 222/3: 616). Artistic production, in other words, synthesizes or unites the free, conscious productivity of the self with the unconscious productivity of nature (the Spinozist '*natura naturans*' that plays a prominent role in Schelling's nature-philosophy of that time). Though both practical reason and aesthetic intuition mediate the contradiction between freedom and necessity, their activities end in different results. The activity of practical reason separates willing and object, but this separation traps it in the infinite task of attempting – but never realizing – to make the object conform to the will. Aesthetic intuition, by contrast, produces a sensible presentation of the infinite in the artwork.

After showing how aesthetic intuition produces, through the power of the imagination, the unity of opposites such as freedom and nature or subjectivity and objectivity, Schelling defines the 'absolute' attributes of the work of art. He differentiates the work of art from two other objects: natural objects and 'common artifacts'. The artwork demonstrates the same identity of intelligibility and necessity as a natural object, but the former shows conscious intent. The artwork differs from 'common artifacts' because the value of the artwork is not derived from any other end; it is neither a means for economic exchange, nor an object for moral or scientific ends (1800, 226–7/3: 622–3). Instead, the work of art is a singular object for three reasons. First, the artwork is a work of beauty, which is the 'infinite finitely presented;' it presents the infinity of identity in sensible, finite form. Second, while artistic production proceeds from the feeling of an 'infinite contradiction' between freedom and necessity, the completion of the artwork resolves this contradiction. The completion of the artwork, then, is accompanied by the feeling of 'infinite satisfaction' rather than a feeling of necessity (1800, 225tm/3: 620).

Finally, the artwork presents its own rule that mediates content and form rather than reflecting an external rule that had guided its creation. More importantly, while the artwork presents its own rule, the meaning of the work is irreducible to the artist's conscious intention. Indeed, Schelling argues that the meaning of the work is elaborated in relation to its (universal) audience in ways that this audience is not necessarily conscious of. He likens the artwork to Greek mythology:

> the mythology of the Greeks, which undeniably contains an infinite meaning and a symbolism for all ideas, arose among a people, and in a fashion, which both make it impossible to suppose any comprehensive forethought in devising it, or in the harmony whereby everything is united into one great whole. (1800, 225/3: 619–20)

This social and mythological aspect of art is not, for Schelling, a thing of the past. In the lectures published as *The Philosophy of Art*, he claims that the novel 'should be a mirror of the world, or at least of the age, and thus become a partial mythology' (1802–5, 232/5: 676). The role of the contemporary artist is to create new materials that open the possibility of a new mythology that would unite the fragmentary parts of society into a singular social life – this new mythology 'shall be the creation, not of some individual author, but of a new race, personifying, as it were, one single poet' (1800, 233/3: 629). It is through the idea of the new mythology that Schelling's Platonic regime of art formulates the politics of art in a monumental and evental form.

While Schelling recognizes the value of art as an end in itself, distinct from the utility that determines the value of commodities or common artifacts, and as a non-fragmentary object around which a social community gathers, the ultimate value of art lies primarily in its relation to philosophy. The artwork is both autonomous end in itself and a symbol of the community insofar as it presents the ideas of philosophy in concrete form. Therefore, Schelling's Platonism maintains that the ontological veracity of art is established in relation to the Idea – art is art because it presents the Idea in sensible form. Indeed, in *The Philosophy of Art*, Schelling organizes the significance of the arts according to the way in which they express the absolute, with the highest form of art being Greek tragedy, which enacts or presents (*darstellen*) a movement that leads from the conflict between freedom and necessity to the restoration of their identity. Thus, Schelling writes, when, in *Oedipus at Colonus*, Oedipus disappears from the eyes of mortals, his sublime acceptance of his destiny – that is, of being punished for an involuntary transgression – brings about the 'inner reconciliation' and the restoration of the indifference and identity of freedom and necessity, the transfiguration of freedom itself 'into the highest identity with necessity' (1802–5, 258; 255/5: 703–4; 699).

4.4. Monuments and micropolitics

We have now examined both the impasse between Rancière's aesthetics and Badiou's inaesthetics and Schiller's and Schelling's competing accounts of how artistic production is a free activity that overcomes the formalism of Kant's practical reason. Having done so, we can now interrogate how the aesthetic regime of art and the Platonic regime of art think the politics of art.

In Part II, I have followed the hypothesis that the politics of the aesthetic regime of art is a micropolitics that operates in the intervals of the heterogeneity of egalitarian politics and policing. At some points I have used textual evidence from Rancière's work to support this hypothesis, and at others I have argued that thinking artistic practices and discourses in micropolitical forms contributes to understanding Rancière's criticisms of several major figures in art theory, such as Walter Benjamin and Clement Greenberg. To conclude this chapter and Part II, I will argue that the differences between Rancière's aesthetics and Badiou's inaesthetics are based on their differences over the politics of art. I think that Rancière attacks Badiou's inaesthetics on political grounds in order to demonstrate that Badiou's work lacks a micropolitics that could supplement his eventual politics. Given that Badiou maintains, even after conceding that an immanent and singular account of art must account for its politics, that 'Today *we know*' art and politics 'constitute two distinct truth procedures, two heterogeneous confrontations between the thinking invention of forms and the indistinctness of the real,' it is unsurprising that he does not take Rancière's objections seriously (Badiou, 2005, 152, my emphasis). *We know*, Badiou claims, because the politics of the avant-gardes, their 'splendid and violent ambition' to destroy art to revolutionize everyday life, their passion for the real, resulted in, first, a merely allegorical commitment to communism and, later, their self-destruction or exhaustion.

To fully appreciate their differences concerning the politics of art, we should situate the impasses of Rancière's aesthetics and Badiou's inaesthetics within the conflict between the aesthetic regime of art and the Platonic regime of art. This requires considering aesthetics as a scene instead of a regime; like Badiou's inaesthetics, it would then describe *some* works of art rather than a general domain of art. Rancière's discussions of aesthetics shift between the aesthetic regime of art as a regime – that is, a general *dispositif* that organizes artistic production – and a scene, which considers aesthetics as a particular staging of practical and discursive relations that introduces new modes of intelligibility, sensibility, or visibility within a given practico-inert social space. Rancière's recent work suggests that the aesthetic '"counter-history" of artistic modernity' intervenes against a given set of artistic social conventions (Rancière, 2011a, xiii). In this regard, Rancière's work is more explicitly prescriptive; it exhibits, as Joseph Tanke summarizes, the 'idea that art and the experiences it occasions can be the proving grounds for the equality of intelligences ... that [works] posit the intelligence and agency of their viewers' (Tanke, 2011, 89). Furthermore, Tanke notes that at points Rancière also criticizes 'the logic of stultification found in many quarters of contemporary art' in works by Paul McCarthy and Jason Rhoades or by Josephine Meckseper, who – for differing reasons – 'reproduce the model of explication' (Tanke, 2011, 90).

The Platonic regime maintains that art, to be monumental, must relate to the Idea. Both Schelling and Badiou make recourse to the Idea to name the truth of art, even though they do not define the Idea in the same terms. That monumental art relates to the Idea does not mean that monumentality is a consequence of the Idea. Instead, the Idea names the cut that produces the relation of rupture that breaks with a given state of the situation or – in Rancière's terms – a given regime of policing. For Schelling, modern social relations reduce humanity to fragmented individuals who relate to one another as a society through mechanistic and formal institutional relations, and the art of a new mythology would signal a relation of rupture with this fragmented state of humanity. This monumental art, which – like Greek tragedy before it – would exhibit the indifference or identity of freedom and necessity, of the self and nature, would call forth a new humanity that, as it is phrased in the 'System Program', would realize the equal formation and cultivation of all capacities of intellectual equality. Later, in the *System der gesamten Philosophie und der Naturphilosophie insbesondere* (1804), Schelling argues that a nation and a national art emerge simultaneously:

> Lyrical poetry lives and exists truthfully only in a universally public life. Where all public life collapses into the particulars and dullness of private life, poetry more or less sinks into this same sphere. Epic poetry requires chiefly mythology and is nothing without it. But even mythology is not possible in the particular; it can only be born in the totality of a nation that as such acts simultaneously as identity and individuality. In dramatic poetry, tragedy grounds itself in the public law, in virtue, religion, heroism – in a word – in the holiness of the nation. A nation that is not holy, or which was robbed of its holy relics, cannot have true tragedy ... The question of the possibility of a universal content of *poesie*, just as the question of the objective existence of science and religion, impels us to something higher. Only in the spiritual unity of a people, in a truly public life, can true and generally valid *poesie* arise – as only in the spiritual and political unity of a people can science and religion find its objectivity. (6: 572–3)

Here Schelling's politics of a new mythology has lost its radical utopian complexion. He no longer opposes the mechanism of the state to the organic community. Whereas he once opposed the state qua form, he now contends that with truly public sphere, and with a new mythology, emerges the state as organic community. Indeed, in 'Concerning the Relation of the Plastic Arts to Nature', Schelling praises Bavarian paternalism for allowing the cultivation of the firmly established taste and public opinion of a whole people that avoids the pitfalls of the levelling of popular opinion that he associates with the French Revolution and democracy (Schelling, 1807, 355–6/7: 327; 1803, 52–5/5: 258–61).[30] Though Schelling thinks the Idea as organic totality, to which Badiou opposes the thematic of subtraction, and despite their opposed political commitments, both think the Idea as a relation of rupture. While for Schelling, a monumental work brings forth, by way of the rupture with the mechanisms structure of modern society, an organic community, Badiou affirms that monumental work subtracts itself from the circulation of commodities and democratic consensus.

After the publication of *Handbook of Inaesthetics*, Badiou has formulated an explicitly monumental politics of art, even while paradoxically maintaining the strict separation between the four conditions of philosophy. In the 'Manifesto of Affirmationist Art', he demands an art that makes visible that which the powers of capitalism and democratic consensus declare inexistent: 'monumental construction, projects, the creative force of the weak, [and] the overthrow of established powers' (2004, 133). In both the 'Manifesto of Affirmationist Art' and *The Century*, Badiou defines the monumental Idea by reference to subtraction. In other words, it is the process of subtraction that instigates the relation of rupture by which monumental art becomes visible.

In *The Century*, Badiou aims to demonstrate how the radical movements of the twentieth century subjectively thought their political and artistic praxes. He identifies two forms of subjective praxis, both of which maintained a militant fidelity to inventing and inaugurating an alternative to the hegemony of capitalism and Western parliamentarianism. He characterizes one practice as a 'passion for the real' (a phrase that he appropriates from Lacan) and the other as a fidelity to subtraction. While Badiou ultimately claims that the political and artistic avant-gardes that sought to realize the passion for the real are exhausted or saturated, he affirms their legacy in opposition to democratic consensus. It is, for Badiou, better to destroy the reified structures of consensus than to accept them, but it is even better to subtract militant fidelity from the established powers of democratic materialism.[31] He affirms, in opposition to democratic materialism, the radical legacy of the twentieth century's avant-gardes while attempting to treat their contradictions by resolving 'the conflict between formalization and destruction by means of formalization' (Badiou, 2005, 110). The procedure of those militants committed to the passion for the real, on Badiou's account, engaged in the task of destroying or purging all forms of semblance in order to actualize the real – the source of horror, enthusiasm and invention that cannot be symbolized by discourse. Thus the avant-gardes, by attempting to destroy all forms of semblance and imitation in order to realize an aesthetic revolution of everyday life, would 'sacrifice art' rather than 'give up on the real' (Badiou, 2005, 131).

While Badiou holds that the avant-garde sequence of the passion for the real is exhausted or saturated, he argues that there is a competing tendency of militant subjectivity within the twentieth century that still carries prescriptive force today: 'a subtractive thinking of negativity can overcome the blind imperative of destruction and purification' (Badiou, 2005, 55). The subtractive orientation, instead of attempting to identify the real itself, attempts to show the minimal difference between the place and the taking-place of the event (note the Mallarmean phrasing) – to show this gap itself as real. Badiou provides the example of Malevich's painting *White on White* (1918), which retains, through purification, only the difference between background and form and the 'null difference' between white and white. But this painting should not be seen as destructive but subtractive: 'instead of treating the real as identity, it is treated right away as a gap. The question of the real/semblance relation will not be resolved by a purification that would isolate the real, but by understanding that the gap itself is real' (Badiou, 2005, 56). Therefore the monumental form of art is not determined by the unique medium of the work, as modernist critics would have it. Badiou explicitly rejects the modernist emphasis on how each art interrogates its unique and opaque medium (Badiou, 2005, 36). Instead, it is the subtractive thinking of the work, the Idea, that constitutes the relation of rupture between the work and a given state of the situation.

In *Aesthetics and Its Discontents*, Rancière adds to the critique of inaesthetics found in 'Aesthetics, Inaesthetics, Anti-aesthetics' a final objection against Badiou's monumentalism. He contends that the 'Manifesto of Affirmationist Art' reaffirms the modernist emphasis on the autonomy and specificity of art. However, Rancière writes,

> the more one emphasizes art in its specificity, the more one is led to identify that 'specificity' with the experience of radical heterogeneity, whose ultimate model is Paul's disconcerting shock-encounter with God or God's speaking to Moses in the cloud. As it says in the 'Manifesto of Affirmationist Art', 'The art that is, and the art that is to come, should hang together as solidly as a demonstration, be as surprising as a night-time ambush, and be as elevated as a star' [see Badiou, 2004, 147]. This formulation is by no means a simple rhetorical approximation. It points in exemplary fashion to the heart of Badiou's problematic: the double transformation of the revolutionary cut into a Lacanian encounter with the face of the Gorgon and of the Gorgon into the Platonic call of the Idea. To posit an identity between the art which is and that which ought to be, art must be made the pure experience of the imperative dictated by the sudden encounter with the Other. On this point, the assertion proper to inaesthetics of the Idea's Platonic

> force joins with the proclamation of the Other's commandment proper to the aesthetics of the sublime. Each of them isolates art from aesthetics, only to prostrate it before the indistinction of ethics. (Rancière, 2004a, 87tm)

In this passage, it is necessary to separate Rancière's critique of alterity and his critique of monumentality. The critique of alterity seeks to bind Badiou to Lyotard's ethics of the sublime. But, in order to link Badiou's thought to Lyotard's, Rancière elides between Lyotard's concept of the Other (which draws on Lévinas) and Lacan. This quiet elision can be seen in the reference to the 'Lacanian encounter with the face of the Gorgon'. *If* one wants to use Lacan against Badiou, one should distinguish between the Other and the Real: the Real is the domain of the traumatic encounter, of symbolic deadlocks, while the Other designates the locus of the symbolic order, or the mediation of meaning and the social bond. Lacan's Other is not the Lévinasian Other. While the latter is the transcendental imperative which calls one to ethical respect, the former is the symbolic fiction *par excellence*: for Lacan, the Other, strictly speaking, does not exist; it functions only insofar as subjects attribute to it symbolic efficacy.

Badiou has also made it clear that his concept of the event is tied to the subject, and not the Other. To avoid any confusion, or 'ethical indistinction', Badiou clarifies his position *vis-à-vis* Lévinas in the second chapter of his *Ethics*. For Lévinas, 'I experience myself ethically as "pledged" to the appearing of the Other, and subordinated in my being to this pledge' (Badiou, 1993, 19–20). Like Rancière, Badiou finds this phenomenological account ethically ambiguous, and both claim that the ethics of the Other conveniently conforms to consensus and the nullification of politics (Badiou, 1993, 23–5; Rancière, 2004a, 109–17). Badiou explicitly states, time and again, that infinity is not the transcendental power of God, but 'the banal reality of every situation' (Badiou, 1993, 25). The event cannot be guaranteed by the Other; it can only be wagered on by a subject.

I think Rancière's final objection is, if we leave aside the finer points of Lacanian theory, much more straightforward: by separating the conditions of philosophy, and by conceptualizing each as evental, Badiou ends up with a politics and an inaesthetics that are both too narrow. Rancière's politics of aesthetics describes a series of heterotopian practices that invent social change in the interval between politics and policing, while Badiou concludes that it is better to do nothing than work in the intervals of visibilities, discourses, and places.

Schiller raises a similar criticism against Schelling. Therefore we should neither, like Hegel, treat Schiller's aesthetics as merely a predecessor to the 'absolute standpoint' of Schelling's philosophy of art, nor, like Rancière, assimilate Schelling's Platonist principles to the aesthetic regime. In a letter to Goethe, dated 27 March 1801, Schiller expresses a fundamental disagreement with Schelling's philosophy. He states that some critics have taken up 'their position on the vague domain of the Absolute', which leads them to confuse the activity of artistic production with the activity of producing excellent art (in Schiller and Goethe, 1890, 373). Critics like Schelling maintain a philosophy of monumental art that lacks a concept of degree. Art, Schiller continues, can be practised by anyone and everyone, though with varying degrees of success:

> Any one who is able to place his own feelings into an object so that this object compels me to pass over into that state of feeling, and, accordingly, works actively upon me, him I call a poet, a maker. But every poet is not on this account – according to *rank* – an excellent one. (in Schiller and Goethe, 1890, 372)

While the 'perfect poet ... gives expression to the entirety of humanity', that is, gives expression to both the sensible and formal drives of human nature, this does not mean that the so-called lesser poet who does not is not a poet (in Schiller and Goethe, 1890, 373tm). In other words, by thinking artistic production as an event, Schelling relegates minor works to the domain of insignificance. This objection is, in fact, not entirely insignificant concerning Schelling, who claims, in his *Philosophy of Art* that from an absolute standpoint 'it is not too much to assert that until now there have been only two novels': Cervantes's *Don Quixote* and Goethe's *Wilhelm Meister* (Schelling, 1802–5, 234/5: 679). Therefore, from Schiller's standpoint, Schelling's philosophy of art makes of artistic production an event or monument rather than a form of micropolitics, which means that, by thinking art monumentally, Schelling's Platonism will miss the molecular social transformations brought about by aesthetics – which also means that when art in general, rather than monumental or evental art, fails to live up to its absolute task of presenting the sensibility of the Idea, it loses its significance for philosophy.

4.5. Heterotopias: One world divides into two

The disagreements between Badiou and Rancière, even concerning art, are political. For Badiou, art must be monumental or it will not be at all. An art that merely makes visible that which already exists within the world of democratic materialism is not monumental; it is merely culture. The Platonism of Badiou and Schelling is of interest for thinking through the problem of the relation of rupture by which art becomes monumental. But, conceptualized in its Platonic form, the idea of monumental art concedes too much to a given hegemonic practico-inert world by dismissing all artistic production that is not monumental as already counted in the 'recycled obsolescences' of culture or the levelling forces of the circulation of commodities and readily available pleasures – in a word, as kitsch (Badiou, 2005, 143; 1997, 12). This account neglects the possibility of micropolitical practices. The very practice of the micropolitics of aesthetics aims to invent, in the intervals of politics and the practico-inert, new modes of visibility, intelligibility, and place.

Both Badiou and Rancière contend that politics divides the world into two. For Badiou, one world is divided between being and event, and for Rancière, one world is divided into the two worlds of egalitarian politics and policing (Rancière, 1995, 42/67; 1998e, 36–7). But where Badiou opposes monumental art and kitsch, Rancière proposes a heterotopian micropolitics of aesthetic egalitarianism that takes place in the interval between the heterogeneity of politics and policing. Like politics, this micropolitics begins with a dynamic – or 'aesthetic effect' – of disidentification (Rancière, 2009a, 73), which precipitates a political or aesthetic practice that challenges those partitions that organize our 'polemical common world' with another, more egalitarian distribution of the sensible. Whereas politics is the heterogeneous interruption of policing by the activation of the supposition of equality, aesthetics works in the interstices of this heterogeneity. Again, there is a continuity between Rancière's work on workers' history and his aesthetics. In *Proletarian Nights* there are numerous references to one world dividing into two. On the one hand, Rancière describes ways that 'an exceptional group of worker-writers remained awake in order to compose their tracts and treatises, novels and poems, encroaching as they did so into the time allotted for them to rest after one working day of manual labour and [to] prepare for the next' (Davis, 2010, 52). These workers, then, challenged the presumption that their lives were necessarily divided between days of work and nights of rest. But Rancière also contends that these workers, in formulating their sense of subjectivity – a subjectivation that recognizes a wrong in the way that their world is organized and policed – through writing poetry and metaphysics, laid claim to worlds that were not theirs, worlds of those whose task it is to think, not of those whose task it is to work. Those other worlds, Rancière writes, 'which supposedly anaesthetize the sufferings of the workers, can actually be the thing that sharpens their awareness of such sufferings' (Rancière, 1981, 19). For critics such as Eagleton (as we saw in Chapter 3) or Badiou, this aesthetic interpellation would merely reiterate the ideology of consensus. But for Rancière, these workers, split between days of work and nights of autodidactic freedom, make of borrowed words, homonyms, and misunderstandings new forms of dissensus that transform the ways we speak, think, and act. Although, for analytic purposes, we have separated Rancière's egalitarian politics and his micropolitics of aesthetics, we should not overlook the fact that both emerge from practices of dissensus, suggesting that dynamics of collective political subjectivation could – although not necessarily – begin with the seemingly imperceptible transformations of the aesthetic coordinates of socially lived experience.

There is, nonetheless, no need to choose *either* Rancière's aesthetics *or* Badiou's inaesthetics, just as there is no need to decide between Schiller and Schelling. Instead, I have argued that: first, both an aesthetic regime of art and a Platonic regime of art become possible with the collapse of the mimetic norms that structure the representative regime of the arts; and, second, the fundamental conflict between aesthetics and Platonism concerns the political scope of art. If Platonism remains persuasive, it is because Badiou and Schelling insist on the monumental and eventual character of some works of art. But if I side with Rancière or Schiller, it is because I think it is necessary to think the relation of rupture beginning with concrete micropolitical practices rather than the Idea. Thinking the politics of art after Rancière and Badiou, then, requires beginning at the micropolitical level without excluding the possibility of conceptualizing art monumentally. The politics of art – if art is to be political – inscribes the discourses and practices of art between the intervals of egalitarian politics and policing and the momentary and monumental ruptures that make visible that inexistent space independent of commodification and consensus. From Schiller to Rancière, if art has been linked to the possibility of radical social transformation and the inventive capacities of political subjects, then art is, in effect, sensible imbrication of emancipatory practices of good sense and, as William Wordsworth writes, 'just sentiments'. To think art politically affirms the possibility of making visible utopian and heterotopian worlds that work to reconfigure and transform – again, in the words of Wordsworth – 'the very world which is the world / Of all of us', the only place that 'We find our happiness, or not at all'.

Notes

1   Many of the claims that follow about Schelling are elaborated and defended in more detail in Shaw 2010 and 2014.

2   The irony is that Rockhill intends this passage as a criticism of, rather than an elaboration upon, Rancière's theses on aesthetics.

3   Here we will not deliberate over whether Rancière's interpretations of Brecht and Debord are accurate. We are interested in showing how the Platonic regime of art does not fall into the problem of the paradox of the spectator, which requires first elaborating – in albeit simplified and schematic terms – Rancière's account of this paradox.

4   From this point forward, aside from references to what Rancière calls 'Platonic modernism', when I say *Platonism* or that something is *Platonic* I'm using the terms technically to mean 'of the Platonic regime of art'.

5   Peter Hallward coins 'evental' as an adjectival neologism that translates Badiou's technical use of the term *événementiel*. He notes that a more common term like 'eventful' invites misleading associations such as plenitude, bustle, or familiarity (Hallward, 2003, xviii).

6   I am not, like Rancière, using 'politics of aesthetics' as a synonym for 'the politics of art'. Instead, the politics of art is the locus of the debate between proponents of the aesthetic regime and those of the Platonic regime.

7   Nor am I making any claim that the conflict between aesthetics and the Platonic regime exhausts the possible conflicts over relating art, politics, and social transformation. Far from it – one need only consider how Proudhon's *Du principe de l'art et de sa destination social* (published in 1865 after Proudhon's death) fits in this context. It might even be that this conflict is more limited, localized to theorizing or philosophizing about art – that is, the reception of art – rather than artistic production, though the theories of each of the figures in question have made varying degrees of impact in the artworld. It seems inaccurate – or at least over-concerned with disciplinarity – to claim that these debates are *merely* about philosophy or *merely* about discourse.

8   Both have, moreover, retrospectively related a youthful exuberance for Sartrean existentialism (q.v. Chapter 2).

9   Note that I am not using 'disagreement' in the technical sense that Rancière gives the term when I describe their debate.

10 For Badiou's critique of Rancière's, see *Metapolitics* (1998c, 107–23) and 'The Lessons of Jacques Rancière: Knowledge and Power after the Storm' (2006a); for Rancière's critique of Badiou, see 'Aesthetics, Inaesthetics, Anti-aesthetics' (2002a), which was published in revised form in *Aesthetics and Its Discontents* (2004a), and the chapter 'The Poet at the Philosopher's: Mallarmé and Badiou' in *The Politics of Literature* (2006b, 183–205). Note that the present interpretation is concerned only with Badiou's theoretical work on art published between *Being and Event* (1988) and *The Century* (2005). In *Logics of Worlds*, Badiou's discussion of art reverts to something like Plato's distinction between model and copy, e.g. between

the Idea of Horseness and the image of a horse, such that he writes: 'The drawing must inscribe the intelligible cut, the separate contemplation of the Horse which is presented by all drawn horses' (2006b, 19).

11 Rancière rightly ignores these accusations for the following reasons. Badiou faults Rancière for neglecting ontology, and more specifically an ontology of the political procedures that grounds militant fidelity. Rancière, however, rejects the method whereby one does ontology first and politics later. And for good reasons: if politics is a dissensus over speech, rationality, and social practices how can one understand new claims to equality – who speaks, how they speak or act – if these new claims must be judged by a system that has already established the rationalities of these practices? (See Rancière's comments criticizing the priority of ontology at 2006a, 476–7; 2011b, 11–16.)

12 Terry Eagleton states, in Lacanian terms, 'We can vicariously gratify our self-destructive drives, at the same time as we can indulge in a certain sadistic pleasure at the prospect of others' pain. Tragedy is in this sense a gentrified, socially acceptable version of obscene enjoyment' (2005, 26–7).

13 In *The Aesthetic Unconscious*, Rancière shows how Freud's approach to art wavers between maintaining the norms of the representative regime and an aesthetics of symptomology (Rancière, 2001, 67, 86).

14 As Robert Lehman points out, Badiou also omits the development of modern aesthetics that occurred in Germany between 1735 (with Alexander Baumgarten's *Reflections on Poetry*) and 1790 (with Immanuel Kant's third *Critique*) (Lehman, 2010, 172).

15 Despite Badiou's characterization of Brecht as a practitioner of a 'Stalinized Platonism', the latter's influence is patent. In *The Century*, Badiou praises Brecht as 'the most universal and most indisputable among those artists who explicitly linked their existence and creativity to so-called communist politics' (Badiou, 2005, 43).

16 See Rancière, 1998d, 73–85. See also A. Ross 2012 for an account of the ways that Rancière critiques and appropriates Hegel's account of romanticism.

17 I am assuming here that Badiou would treat the authors discussed in Lacoue-Labarthe and Nancy's *The Literary Absolute* as romantics. They note, however, that neither Schelling, nor Hölderlin, nor Hegel 'can be characterized, rigorously speaking, as romantic' (1978, 27). Nonetheless, if Badiou held that Schelling is romantic, namely that the Schelling of the *System of Transcendental Idealism* maintains that art presents a truth to which philosophy can only point, this would not be idiosyncratic to Badiou. This position is the received view of Schelling's philosophy of art that I challenge here and, in more detail, in Shaw 2010, especially Chapter 3.

18 As Jeremy F. Lane argues, for Bourdieu, 'Kantian aesthetics enables certain

aptitudes and practices that are the preserve of the bourgeoisie to be misrecognized as objective measures of that class's inherent intellectual and moral worth. Thus Kantian aesthetics formalizes that process whereby "legitimate" aesthetic taste serves to naturalize and reproduce class divisions. The actions of Gauny, or of the other worker-poets featured in [*Proletarian Nights*], who were all determined to manifest their capacity for disinterested aesthetic contemplation *despite* their material impoverishment, are thus strictly unthinkable within the Bourdieusian problematic' (Lane, 2013, 31).

19 Rancière cites the following passage from *The Critique of the Power of Judgment*, where Kant argues that the constitution of lawful sociability 'wrestled with great difficulties surrounding the difficult task of uniting freedom (and thus also equality) with coercion (more from respect and subjection to duty than from fear): such an age and such a people had first of all to discover the art of reciprocal communication of the ideas of the most educated part with the cruder, the coordination of the breadth and refinement of the former with the natural simplicity and originality of the latter, and in this way to discover that mean between higher culture and contented nature which constitutes the correct standard, not to be given by any universal rule, for taste as a universal human sense' (1790, 5: 355–6; cf. Rancière, 1983, 208).

20 This, in fact, is a reversal of his position on Schiller in *The Philosopher and His Poor*. There, Rancière writes, 'Schiller cannot propose any other model [of aesthetic equality] than divine leisure and play for the aesthetic education that must redeem the fragmented society' (Rancière, 1983, 209).

21 In Letter VI, Schiller opposes what he considers to be the virtues of ancient Greek community to modern society. This account wavers between opposing the Greek state to the modern state and opposing the simplicity of Greek community to the complexity of the modern state form.

22 By establishing these differences, we avoid Rockill's conclusion that, for Rancière, 'aesthetics is, in fact, consubstantial with the police or the given order of beings, discourse and perception, which is … the very opposite of politics' (Rockhill, 2011, 32).

23 Schiller stipulates that there is a difference between aesthetic semblance and logical semblance. Aesthetic semblance is an object of play, while logical semblance dissimulates falsity under the semblance of truth (Schiller, 1795, 193). In Letter XXVII, Schiller writes that while some fear that semblance would overtake reality, reality is a greater threat to semblance, for 'chained as he is to the material world, man subordinates semblance to ends of his own long before he allows it autonomous existence in the ideal realm of art' (205).

24 When describing moral judgements, which are 'guaranteed by Personality', Schiller writes: 'once the moral feeling says: this shall be, it decides for ever and aye – once

you confess truth because it is truth, and practice justice because it is justice, then you have made an individual case into a law for all cases, and treated one moment of your life as if it were eternity' (1795, 83).

25   In Letter XIX, Schiller reiterates that he considers this question to be transcendental rather metaphysical: 'How far two such opposed tendencies can co-exist in the same being is a problem which may well embarrass the metaphysician, but not the transcendental philosopher. The latter does not pretend to explain how things are possible, but contents himself with determining the kind of knowledge which enables us to understand how experience is possible' (1795, 133).

26   Though Rancière's aesthetics is not regulative in the Kantian sense, he does adopt Schiller's phrasing at one point: 'The set of relations that constitutes the work operates *as if* it had a different ontological texture from the sensations that make up everyday experience' (2009a, 67).

27   I take Schiller's acknowledgement, in Letter XVI (rather than XVII, given that the two letters are inconsistent), that our accounts of beauty will vacillate between the concepts of melting beauty and energizing beauty to be an expression of the dissensus generated by its regulative status.

28   I use 'aesthetic intuition' and 'artistic production' as synonyms here, although it seems that, for Schelling, the activity of aesthetic intuition encompasses both artistic production and the capacity of the spectator to recognize the 'absolute' value of the artwork.

29   Schelling subsequently maintains that the *System*, despite its subjective ground, establishes the general schematism of his philosophical system of absolute idealism developed between 1801 and 1806 (Schelling, 1802, 224/4: 410).

30   Concerning the politics of Schelling's new mythology, see Shaw, 2010, 135–41 and Shaw, 2014, 533–6 (which addresses Rancière's interpretation of the 'System Program').

31   Badiou argues that purification demanded by the passion for the real is marked by destruction, violence, and 'the realm of suspicion [where] a formal criterion is lacking to distinguish the real from semblance' (Badiou, 2005, 54). The strength of this destructive passion for purification, including the philosophical theme of authenticity found in Heidegger and Sartre, lies in the fact that 'many things deserved to be destroyed' (Badiou, 2005, 56). But the attempt to identify a commitment to actualizing the real is indefinite; there is always a chance that it is a semblance of the real.

Conclusion: The Politics of *Aisthesis*

The work of Jacques Rancière brings equality to the forefront of radical political thought. Rancière insists that emancipatory politics and political subjectivation involve supposing – and pursuing – the equality of the intelligences of anybody and everybody. This egalitarian supposition interrupts the modes of stratification that organize and police social life. Thus politics is not the seizure of state or institutional power; it is a set of practices and discourses based on the supposition that equality invents, in ways that may be transitory, social relations of solidarity and reciprocity that both contest how the parts of society are counted and affirm how the part of those who have no part come to give an account of themselves, to combat a wrong, to speak and act as political agents, as subjects and not others. Given that it introduces new ways of speaking, acting, and delimiting place, politics is integrally aesthetic. But there is also, according to Rancière, a politics of aesthetics. If egalitarian politics is an activity of political subjectivation, and if egalitarian politics – in its discourses and practices – is heterogeneous to apparatuses of policing, then the micropolitics of aesthetics takes place in and situates social spaces in the interstices of policing and politics.

This disjunction between the politics of equality and the micropolitics of aesthetics allows us to trace the dynamics of social change in everyday life since the emergence of the aesthetic regime of art while acknowledging the difficult and transitory character of political subjectivation. And yet, given that Rancière demonstrates that there is the same supposition of equality at the basis of Descartes's good sense and Kant's aesthetic *sensus communis*, we must admit that the strict distinction between the politics of equality and the micropolitics of aesthetics that has oriented this study is artificial to a degree. Though such a distinction is useful for situating the conceptual and discursive decisions made in egalitarian moments of philosophy, it would be difficult, in recounting a historical scene of egalitarian struggle, to demarcate where aesthetics ends and politics begins.

The significance of the imbrication of politics and aesthetics is especially pressing in the case of writing. An author such as Rancière writes about politics, but writing isn't an expressly political act in the sense he defines it, as a collective practice of political subjectivation. Yet the 'errant democrat' that is writing is nonetheless political as a kind of aesthetics. Furthermore, philosophical or theoretical writing – insofar as it concerns concepts and arguments rather than percepts and affects – isn't exactly an aesthetics, though 'a theoretical discourse is always simultaneously an aesthetic form, a sensible reconfiguration of the facts it is arguing about', which is precisely why it is simultaneously political (Rancière, 2004b, 65). In *Short Voyages to the Land of the People,* Rancière reflects upon his intellectual formation during the reinvention of Marxism in the 1960s through the work of Althusser, who insisted upon paying attention 'to the simple gestures that are so natural that we neglect to reflect upon them – seeing, hearing, reading, [and] writing' (1990, 118). Though he later concludes that Althusser silences the voices and forestalls the political agency of those who are not politicized through the detour of the science of philosophy, Rancière has remained attentive to those simple gestures of reading and writing, seeing and hearing, discovering in the 'babbling' of workers' archives a lesson of equality. Beginning with the marginalized voices of those workers who had taken themselves as philosophers, 'poets or knights, priests or dandies', Rancière has pursued the consequences of the supposition of equality to contest the assumptions that partition, through opposing science to ideology, truth to appearances, speech to noise, those who think and those who work (Rancière, 1983, 200).

We have approached the work of Rancière by situating it within the historical fiction of the philosophy of equality. I call it a historical fiction for two reasons. First, we know that Rancière's method was developed through a critique of Marxism and sociology and a project of conceptualizing a radical account of political subjectivation that he comes to call the politics of equality. Rather than recount Rancière's intellectual formation, I have reinscribed his work within a history of the philosophy of equality that includes Descartes, the existentialism of Beauvoir and Sartre, and the aesthetics of Kant, Schiller, and Benjamin. This history, too, is a type of fiction. The philosophers we have considered do not foreground their work as a philosophy or politics of equality. Nonetheless equality is a fundamental supposition that situates – positively, negatively, or ambiguously – their respective projects of metaphysics, ontology, ethics, or aesthetics.

In Part I, I argued that Rancière's account of the subject of equality is indebted to both Cartesian egalitarianism and existentialism. Those thinkers that I have defined as Cartesian egalitarians – Poullain de la Barre, Jacotot, and Beauvoir – politicize the fundamental supposition of Descartes's philosophy:

that 'good sense' or reason is equally distributed to all human beings. While Descartes introduces this supposition in order to disentangle the threads that tie together philosophy, habit, and prejudice, he limits the egalitarianism of his philosophical meditations to metaphysical and epistemological problems. Later, these Cartesian egalitarians politicize the supposition of good sense to criticize how philosophy can be used to reinforce the social prejudices and practices that subjugate certain parts of society. For these Cartesian egalitarians, the supposition of equality demonstrates a wrong that is committed against these parts of society that have no part. As Poullain argues, in a passage that Beauvoir paraphrases as an epigraph to *The Second Sex*, the historical and intellectual record shows that:

> Women were judged in former times as they are today and with as little reason, so whatever men say about them should be suspect as they are both judges and defendants. Even if the charges brought against them are backed by the opinions of a thousand authors, the entire brief should be taken as a chronicle of prejudice and error. (1673, 76)

While Poullain embraces the metaphysics of Descartes, he stages Descartes's dualism as an argument that demonstrates how patriarchal prejudices and practices wrong women: that the mind has no sex and that intellectual capacities are equally distributed to all human beings shows that the exclusion of women from intellectual pursuits is a wrong, while the claims that give a sex to virtue confuse the powers of thought and capacities of the body. Likewise, Beauvoir politicizes the individualist ethics of Sartre's existentialism. While both Sartre and Beauvoir maintain that freedom is the basis of all human activity, Beauvoir contends that not all types of free activity – that is, not all free projects – are equivalent; an egalitarian sense of freedom requires that one act in such a way so as to work toward the freedom of others. A philosophical account of freedom must remain attentive to social perceptions and social relations, including the ways that in relations of oppression, domination, or exploitation, some human beings – such as women, the colonized, or African Americans – are forced to assume their freedom as others rather than subjects. In a word, the dynamic of political subjectivation must remain attentive to *l'expérience vécue*: the socially lived experience of giving an account of oneself within a historically concrete situation.

Rancière argues that Descartes's *ego sum, ego existo* is the prototype of egalitarian political subjectivation. This collective practice – a *nos sumus, nos existimus* – produces new modes of experience, speaking, acting, or place (Rancière, 1995,

35–6/59). These new modes of experience, which are invented through the supposition of equality, are interruptive and transformative. The dynamic of political subjectivation is heterogeneous to techniques of policing. And while politics is rare and transitory, political practices nevertheless transform a given distribution of the sensible – even in its policed forms – toward new, egalitarian possibilities: both 'new inscriptions of equality within freedom and a new sphere of visibility for further demonstrations' (1995, 42/67tm).

In Chapter 2, I argued that Rancière's account of political subjectivation is indebted to the work of Sartre. Both maintain that the dynamic of subjectivation begins with the disidentification of self-politicizing subjects from the policing of the roles, occupations, and identities that structure the practico-inert world. And both maintain that politics interrupts these practico-inert structures of policing. This does not mean that politics is a movement divorced from historical contexts. Instead, politics is defined by the reciprocal play of practice and discourse, of a logic or rationality and of modes of acting, all of which are historically situated – that is to say, historically contingent. Where Sartre and Rancière differ is the definition of the logic and praxis of politics. For Sartre, radical politics becomes a force when political agents come to freely totalize their practices and oppose their tactics and strategies against sedimented and practico-inert forms of exploitation and domination. While Rancière's radical egalitarianism also contests and interrupts forms of exploitation and domination, he argues that Sartre's emphasis on the stabilization of political struggle through the pledge, organization, and totalization hyperinstrumentalizes political freedom. According to Rancière, by the time of the pledge, politics is already over. Therefore he argues that the political subjectivation through dissensus takes equality as both its means and its ends: egalitarian relations must structure the means – the discourses (logics) and the practices of equality – and the ends of politics, however temporary and transitory they may be.

In Part II, I proposed and defended the hypothesis that Rancière's politics of aesthetics names a network of micropolitical practices that transform relations between words, things, and affects; these practices and the discourses introduce new sensible forms of visibility, intelligibility, and place. This hypothesis is situated by Rancière's politics of equality. Politics, he insists, is both heterogeneous to policing and, given that moments of politics are singular events, rare. I have proposed that the politics of literature or the politics of aesthetics are forms of micropolitical contestation in order to account for the emancipatory social and political transformations of everyday life that have taken place since the emergence of the aesthetic regime of art. Moreover, I have maintained that considering aesthetics as micropolitics casts in stark relief Rancière's differences with Badiou, Greenberg, and Benjamin.

As we have seen, Rancière argues that art is political by virtue of being art. Art, he contends, is not a transhistorical form of cultural production. Instead, it names a singular domain of production and experience that emerges with the collapse of the representative regime of the arts, which is governed by a series of mimetic norms that maintain – by establishing a parallel between the values of social hierarchies and those of artistic hierarchies – the boundaries between the fine arts (and the genres of the fine arts) and the lesser arts, as well as the forms of technical and moral proficiency adequate to each fine art or genre. The representative regime is a form of policing the arts to reinforce both artistic and social hierarchies. The aesthetic regime of art erodes these mimetic norms, not by critiquing representation *tout court* (*à la* Greenberg), but rather by challenging the practico-inert forms of representing the various parts of society. Art, as a singular domain, interrupts and reinscibes the relations between words, things, affects, and values. Like Benjamin, Rancière avers that art is imbricated in social life; the aesthetic revolution and literarization transform the coordinates of everyday life, subverting and reinscribing the 'conventional distinctions between genres, between writer and poet, between scholar and populizer ... even the distinction between author and reader' (Benjamin, 1934a, 772). Nevertheless, Rancière contends that the aesthetic revolution can neither be sufficiently explained by reference to technological change nor subsumed under the teleology of messianism. Finally, both Badiou and Rancière hold that artistic novelty breaks with the established forms and visibilities of a given distribution of the sensible. However, for Rancière, Badiou's monumental and evental idea of art cannot account for micropolitical change. If there is a modernist aspect to Badiou's inaesthetics, it is his contempt for all art that is not monumental. What Badiou calls culture is similar to what Greenberg calls kitsch. But, where Badiou posits inaesthetics or affirmationism as a universal 'proletarian aristocratism' available to all, Greenberg asserts that the modernist avant-garde is tasked with preserving living culture against bourgeois philistinism and proletarian kitsch. For Greenberg, only the avant-garde artist has the social consciousness to match his or her leisure; the bourgeois has leisure but bourgeois values, while the proletarian lacks the leisure to cultivate an aesthetic experience divorced from kitsch. For Rancière, Greenberg's modernism is politically and aesthetically stultifying.

Given that Rancière's politics and aesthetics remain open to revision and reconsideration, I would like to conclude by addressing how his recent book

Aisthesis at once confirms and challenges several of the claims that I have made here. The framework of *Aisthesis* is familiar. Rancière argues that, over the last two hundred years, the practices and discourses of art within the aesthetic regime have worked to produce a 'sensible fabric of experience' that weaves together artistic novelty and life (Rancière, 2011a, x). Rancière situates aesthetics between three different forms of policing what is proper to art: the ethical regime of images, the representative regime of the arts, and modernism. As we have seen, Rancière's aesthetics and Greenberg's modernism are both premised on the critique of mimesis, though they draw radically different consequences from the collapse of the mimetic norms that govern the representative regime. For Greenberg, each art is autonomous insofar as it interrogates its own unique and opaque medium – any remaining use of representation or figuration within the work is residual and accidental. On Greenberg's account, the history of painting since Manet has been governed by the task of interrogating the flatness and two-dimensionality of the painting surface, which required gradually divesting painting of characteristics of the other arts, such as sculptural modelling and literary or narrative techniques.

For Rancière, by contrast, art is aesthetic and political insofar as it interrupts, subverts, and gradually erodes the mimetic norms that governed the representative regime of the arts. The mimetic norms of the representative regime produce the fiction of a social body divided between great men who act and shape history and those anonymous masses who are relegated to the prosaic life of meeting needs and producing useful things. The norms of the representative regime establish a fiction of causality whereby the acts and deeds of the characters of an artwork impart the proper moral lessons to an audience. The representative order, Rancière writes, defines

> discourse as a body with well-articulated parts, the poem as plot, and a plot as an order of actions. This order clearly situated the poem – and the artistic productions for which it functioned as a norm – on a hierarchical model: a well-ordered body where the upper part commands the lower, [elevating] the privilege of action, that is to say of the free man, capable of acting according to ends, over the repetitive lives of men without quality. (Rancière, 2011a, xiv)

Both Greenberg and Rancière contest the priority of plot and the order of actions that structure mimetic effects. However, on Greenberg's account, the priority of plot and the order of actions defines the literary confusion that perverts and distorts other, non-literary arts, when they suppress the opacity of their respective media in order to imitate literary techniques (Greenberg, 1940,

26). According to Rancière, by contrast, literature emerges with the collapse of the mimetic norms through which plot and the order of actions establish social and artistic fictions that distinguish between two types of humanity: those whose occupation is to act and pursue grand designs, and those whose lot in life it is to do an occupation that meets their individual needs (Rancière, 2011a, 46). Through literature and aesthetics emerge those words, bodies, places, and affects that had been relegated, in the ethical regime of images and the representative regime of the arts, to a world of prosaic life that remained below the threshold of great art and the deeds of great men. Rancière's point, however, is not that the representative regime cannot accommodate all the new subjects who had not yet been represented according to its mimetic norms. More specifically, he argues that aesthetics and literature name new practices and discourses of relating the worlds of art, the arts, and non-art, of relating words, bodies, places, and affects.

Given that it introduces new relations between art and non-art, affect and intelligibility, aesthetics is political. Rancière argues that the aesthetic regime opens a singular experience of art that is unbound from social and political hierarchies and practico-inert modes of valuation. But it is crucial to underline that there is no *one* politics of aesthetics. The aesthetic regime includes several sometimes paradoxical politics that relate art and social life: among them, Rancière discusses symptomological metapolitics, a politics of resistant form, and a politics of emancipated spectators in which artistic practices and discourses suppose the intellectual and aesthetic equality of anybody and everybody. If *Aisthesis* constitutes a significant departure from Rancière's previous works on aesthetics, it is because he advances what I will refer to as a *politics of life* to situate the 'history of the paradoxical links between the aesthetic paradigm and political community' (Rancière, 2011a, xiv).

Admittedly, Rancière has consistently argued in his work on aesthetics that the aesthetic regime of art includes artistic practices and discourses that have sought to revolutionize the relation between art and life as a form of politics. Benjamin, for example, argues that early twentieth-century historical avant-gardes had sought to produce new artistic forms as emancipatory forms of everyday life. In Benjamin's phrasing, to demand that art becomes life is to demand that art revolutionizes socially lived experience – new, emancipatory forms of art would dispense with prior artistic hierarchies and political forms of domination and oppression. In other words, the significance of emancipatory art is situated between regimes of art and the heterogeneity of the politics of equality and policing. This is the type of phrasing that situates Rancière's interpretation of Schiller's micropolitics in *Aesthetics and Its Discontents*. In *Aisthesis*, however, Rancière's politics of life is political solely by virtue of being neither the representative regime of the art nor the ethical regime of images. In each of the scenes that constitute the history of the aesthetic regime, Rancière underlines how *aisthesis* interrupts or upsets the ways that these other regimes of art assign a form of social causality to art. Both Plato's ethical regime of images and Aristotle's representative regime of the arts provide an account for what an art does and how it affects – interferes with or reinforces the structures of – the political community. In the *Republic*, Plato avers that the arts of the pleasure-giving muse incite both a rebellion in the soul and a rebellion in the city; these arts arouse the desires against reason and the freedom of the *demos* against the proper order of the city. In the *Poetics*, Aristotle argues that the proper use of the arts can reinforce the order of the city; indeed, the effects of catharsis are predicated on a moral universe in which virtue begets eudaimonia. Both regimes work to police the arts and the relation between the arts and society. In the representative regime, as we have seen, the fiction of plot and the order of actions produce a sensibility that eulogizes the historical efficacy of great men who act while inculcating, like an orator, the morality of the wills of the members of the audience.

The aesthetic regime of art abolishes these attempts to establish a direct social causality of art. Instead, the aesthetic regime articulates the figure of activity that is inactivity, freed from teleology and effectivity. This aesthetic indifference of activity and inactivity, Rancière writes,

> means two things: first, it is the rupture of all specific relations between a sensible form and the expression of an exact meaning; but it is also the rupture of every specific link between a sensible presence and a public that would be its public, the sensible milieu that would nourish it, or its natural addressee. (2011a, 18)

The aesthetic regime dismisses the social causalities that bind a sensible form to a univocal meaning and interrupts assumptions about the relationships – such as: the spectator is by definition a passive participant – between art and addressee. Moreover, as Rancière had established already in *The Philosopher and His Poor*, the Kantian aesthetic *sensus communis* undermines the distinction between a humanity who has the leisure to cultivate the capacity for taste and aesthetic judgement and those who do not, that is, those who work and live a life of utility. Aesthetic equality, first, names that sensible experience through which anyone and everyone can disidentify with everyday interests and exigencies, 'where one *does nothing*' (Rancière, 2011a, 46). But this equality also makes possible a distribution of the sensible whereby anything can be art, where no situation or subject is preferable, whereby 'anyone can grab a pen, taste any kind of pleasure, or nourish any ambition whatsoever' (2011a, 51).

Again, much of this account of aesthetics has been anticipated in Rancière's other works. In *Aisthesis*, though, *life* is treated as a metonymy for the micropolitics of aesthetics that binds the various aesthetic scenes together. Whereas life, in other works, is defined as socially lived experience, much as it is by Sartre, Beauvoir, or Fanon, in *Aisthesis* aesthetic discourses and practices are socially valuable insofar as they exhibit the singular events of life: Winckelmann 'inaugurates the age during which artists were busy unleashing the sensible potential hidden in inexpressiveness, indifference or immobility' (2011a, 9); Stendhal's *Red and Black* is emblematic of the literary revolution that substitutes for the revolutions of state power the 'pure nonsense of life, the obstinate will that wants nothing' (52); the pages of Whitman's *Leaves of Grass* 'must be considered like the detached leaves of any tree whatsoever, emanations of universal anonymous life' (71); while James Agee's account of destitute sharecroppers inventories each of those parts of 'an existence that is entirely actual, inevitable and unrepeatable' (250).

Despite Rancière's attention to the detailed contexts of each aesthetic scene, his descriptions and interpretations return, again and again, to life. This metonymic device makes visible a politics phrased in quasi-vitalist terms – as Donna V. Jones phrases it, in terms of a 'cultural vitalism' that 'urges a return to raw, unverbalized lived experience through a bracketing of the sedimented categories and schema by which we reflect on and "deaden" it' (Jones, 2010, 4). Rancière's analyses in *Aisthesis* come to resemble those of contemporary vitalists such as Deleuze and Agamben, who contend that *a* life manifests a singular haecceity that is antecedent to any particular subjectivity or objectivity to which *a* life gives rise. Deleuze points to an incident found in Charles Dickens's *Our Mutual Friend* to illustrate the meaning of a life: at the liminal and singular point between life and death even a disreputable man elicits a sense of 'eagerness, respect, even love' from his caretakers (Deleuze, 1995, 28). For Deleuze, *a* life is an immanent moment of beatitude beyond good and evil. On Agamben's account, Deleuze articulates a concept of bare life, which is both subjected to apparatuses of power/knowledge – including, he later adds, language itself ('perhaps the most ancient of apparatuses') (Agamben, 2006, 14) – and the cipher of resistance to these apparatuses, a 'pure potentiality that preserves without acting' (Agamben, 1996, 234).

I do not think that *Aisthesis* commits Rancière to a vitalist ontology. His work persistently resists prioritizing ontology to establish philosophical categories and concepts. Instead, Rancière's work tests the supposition of equality against a number of systems in order to evaluate whether or not they offer new discursive and practical possibilities for thinking emancipation. Moreover, Rancière's aesthetics is not Deleuzian (see 1998b, 146–64; 1998c; 2010b, 169–83). Rancière's account of the politics of life, then, constitutes an attempt to appropriate the term from contemporary vitalism: Deleuze's Christ-like figures – Riderhood (the disreputable man, as Agamben points out, of *Our Mutual Friend*), Bartleby, etc. – around whom crystallize the affective haecceities of art, or Agamben's treatment of bare life as a singular resistance that renders inoperative the apparatuses of capture that foreclose upon the pure potentiality of the Open. To 'do nothing', to put aside the exigencies and interests of the practico-inert in order to pursue the errancy of autodidactic freedom, for Rancière, is neither exceptional nor messianic – it is to pursue the possibilities and passions of everyday life within the aesthetic regime of art (Rancière, 2011a, 51). Nonetheless, given that he contends that *aisthesis* 'loses its simplicity in the aesthetic age' insofar as it is unbound from the mimetic norms that attached meanings to affects, Rancière could have emphasized, like Beauvoir, Sartre, or Fanon, the socially mediated character of lived experience (2011a, 119). From their standpoint, Deleuze's immanent vital force would be an appeal to a transcendent value that precedes the social mediation of human practices. This is, in fact, Rancière's critique of Deleuze found in 'The Monument and Its Confidences' (2010b, 180). This is clearly not the case with Rancière's aesthetics, which despite the repeated reference to life, remains sensitive to its historical contexts.

I have addressed the problem of vitalism and the politics of life because I am interested in how Rancière's discourse in *Aisthesis* – the act of writing a particular historical narrative that, he notes, could be otherwise (2011a, xiii) – is simultaneously an aesthetic form and political intervention, and 'a sensible reconfiguration of the facts it is arguing about' (Rancière, 2004b, 65). Peter Gratton worries that the quasi-vitalism of *Aisthesis* works to depoliticize the aesthetic scenes found therein:

> Rancière privileges the clown, the prisoner awaiting execution, the de-gendered dancer, and so on, all in the name of an inactivity that is but another name for the pure vital force of living, while calling for an indifference to differences that for the author would only be hierarchical and power driven. Indeed they are and have been, but isolating non-hierarchical moments in some sort of *eidos* of pure

inactivity in these descriptions becomes a phenomenological *epoché* that has to bracket so much away from given [social] contexts. (2014)

The 'de-gendered dancer' in question is Loïe Fuller. Rancière recounts how a New York court, using a terminology of the representative regime, denied the copyright for a composition in dance on the grounds that it is a series of graceful gestures rather than dramatic composition. He contraposes a passage from the court's decision with a description from Mallarmé, who writes that

> *the dancer is not a woman dancing*, for these juxtaposed reasons: that *she is not a woman*, but a metaphor summing up one of the elementary aspects of our form: knife, goblet, flower, etc., and that *she is not dancing*, but suggesting through the miracle of bends and leaps a kind of corporeal writing. (quoted in Rancière, 2011a, 103)

On Rancière's account, Mallarmé offers a description of an aesthetic experience of art that challenges the boundaries between art and non-art and the representative separation of the arts. He writes that

> Fuller's dance is not only an art, but an illustration of a new paradigm of art: it is not a dance anymore, but the performance of an unknown art, or rather a new idea of art: a writing of forms determining the very space of its manifestation. (Rancière, 2011a, 103)

Nonetheless, the aesthetic context does not exhaust the politics of aesthetics. While Mallarmé offers an interpretation that differs from the logic of the representative regime of the arts, it remains within those discourses, including literary discourses, that – as Beauvoir would say – explicitly 'other' women and women's bodies through idealization (Beauvoir, 1949, 214–74/1: 311–95). Thus determining the politics of art by reference to its relation to the representative regime of the arts or the ethical regime of images produces an incomplete account of the ways that art is politicized within socially lived experience. The micropolitics of aesthetics not only challenges and disrupts the other regimes of identifying art, it also interrupts the practico-inert structures of the apparatuses of policing a given distribution of the sensible. While the politics of equality is heterogeneous to policing, the micropolitics of aesthetics works in the intervals of heterogeneity. Aesthetics is constituted by practices and discourses that introduce new forms of visibility, intelligibility, and place.

The micropolitics of aesthetics, I have argued, traverses a polemical common world of various regimes of arts, apparatuses of policing, and dissensual claims to equality. In *Aisthesis*, Rancière's politics of life affirms the teeming pluralities of Whitmanian cultural democracy. Each of the scenes that constitute the history of *Aisthesis* repeatedly affirm that *life is something, isn't it?* and at points illustrate delight in the emancipation of words, bodies, affects, and places. But this narrative risks, to paraphrase Rancière's critique of Deleuze, returning political and artistic invention to one and the same sensible experience (see Rancière, 2010b, 182). We must insist, then, that these affirmations of life exhaust neither politics nor aesthetics. The micropolitics of aesthetics can also invent, beginning with the supposition of aesthetic and intellectual equality, forms of making visible and intelligible those forms of injustice, oppression, and exploitation that mar the world we tenuously have in common.

To conclude with but one example: Rancière points, in *The Emancipated Spectator*, to a photograph that shows a pile of stones 'harmoniously integrated into an idyllic landscape of hills covered with olive trees, a landscape similar to that photographed by Victor Bérard to display the permanence of the Mediterranean of Ulysses' voyages' (2009a, 103; the photograph is reproduced on 104). This photograph, however, is part of a series assembled by Sophie Ristelhueber collected under the title 'WB' (West Bank), and it captures, from a bird's-eye view, an Israeli roadblock constructed on a Palestinian road. According to Rancière, Ristelhueber's photographs do not oppose the appearance of idyll to the reality of conflict, but rather play on discordances and indeterminations that require the attention of the spectator to make sense of the image – the affects of the juxtaposition of idyllic landscape and the discursive context interrupt a univocal social causality between aesthetics and politics. There is a moment of indetermination, of 'doing nothing' perhaps, but it is left to the spectator who, like all of us, shares in the intellectual and aesthetic equality of anyone and everyone, to decide what is to be done. If aesthetics does anything, it invents new and more egalitarian ways to visualize and verbalize the travails and frustrations, the joys and hopes, and the sense of justice and injustice that guide dissensus.

Bibliography

I have tried as much as possible to supply the original dates of publication in the case of each bibliographical entry, although occasionally I have had to make decisions concerning dates when choosing, for example, between first and subsequent dates of publication (e.g. supplying the date of the original publication of Schiller's *Ästhetische Briefe* though the translation is based on a later edition) or between original and revised texts (e.g. some texts by Rancière have different contents in translation). I hope that these choices allow the reader to consider relations of historical proximity and distance in the material discussed. I must add that, in dating Rancière's texts, Cody Hennesy's 'The published works of Jacques Rancière,' in *Symposium*, 15, 2 (2011), 120–49 has been indispensible. I have used, as much as possible, extant translations of texts published in languages other than English, though I have at times I have modified translations and signaled these passages with 'tm.' Any errors remain my own.

Jacques Rancière

Faure, Alain and Jacques Rancière (eds.) [1976], *La parole ouvrière*. Paris: La fabrique editions, 2007.

Rancière, Danielle and Jacques Rancière [1978], 'The Philosophers' Tale: Intellectuals and the Trajectory of *Gauchisme*,' in *The Intellectual and His People: Staging the People Vol. 2*. Trans. David Fernbach. London: Verso, 2012, pp. 74–100.

Rancière, Jacques [1974], *Althusser's Lesson*. Trans. Emiliano Battista. London: Continuum, 2011.

Rancière, Jacques [1978], 'Good Times, or, Pleasure at the Barrière,' in *Staging the People: The Proletarian and His Double*. Trans. David Fernbach. London: Verso, 2011, pp. 175–232.

Rancière, Jacques [1981], *Proletarian Nights*. Trans. John Drury. London: Verso, 2012.

Rancière, Jacques [1983], *The Philosopher and His Poor*. Ed. Andrew Parker. Durham, NC: Duke University Press, 2003.

Rancière, Jacques [1987], *The Ignorant Schoolmaster*. Trans. Kristin Ross. Stanford: Stanford University Press, 1991.

Rancière, Jacques [1990], *Short Voyages to the Land of the People*. Trans. James B. Swenson. Stanford: Stanford University Press, 2003.

Rancière, Jacques (1991), 'After What,' in Eduardo Cadava, Peter Connor and Jean-Luc Nancy (eds.), *Who Comes After the Subject?* London: Routledge, pp. 246–52.

Rancière, Jacques [1992], *The Names of History*. Trans. Hassan Melehy. Minneapolis: University of Minnesota Press, 1994.

Rancière, Jacques [1995], *Disagreement: Politics and Philosophy*. Trans. Julie Rose. Minneapolis: University of Minnesota Press, 1999. All citations give the pagination of the English translation followed by the pagination of *Mésentente: Politique et philosophie*. Paris: Galilée.

Rancière, Jacques (1996a), 'The Archaeomodern Turn,' in Michael P. Steinberg (ed.), *Walter Benjamin and the Demands of History*. Ithaca, NY: Cornell University Press, pp. 24–40.

Rancière, Jacques [1996b], *Mallarmé: The Politics of the Siren*. Trans. Steven Corcoran. London: Continuum, 2011.

Rancière, Jacques [1997], 'The Cause of the Other,' *Parallax* 4 (2) (1998): 25–33.

Rancière, Jacques (1998a), *Aux bords du politique*. Paris: Gallimard.

Rancière, Jacques [1998b], *The Flesh of Words*. Trans. Charlotte Mandell. Stanford: Stanford University Press, 2004.

Rancière, Jacques [1998c], 'Is there a Deleuzian Aesthetics?' *Qui Parle* 14 (2) (2004): 1–14.

Rancière, Jacques [1998d], *Mute Speech*. Trans. James Swenson. New York: Columbia University Press, 2011.

Rancière, Jacques [1998e], 'Ten Theses on Politics,' in Rancière 2010b, pp. 27–44.

Rancière, Jacques [1999], 'Politique et identité,' in *Moments politiques*. Montréal: Lux Éditeur, 2009, pp. 105–13.

Rancière, Jacques [2000], 'Biopolitics or Politics?' in Rancière 2010b, pp. 91–6.

Rancière, Jacques [2001], *The Aesthetic Unconscious*. Trans. Debra Keates and James Swenson. Cambridge: Polity Press, 2009.

Rancière, Jacques [2002a], 'Aesthetics, Inaesthetics, Anti-aesthetics,' in Peter Hallward (ed.), *Think Again: Alain Badiou and the Future of Philosophy*. London: Continuum, 2004, pp. 218–31.

Rancière, Jacques [2002b], 'The People or the Multitudes?' in Rancière 2010b, pp. 84–90.

Rancière, Jacques [2003], *The Future of the Image*. Trans. Gregory Elliott. London: Verso, 2007.

Rancière, Jacques [2004a], *Aesthetics and Its Discontents*. Trans. Steven Corcoran. Cambridge: Polity Press, 2009.

Rancière, Jacques (2004b), *The Politics of Aesthetics*. Trans. Gabriel Rockhill. New York: Continuum.

Rancière, Jacques [2004c], 'Who is the Subject of the Rights of Man?' in Rancière 2010b, pp. 62–75.

Rancière, Jacques [2005a], 'L'actualité du *Maître ignorant*,' in *Et tant pis pour les gens fatigués*. Paris: Editions Amsterdam, 2009, pp. 409–27.
Rancière, Jacques [2005b], *Hatred of Democracy*. Trans. Steve Corcoran. London: Verso, 2006. Quotations that provide the translation and the French text will provide the pagination of the translation followed by that of *La haine de la démocratie*. Paris: La Fabrique.
Rancière, Jacques [2006a], 'Jacques Rancière et l'a-disciplinarité' in *Et tant pis pour les gens fatigués*. Paris: Editions Amsterdam, 2009, pp. 474–89.
Rancière, Jacques [2006b], *The Politics of Literature*. Trans. Julie Rose. Cambridge: Polity Press, 2011.
Rancière, Jacques (2007), *On the Shores of Politics*. Trans. Liz Heron. London: Verso.
Rancière, Jacques [2008], 'The Politics of Disagreement,' in *Moments Politiques: Interventions 1977–2009*. Trans. Mary Foster. New York: Seven Stories Press, 2014, pp. 153–66.
Rancière, Jacques (2009a), *The Emancipated Spectator*. Trans. Gregory Elliott. London: Verso.
Rancière, Jacques [2009b], 'Preface,' in *Moments Politiques: Interventions 1977–2009*. Trans. Mary Foster. New York: Seven Stories Press, 2014, pp. vii–xiii.
Rancière, Jacques (2010a), 'The Aesthetic Heterotopia,' *Philosophy Today* 54 (SPEP Supplement): 15–25.
Rancière, Jacques (2010b), *Dissensus*. Ed. Steven Corcoran. New York: Continuum. Includes these chapters, first published in this volume: 'The politics of literature,' pp. 152–68; 'The Monument and its Confidences; or Deleuze and Art's Capacity of "Resistance,"' pp. 169–83.
Rancière, Jacques [2011a], *Aisthesis: Scenes from the Aesthetic Regime of Art*. Trans. Zakir Paul. London: Verso, 2013.
Rancière, Jacques (2011b), 'The Thinking of Dissensus: Politics and Aesthetics,' in Paul Bowman and Richard Stamp (eds.), *Reading Rancière*. London: Continuum, pp. 1–17.
Rancière, Jacques (2012a), *La method de l'égalité: Entretien avec Laurent Jeanpierre et Dork Zabunyan*. Montrouge: Bayard.
Rancière, Jacques (2012b), 'Work, Identity, Subject,' in Jean-Philippe Deranty and Alison Ross (eds.), *Jacques Rancière and the Contemporary Scene: The Philosophy of Radical Equality*. London: Continuum, pp. 205–16.
Rancière Jacques and Oliver Davis (2013), 'On aisthesis: an interview,' in Oliver Davis (ed.), *Rancière Now*. Cambridge: Polity Press, pp. 202–18.

Additional Works Cited

Abensour, Miguel [1997], *Democracy against the State*. Trans. Max Blechman and Martin Breaugh. Cambridge: Polity Press, 2011.

Agamben, Giorgio [1996], 'Absolute Immanence,' in *Potentialities: Collected Essays in Philosophy*. Ed. Daniel Heller-Roazen. Stanford: Stanford University Press, 1999, pp. 220–39.

Agamben, Giorgio [2000], *The Time That Remains*. Trans. Patricia Dailey. Stanford: Stanford University Press, 2005.

Agamben, Giorgio [2006], 'What is an Apparatus?' in *What is an Apparatus? and Other Essays*. Trans. David Kishik and Stefan Pedatella. Stanford: Stanford University Press, 2009, pp. 1–24.

Agamben, Giorgio [2008], *The Signature of All Things: On Method*. Trans. Luca D'Isanto with Kevin Attell. New York: Zone Books, 2009.

Althusser, Louis [1965], *For Marx*. Trans. Ben Brewster. London: Verso, 2005.

Althusser, Louis [1970], 'Ideology and Ideological State Apparatuses,' in *Lenin and Philosophy*. Trans. Ben Brewster. New York: Monthly Review Press, 1971, pp. 127–86.

Aristotle (2001), *The Basic Works of Aristotle*. New York: The Modern Library. All citations provide the Bekker numbers as reproduced in this translation.

Aronson, Ronald (1980), *Jean-Paul Sartre: Philosophy in the World*. London: Verso.

Atherton, Margaret (1993), 'Cartesian Reason and Gendered Reason,' in Louise M. Antony and Charlotte Witt (eds.), *A Mind of One's Own: Feminist Essays on Reason and Objectivity*. Boulder, CO: Westview Press, pp. 19–34.

Badiou, Alain [1988], *Being and Event*. Trans. Oliver Feltham. London: Continuum, 2005.

Badiou, Alain [1989], *Manifesto For Philosophy*. Trans. Norman Madarasz. Albany, NY: SUNY Press, 1999.

Badiou, Alain (1992a), 'L'âge des poètes,' in Jacques Rancière (ed.), *La politique des poètes: Pourquoi des poètes en temps de détresse*. Paris: Albin Michel, pp. 21–38.

Badiou, Alain [1992b], *Conditions*. Trans. Steven Corcoran. London: Continuum, 2008.

Badiou, Alain [1993], *Ethics: An Essay on the Understanding of Evil*. Trans. Peter Hallward. London: Verso, 2001.

Badiou, Alain [1997], *Saint Paul: The Foundation of Universalism*. Trans. Ray Brassier. Stanford: Stanford University Press, 2003.

Badiou, Alain [1998a], *Briefings on Existence: A Short Treatise on Transitory Ontology*. Ed. Norman Madarasz. Albany, NY: SUNY Press, 2006.

Badiou, Alain [1998b], *Handbook of Inaesthetics*. Trans. Alberto Toscano. Stanford: Stanford University Press, 2005.

Badiou, Alain [1998c], *Metapolitics*. Trans. Jason Barker. London: Verso, 2005.

Badiou, Alain [1999], 'Philosophy and Cinema,' in *Infinite Thought*. Eds. Oliver Feltham and Justin Clemens. London: Continuum, 2003, pp. 109–25.

Badiou, Alain [2004], 'Third Sketch of a Manifesto of Affirmationist Art,' in *Polemics*. Trans. Steve Corcoran. London: Verso, 2006, pp. 133–48.

Badiou, Alain [2005], *The Century*. Trans. Alberto Toscano. Cambridge: Polity Press, 2007.

Badiou, Alain [2006a], 'The Lessons of Jacques Rancière: Knowledge and Power after the Storm,' in in Gabriel Rockhill and Philip Watts (eds.), *Jacques Rancière: History, Politics, Aesthetics*. Durham, NC: Duke University Press, pp. 30–54.

Badiou, Alain [2006b], *Logics of Worlds*. Trans. Alberto Toscano. New York: Continuum, 2009.

Badiou, Alain [2008], *Pocket Pantheon*. Trans. David Macey. London: Verso, 2009.

Baillet, Adrien (1691), *La Vie de Monsieur Descartes*. 2 volumes. Paris: Chez Daniel Horthemels.

Balzac, Honoré de [1831], *The Wild Ass's Skin*. Trans. Herbert J. Hunt. New York: Penguin Books, 1977.

Balzac, Honoré de [1837–43], *Lost Illusions*. Trans. Kathleen Raine. New York: The Modern Library, 2001.

Baudelaire, Charles [1863], 'The Painter of Modern Life,' in *Selected Writings on Art and Artists*. Trans. P. E. Charvet. Cambridge: Cambridge University Press, 1972, pp. 390–435.

Beauvoir, Simone de [1947], *The Ethics of Ambiguity*. Trans. Bernard Frechtman. New York: Citadel Press, 1976.

Beauvoir, Simone de [1949], *The Second Sex*. Trans. Constance Borde and Sheila Malovany-Chevallier. New York: Vintage, 2009. All citations give the pagination of the English translation followed by the pagination of *Le deuxième sex*. 2 volumes. Paris: Gallimard, 1999.

Beiser, Frederick C. (2005), *Schiller as Philosopher: A Re-Examination*. Oxford: Oxford University Press.

Benjamin, Walter [1931], 'Little History of Photography,' in Michael W. Jennings, Howard Eiland and Gary Smith (eds.), *Selected Writings: Volume 2, 1927–1934*. Cambridge, MA: Belknap/Harvard Unversity Press 1999, pp. 507–30.

Benjamin, Walter [1934a], 'The Author as Producer,' in *Selected Writings: Volume 2, 1927–1934*, pp. 768–82.

Benjamin, Walter [1934b], 'The Newspaper,' in *Selected Writings: Volume 2, 1927–1934*, pp. 741–2.

Benjamin, Walter [1936], 'The Work of Art in the Age of its Technological Reproducibility: Second Version,' in Howard Eiland and Michael W. Jennings (eds.), *Selected Writings: Volume 3, 1935–1938*. Cambridge, MA: Belknap/Harvard University Press, 2002, pp. 101–33.

Benjamin, Walter [1938], 'The Paris of the Second Empire in Baudelaire,' in Howard Eiland and Michael W. Jennings (eds.), *Selected Writings: Volume 4, 1938-1940*. Cambridge, MA: Belknap/Harvard University Press, 2003, pp. 3–92.

Benjamin, Walter [1940], 'On the Concept of History,' in *Selected Writings: Volume 4, 1938-1940*, pp. 389–400.

Benjamin, Walter [1982], *The Arcades Project*. Trans. Howard Eiland and Kevin McLaughlin. Cambridge, MA: Belknap/Harvard University Press, 1999. All citations refer to the German convolute numbers reproduced in this volume.

Bordo, Susan R. (1987), *The Flight to Objectivity: Essays on Cartesiansism and Culture.* Albany, NC: SUNY Press.

Bosteels, Bruno (2009), 'Rancière's Leftism, or, Politics and its Discontents,' in Gabriel Rockhill and Philip Watts (eds.), *Jacques Rancière: History, Politics, Aesthetics.* Durham, NC: Duke University Press, pp. 158–75.

Carriero, John (2009), *Between Two Worlds: A Reading of Descartes's* Meditations. Princeton: Princeton University Press.

Césaire, Aimé [1955], *Discourse on Colonialism.* Trans. Joan Pinkham. New York: Monthly Review Press, 2000.

Chambers, Samuel A. (2013), *The Lessons of Rancière.* Oxford: Oxford University Press.

Clark, T. J. (1999), *The Painting of Modern Life: Paris in the Art of Manet and His Followers.* Revised Edition. Princeton: Princeton University Press.

Craven, David (1996), 'The Latin American Origins of "Alternative Modernism,"' *Third Text* 10 (36): 29–44.

Davis, Oliver (2010), *Jacques Rancière.* Cambridge: Polity Press.

De Gouges, Olympe [1791], 'The Declaration of the Rights of Woman,' in Darline Gay Levy, Harriet Branson Applewhite and Mary Durham Johnson (eds.), *Women in Revolutionary Paris, 1789–1795.* Urbana: University of Illinois Press, 1979, pp. 87–96.

De Man, Paul [1983], 'Kant and Schiller,' in Andrzej Warminski (ed.), *Aesthetic Ideology.* Minneapolis: University of Minnesota Press, 1996, pp. 129–62.

Deleuze, Gilles [1995], 'Immanence: A life,' in *Pure Immanence: Essays on A Life.* Trans. Anne Boyman. New York: Zone Books, 2001, pp. 25–33.

Deleuze, Gilles and Félix Guattari [1980], *A Thousand Plateaus.* Trans. Brian Massumi. Minneapolis: University of Minnesota Press, 1987.

Delon, Michel (1978), 'Cartésianisme(s) et féminisme(s).' *Europe* 56 (594): 73–86.

Deranty, Jean-Philippe (ed.) (2010a), *Jacques Rancière: Key Concepts.* Durham, NC: Acumen.

Deranty, Jean-Philippe (ed.) (2010b), 'Regimes of the Arts,' in Deranty (ed.), 2010a, pp. 116–30.

Derrida, Jacques [1972], *Dissemination.* Trans. Barbara Johnson. Chicago: University of Chicago Press, 1981.

Descartes, René (1984–91), *The Philosophical Writings of Descartes.* 3 Volumes. Eds. John Cottingham, Robert Stoothoff and Dugald Murdoch (and Anthony Kenny in Volume 3). Cambridge: Cambridge University Press. All citations give the Adam and Tannery pagination as reproduced in these translations. Volume 1 contains the *Discourse on the Method* and *Principles of Philosophy*, Volume 2 the *Meditations*, the *Objections and Replies* and 'The Search for Truth,' and Volume 3 the correspondence.

Diagne, Souleymane Bachir [2007], *African Art as Philosophy: Senghor, Bergson and the Idea of Negritude.* Trans. Chike Jeffers. London: Seagull Books, 2011.

Dobie, Madeleine (2010), *Trading Places: Colonization and Slavery in Eighteenth-Century French Culture.* Ithaca, NY: Cornell University Press.

Eagleton, Terry (1990), *The Ideology of the Aesthetic*. Oxford: Blackwell Publishing.
Eagleton, Terry (2005) *Holy Terror*. Oxford: Oxford University Press.
Fanon, Frantz [1952], *Black Skin, White Masks*. Trans. Richard Philcox. New York: Grove Press, 2008.
Fanon, Frantz [1961], *The Wretched of the Earth*. Trans. Richard Philcox. New York: Grove Press, 2004.
Fichte, J. G. [1794–5], *The Science of Knowledge*. Eds. Peter Heath and John Lachs. Cambridge: Cambridge University Press, 1982.
Flynn, Thomas R. (1984), *Sartre and Marxist Existentialism*. Chicago: University of Chicago Press.
Foucault, Michel [1966a], 'L'homme est-il mort?' in Daniel Defert, François Ewald and Jacques Lagrange (eds.), *Dits et écrits*. Volume 1. Paris, Gallimard, 2001, pp. 568–72.
Foucault, Michel [1966b], *The Order of Things*. New York: Vintage Books, 1994.
Foucault, Michel [1972], 'My Body, this Paper, this Fire,' in James D. Faubion (ed.), *Aesthetics, Method, and Epistemology*. New York: The New Press, 1998, pp. 393–417.
Garber, Daniel (1986), '*Semel in vita*: The Scientific Background to Descartes,' in Amélie Oksenberg Rorty (ed.), *Meditations: Essays on Descartes' Meditations*. Berkeley: University of California Press, pp. 81–116.
Gratton, Peter (2014), 'Jacques Rancière, *Aisthesis: Scenes from the Aesthetic Regime of Art*,' *Society and Space*. http://societyandspace.com/reviews/reviews-archive/ranciere/
Greenberg, Clement [1939], 'Avant-garde and Kitsch,' in *Art and Culture: Critical Essays*. Boston: Beacon Press, 1989, pp. 3–21.
Greenberg, Clement [1940], 'Towards a Newer Laocoon,' in John O'Brian (ed.), *The Collected Essays and Criticism, Volume 1: Perceptions and Judgments 1939–1944*. Chicago: University of Chicago Press, 1986, pp. 23–38.
Greenberg, Clement [1953], 'The Plight of Culture,' in *Art and Culture*, pp. 22–33.
Greenberg, Clement [1954], 'Abstract, Representational, and so forth,' in *Art and Culture*, pp. 133–8.
Greenberg, Clement [1958], '"American-type" Painting,' in *Art and Culture*, pp. 208–29.
Greenberg, Clement [1965], 'Modernist Painting,' in Francis Frascina and Charles Harrison (eds.), *Modern Art and Modernism*. New York: Harper and Row, 1982, pp. 5–10.
Greenberg, Clement [1967], 'Manet in Philadelphia,' in John O'Brian (ed.), *The Collected Essays and Criticism, Volume 4: Modernism with a Vengeance*. Chicago: University of Chicago Press, 1993, pp. 240–4.
Guyer, Paul (1997), *Kant and the Claims of Taste*. Second Edition. Cambridge: Cambridge University Press.
Habermas, Jürgen [1985], *The Philosophical Discourse of Modernity*. Trans. Frederick G. Lawrence. Cambridge, MA: MIT Press, 1987.
Hallward, Peter (2003), *Badiou: A Subject to Truth*. Minneapolis: University of Minnesota Press.

Hallward, Peter (2009), 'Staging Equality: Rancière's Theatrocracy and the Limits of Anarchic Equality,' in Gabriel Rockhill and Philip Watts (eds.), *Jacques Rancière: History, Politics, Aesthetics*. Durham, NC: Duke University Press, pp. 140–57.

Hanssen, Beatrice (2005), 'Benjamin or Heidegger: Aesthetics and Politics in an Age of Technology,' in Andrew Benjamin (ed.), *Walter Benjamin and Art*. London: Continuum, pp. 73–92.

Harth, Erica (1992), *Cartesian Women: Versions and Subversions of Rational Discourse in the Old Regime*. Ithaca, NY: Cornell University Press.

Hegel, G. W. F. [1835], *Hegel's Aesthetics*. Volume 1. Trans. T. M. Knox. Oxford: Oxford University Press, 1975.

Heidegger, Martin [1961], 'On the Essence of Truth,' in *Basic Writings*. Second edition. Ed. David Farrell Krell. New York: Harper Collins, 1993, pp. 115–38.

Heidegger, Martin [1962], *What is a Thing?* Trans. W. B. Barton and Vera Deutsch. Chicago: Henry Regnery Company, 1967.

Hobbes, Thomas [1651], *Leviathan*. 2 vols. Eds. G. A. J. Rogers and Karl Schuhmann. London: Continuum, 2005.

House, Jim and Neil MacMaster (2006), *Paris 1961: Algerians, State Terror, and Memory*. Oxford: Oxford University Press.

Howells, Christina (1992), 'Conclusion: Sartre and the Deconstruction of the Subject,' in Christina Howells (ed.), *The Cambridge Companion to Sartre*. Cambridge: Cambridge University Press, pp. 318–52.

Howells, Christina (2011), 'Rancière, Sartre and Flaubert: From *The Idiot of the Family* to *The Politics of Aesthetics*,' *Symposium* 15 (2): 82–94.

Hunt, Lynn (2007), *Inventing Human Rights: A History*. New York: W. W. Norton and Company.

Ishay, Micheline R. (2008), *The History of Human Rights: From Ancient Times to the Globalization Era*. Second edition. Berkeley: University of California Press.

Jones, Donna V. (2010), *The Racial Discourses of Life Philosophy: Négritude, Vitalism, and Modernity*. New York: Columbia University Press.

Kail, Michel (2009), 'Beauvoir, Sartre, and the Problem of Alterity,' in Christine Daigle and Jacob Golomb (eds.), *Beauvoir and Sartre: The Riddle of Influence*. Bloomington: Indiana University Press, pp. 143–59.

Kant, Immanuel [1781/87], *Critique of Pure Reason*. Eds. Paul Guyer and Allen W. Wood. Cambridge: Cambridge University Press, 1998. All references to Kant are cite the English translation followed by the volume and pagination of *Gesammelte Werke* (Berlin: de Gruyter, 1900–) as reproduced in the English translations, with the exception of the *Critique of Pure Reason*, which references the pagination of the 1781 (A) and 1787 (B) editions.

Kant, Immanuel [1788], *Critique of Practical Reason*, in *Practical Philosophy*. Trans. Mary J. Gregor. Cambridge: Cambridge University Press, 1996, pp. 137–271.

Kant, Immanuel [1790], *Critique of the Power of Judgment*. Ed. Paul Guyer. Cambridge: Cambridge University Press, 2000.

Krell, David Farrell (2005), *The Tragic Absolute: German Idealism and the Languishing God*. Bloomington: Indiana University Press.
Lacoue-Labarthe, Philippe and Jean-Luc Nancy [1978], *The Literary Absolute: The Theory of Literature in German Romanticism*. Trans. Philip Barnard and Cheryl Lester. Albany, NY: SUNY Press, 1988.
Lane, Jeremy F. (2013), 'Rancière's Anti-platonism: Equality, the 'Orphan Letter' and the Problematic of the Social Sciences,' in Oliver Davis (ed.), *Rancière Now*. Cambridge: Polity Press, pp. 28–46.
Lecercle, Jean-Jacques (2004), 'Badiou's Poetics,' in Peter Hallward (ed.), *Think Again: Alain Badiou and the Future of Philosophy*. London: Continuum, 2004, pp. 208–17.
Lehman, Robert S. (2010), 'Between the Science of the Sensible and the Philosophy of Art,' *Angelaki: Journal of the Theoretical Humanities* 15 (2): 171–85.
Lloyd, Genevieve (1993), *The Man of Reason: 'Male' and 'Female' in Western Philosophy*. Minneapolis: University of Minnesota Press.
Marx, Karl [1843], 'On the Jewish Question,' in David McLellan (ed.), *Karl Marx: Selected Writings*. Oxford: Oxford University Press, 1977, pp. 39–62.
Marx, Karl [1844], 'Toward a Critique of Hegel's *Philosophy of Right*: Introduction,' in Lawrence H. Simon (ed.), *Selected Writings*. Indianapolis: Hackett Publishing, 1994, pp. 27–39.
Marx, Karl [1859], 'Preface to *A Critique of Political Economy*,' in David McLellan (ed.), *Karl Marx: Selected Writings*. Oxford: Oxford University Press, 1977, pp. 388–92.
Marx, Karl [1867], *Capital*. Volume 1. Trans. Ben Fowkes. New York: Penguin Books, 1990.
Marx, Karl (1977), 'A Correspondence of 1843,' in David McLellan (ed.), *Karl Marx: Selected Writings*. Oxford: Oxford University Press, 1977, pp. 36–8.
May, Todd (2008), *The Political Thought of Jacques Rancière*. University Park: Pennsylvania State University Press.
Mecchia, Giuseppina (2009), 'The Classics and Critical Theory in Postmodern France: The Case of Jacques Rancière,' in Gabriel Rockhill and Philip Watts (eds.), *Jacques Rancière: History, Politics, Aesthetics*. Durham, NC: Duke University Press, pp. 67–82.
Mecchia, Giuseppina (2010), 'Philosophy and its Poor: Rancière's Critique of Philosophy,' in Jean-Philippe Deranty (ed.), *Jacques Rancière: Key Concepts*. Durham, NC: Acumen, pp. 38–54.
Miller, Jacques-Alain (2003), 'Transcription of the J. P. Elkabbach broadcast with J-A. Miller and M. Accoyer on the phone on Europe 1,' available at http://www.lacan.com/europe1.htm
Moi, Toril (1994), *Simone de Beauvoir: The Making of an Intellectual Woman*. Oxford: Blackwell.
Montaigne, Michel de (2003), *The Complete Essays*. Trans. M. A. Screech. New York: Penguin Books. Cited by book number, chapter number, page number.
Moore, Lisa (1989), 'Sexual agency in Manet's *Olympia*,' *Textual Practice* 3 (2): 222–33.

Nancy, Jean-Luc (1991), 'Introduction,' in Eduardo Cadava, Peter Connor and Jean-Luc Nancy (eds.), *Who Comes After the Subject?* London: Routledge, pp. 1–8.

Negri, Antonio [1970], *Political Descartes: Reason, Ideology, and the Bourgeois Project*. Trans. Matteo Mandarini and Alberto Toscano. London: Verso, 2007.

Newmark, Kevin (2011), 'A Poetics of Sharing: Political Economy in a Prose Poem by Baudelaire,' *Symposium* 15 (2): 57–81.

Ngũgĩ wa Thiong'o (2012), *Globalectics: Theory and the Politics of Knowing*. New York: Columbia University Press.

Nochlin, Linda [1965], 'Innovation and Tradition in Courbet's *A Burial at Ornans*,' in *Courbet*. New York: Thames and Hudson, 2007, pp. 19–28.

Noys, Benjamin (2009), '"Monumental Construction": Badiou and the Politics of Aesthetics,' *Third Text* 23 (4): 383–92.

Phillips, John W.P. (2010), 'Art, Politics and Philosophy: Alain Badiou and Jacques Rancière,' *Theory, Culture and Society* 27 (4): 146–60.

Plato (1997), *Complete Works*. Ed. John M. Cooper. Indianapolis: Hackett Publishing. All citations provide the Stephanus numbers as reproduced in this translation.

Pollock, Griselda [1988], *Vision and Difference: Feminism, Femininity and the Histories of Art*. Routledge Classics Edition. London: Routledge, 2003.

Poullain de la Barre, François [1673], *On the Equality of the Two Sexes*, in Poullain 2002, pp. 49–121.

Poullain de la Barre, François [1674], *On the Education of Ladies*, in Poullain 2002, pp. 139–251.

Poullain de la Barre, François (2002), *Three Cartesian Feminist Treatises*. Trans. Vivien Bosley. Chicago: University of Chicago Press.

Pugh, David (1996), *Dialectic of Love: Platonism in Schiller's Aesthetics*. Montreal and Kingston: McGill-Queen's University Press.

Rockhill, Gabriel (2010), 'Recent Developments in Aesthetics: Badiou, Rancière, and their Interlocutors,' in Todd May (ed.), *Emerging Trends in Continental Philosophy*. Durham, NC: Acumen, pp. 31–48.

Rockhill, Gabriel (2011), 'Rancière's Productive Contradictions: From the Politics of Aesthetics to the Social Politicity of Artistic Practice,' *Symposium* 15 (2): 28–56.

Rodis-Lewis, Geneviève (1990), *L'anthropologie cartésienne*. Paris: Press Universitaires de France.

Rodis-Lewis, Geneviève [1995], *Descartes: His Life and Thought*. Trans. Jane Marie Todd. Ithaca, NY: Cornell University Press, 1998.

Ross, Alison (2012), 'Equality in the Romantic Art Form: The Hegelian Background to Jacques Rancière's "Aesthetic Revolution,"' in Jean-Philippe Deranty and Alison Ross (eds.), *Jacques Rancière and the Contemporary Scene: The Philosophy of Radical Equality*. London: Continuum, pp. 87–98.

Ross, Kristin (1991), 'Translator's Introduction,' in *The Ignorant Schoolmaster*. Trans. Kristin Ross. Stanford: Stanford University Press, pp. v–xxiii.

Sartre, Jean-Paul [1943], *Being and Nothingness*. Trans. Hazel E. Barnes. New York: Washington Square Books, 1956. All citations give the pagination of the English translation followed by the pagination of *L'être et le néant*. Ed. Arlette Elkaïm-Sartre. Paris: Gallimard, 1976.

Sartre, Jean-Paul [1947], 'Cartesian Freedom,' in *Critical Essays (Situations I)*. Trans. Chris Turner. Calcutta: Seagull Books, 2010, pp. 498–532.

Sartre, Jean-Paul [1948a], 'Black Orpheus,' in *The Aftermath of War (Situations III)*. Trans. Chris Turner. London: Seagull Books, 2008, pp. 259–329.

Sartre, Jean-Paul [1948b], *What is Literature? and Other Essays*. Cambridge, MA: Harvard University Press, 1988.

Sartre, Jean-Paul [1957a], 'Albert Memmi's *The Colonizer and the Colonized*,' in *Colonialism and Neocolonialism*. Trans. Azzedine Haddour, Steve Brewer and Terry McWilliams. London: Routledge, 2001, pp. 56–62.

Sartre, Jean-Paul [1957b], *Search for a Method*. Trans. Hazel E. Barnes. New York: Vintage Books, 1968.

Sartre, Jean-Paul [1960], *Critique of Dialectical Reason*. Volume 1. Trans. Alan Sheridan-Smith. London: Verso, 2004.

Sartre, Jean-Paul [1961], 'Preface,' in Frantz Fanon, *Wretched of the Earth*. Trans. Richard Philcox. New York: Grove Press, 2004, pp. xliii–lxii.

Sartre, Jean-Paul [1969], 'The Itinerary of a Thought,' in *Between Existentialism and Marxism*. Trans. John Matthews. London: Verso, 2008, pp. 33–64.

Sartre, Jean-Paul [1972], 'The Maoists in France,' in *Life/Situations: Essays Written and Spoken*. Trans. Paul Auster and Lydia Davis. New York: Pantheon Books, 1977, pp. 162–71.

Schelling, F. W. J. [1800], *System of Transcendental Idealism*. Trans. Peter Heath. Charlottesville: University Press of Virginia, 1978.

Schelling, F. W. J. [1802], 'Further Presentations from the System of Philosophy [extract],' in J. G. Fichte and F. W. J. Schelling, *The Philosophical Rupture between Fichte and Schelling: Selected Texts and Correspondence (1800–1802)*. Eds. Michael G. Vater and David W. Wood. Albany, NY: SUNY Press, 2012, pp. 206–25.

Schelling, F. W. J. [1802–5], *The Philosophy of Art*. Trans. Douglas W. Stott. Minneapolis: University of Minnesota Press, 1989.

Schelling, F. W. J. [1803], *On University Studies*. Trans. E. S. Morgan. Athens, OH: Ohio University Press, 1966.

Schelling, F. W. J. [1807], 'Concerning the Relation of the Plastic Arts to Nature.' Trans Michael Bullock, in Herbert Read, *The True Voice of Feeling*. London: Faber and Faber, 1968, pp. 323–64.

Schelling, F. W. J. (1927–59), *Schellings Werke. Nach der Original Ausgabe in neuer Anordnung*. 12 volumes. Ed. Manfred Schröter. Munich: Beck. All references to Schelling cite the English translation, when available, and then the volume and page of *Schellings sämmtliche Werke*, 14 volumes. Ed. K. F. A. Schelling. Stuttgart: Cotta, 1856–61, as reproduced in this edition. All citations are from Part 1.

Schiller, Friedrich [1793], 'On the Pathetic,' in Walter Hinderer and Daniel O. Dahlstrom (eds.), *Essays*. London: Continuum, 1993, pp. 45–69.

Schiller, Friedrich [1795], *On the Aesthetic Education of Man*. Trans. Elizabeth M. Wilkinson and L. A. Willoughby. Oxford: Clarendon Press, 1982.

Schiller, Friedrich and Johann Wolfgang von Goethe (1890), *Correspondence between Schiller and Goethe: From 1794 to 1805*. Volume 2. Trans. L. Dora Schmitz. London: George Bell and Sons.

Scholem, Gershom [1972], 'Walter Benjamin and his Angel,' in Gary Smith (ed.), *On Walter Benjamin: Critical Essays and Recollections*. Cambridge, MA: MIT Press, 1988, pp. 51–89.

Scholem, Gershom [1975], *Walter Benjamin: The Story of a Friendship*. Trans. Harry Zohn. New York: New York Review Books, 1981.

Scott, Joan Wallach (1996), *Only Paradoxes to Offer: French Feminists and the Rights of Man*. Cambridge, MA: Harvard University Press.

Sharpe, Lesley (1995), *Schiller's Aesthetic Essays: Two Centuries of Criticism*. Columbia, SC: Camden House.

Shaw, Devin Zane (2007), 'Inaesthetics and Truth: The Debate between Alain Badiou and Jacques Rancière,' *Filozofski vestnik* 28 (2): 183–99.

Shaw, Devin Zane (2010), *Freedom and Nature in Schelling's Philosophy of Art*. London: Continuum.

Shaw, Devin Zane (2013), 'The Vitalist Senghor: On Diagne's *African Art as Philosophy*,' *Comparative and Continental Philosophy* 5 (1) 92–8.

Shaw, Devin Zane (2014), 'The "Keystone" of the System: Schelling's Philosophy of Art,' in Matthew C. Altman (ed.), *The Palgrave Handbook of German Idealism*. New York: Palgrave Macmillan, pp. 518–38.

Sherman, David (2007), *Sartre and Adorno: The Dialectics of Subjectivity*. Albany, NY: SUNY Press.

Simay, Philippe (2005), 'Tradition as Injunction: Benjamin and the Critique of Historicisms,' in Andrew Benjamin (ed.), *Walter Benjamin and History*. London: Continuum, pp. 137–55.

Simons, Margaret A. (1999), *Beauvoir and the Second Sex: Feminism, Race, and the Origins of Existentialism*. Lanham, MD: Rowman and Littlefield.

Stuurman, Siep (2004), *François Poulain de la Barre and the Invention of Modern Equality*. Cambridge, MA: Harvard University Press.

Swenson, James (2009), '*Style indirect libre*,' in Gabriel Rockhill and Philip Watts (eds.), *Jacques Rancière: History, Politics, Aesthetics*. Durham, NC: Duke University Press, pp. 258–72.

Tanke, Joseph J. (2009), 'Reflections on the Philosophy and Anti-philosophy of Art,' *Philosophy Today* 53 (3).

Tanke, Joseph J. (2011), *Jacques Rancière: An Introduction*. London: Continuum.

Tanke, Joseph J. (2013), 'Why Julien Sorel had to be Killed,' in in Oliver Davis (ed.), *Rancière Now*. Cambridge: Polity Press, pp. 123–42.

Tiedemann, Rolf [1983], 'Historical Materialism or Political Messianism? An Interpretation of the Theses "On the Concept of History,"' in Gary Smith (ed.), *Benjamin: Philosophy, Aesthetics, History*. Chicago: University of Chicago Press, 1989, pp. 175–209.

Vallury, Raji (2009), 'Politicizing art in Rancière and Deleuze: The Case of Postcolonial Literature,' in Gabriel Rockhill and Philip Watts (eds.), *Jacques Rancière: History, Politics, Aesthetics*. Durham, NC: Duke University Press, pp. 229–48.

Van de Weyer, J. S. (1822), *Sommaire des leçons publiques de M. Jacotot sur les principes de l'enseignement universel*. Louvain: Chez Vanlinthout et Vandenzande.

Vaneigem, Raoul (1977), *A Cavalier History of Surrealism*. Trans. Donald Nicholson-Smith. San Francisco: AK Press, 1999.

Wohlfarth, Irving (2006), 'Et cetera? The historian as chiffonnier,' in Beatrice Hanssen (ed.), *Walter Benjamin and The Arcades Project*. London: Continuum, pp. 12–32.

Wollstonecraft, Mary (1792), 'A Vindication of the Rights of Woman', in Janet Todd (ed.), *A Vindication of the Rights of Woman* and *A Vindication of the Rights of Men*. Oxford: Oxford University Press, 1994, pp. 63–283.

Wordsworth, William (1805), *The Prelude, or, Growth of a Poet's Mind (Text of 1805)*. Ed. Ernest de Selincourt. London: Oxford University Press, 1933.

Žižek, Slavoj (1999), *The Ticklish Subject*. London: Verso.

Žižek, Slavoj (2004), *Iraq: The Borrowed Kettle*. London: Verso.

Index

Abensour, Miguel 9
absurdity 55, 67–8, 78 n.18
aesthetic equality 10, 15, 18, 92, 104, 112, 118, 120, 125 n.26, 131, 134, 172 n.20, 181–2, 186
aesthetic regime of art 13–18, 86–7, 90–4, 97, 104, 109, 111–12, 118, 127, 129, 132–6, 142–4, 146–7, 149–54, 157, 161–2, 167, 169, 170 n.6, 175, 179–82, 184
aesthetic revolution 13–15, 93, 104, 112, 143, 149–51, 153, 164, 179, 181 *see also* literary revolution
Aesthetics and Its Discontents (Rancière) 21 n.9, 108, 120, 127–9, 132–4, 142–5, 147–9, 151–4, 157, 165, 170 n.10, 182
aesthetic suspension 83, 85, 94, 121, 148, 154
Aesthetic Unconscious, The (Rancière) 21 n.9, 94, 171 n.13
Agamben, Giorgio 53, 70–1, 79 n.4, 115, 126 n.29, 183–4
aisthesis 15, 25–6, 57, 93–4, 100, 112, 182, 184
Aisthesis (Rancière) 18, 90, 92, 94–5, 103–4, 107–8, 118, 124 n.21, 125 n.21, 133, 162, 180–6
Algerians (in France) 73–4, 81 n.30
Algerian War for Independence 73–4, 76 n.1,
'Älteste Systemprogramm des deutschen Idealismus' 113, 131–3, 152–3, 163, 173 n.30
Althusser, Louis 3, 12, 20 n.3, 47 n.5, 58, 76 n.1, 119, 121, 135, 145, 176
Althusser's Lesson (Rancière) 21 n.9, 76 n.1
ambiguity 78 n.18
anticolonialism 52, 57, 68, 73, 76 n.1
archaeology 23, 86–7, 90, 93, 110, 118, 133–4, 139, 149

archaeomodernism 109, 111, 114–18
'Archaeomodern Turn, The' (Rancière) 15–16, 91, 114–18
archipolitics 5–7, 86, 99, 127, 129, 131
Arendt, Hannah 70–1
Aristotle 6–7, 13, 20 n.6, 25–6, 35, 37, 46 n.1, 48 n.15, 57, 86, 95–8, 140, 142, 182
 Poetics 13, 95–8, 142, 182
 Politics 6–7, 20 n.6, 25–6, 35, 46 n.1, 57
Aronson, Ronald, 67
art
 autonomy of 14, 89, 94, 101–7, 143–4, 148–50, 154–5, 157, 165
 monumental art 17–18, 83, 132–5, 142–3, 145, 153, 161–9, 179
Atherton, Margaret 46 n.3
avant-garde
 historical 91–2, 107–8, 123 n.8, 140–1, 162, 164, 181
 modernist 15, 91–2, 102, 104–9, 123 n.8, 145, 179

Badiou, Alain 3, 16–18, 23, 29–30, 47 n.5, 77 n.6, 83, 87, 90, 129, 132, 134–48, 161–9, 170 n.5, 171 n.14, 171 n.15, 171 n.17, 173 n.31, 179
 Being and Event 136–8
 Century, The 135–6, 144, 162, 164–5, 168, 171 n.15, 173 n.31
 classicism 138, 140–2
 critique of Heidegger 30, 47 n.5, 90, 137, 139–41, 173 n.31
 democratic materialism 17, 30, 132, 145, 164, 167
 didacticism 138–42
 Ethics 166
 event 17, 83, 132, 134–7, 142–5, 153, 161–2, 165–9, 170 n.5, 179
 Handbook of Inaesthetics 135, 138–46, 164

inaesthetics 10, 13, 83, 134–6, 138–47, 161–2, 165–6, 179
Logics of Worlds 30, 132, 170 n.10
Manifesto for Philosophy 47 n.5, 90, 139
Metapolitics 135, 170 n.10
ontology 136–8, 171 n.11
passion for the real 162, 164–5, 173 n.31
subtraction 17, 136, 138, 143, 164
'Third Sketch of a Manifesto of Affirmationist Art' 17–18, 142–3, 164–5
Baillet, Adrien 1, 2, 4, 42
Balzac, Honoré de 94, 101, 116, 124 n.15
La Peau de chagrin 116
Lost Illusions 101, 124 n.15
'Banquet des Travailleurs socialistes' 121
Baudelaire, Charles 90–1, 102, 110–11, 120, 148
Beauvoir, Simone de 11, 27–9, 37–42, 46, 48 n.15, 48 n.20, 48 n.21, 54, 77 n.5, 78 n.18, 86, 176–7, 183–5
Ethics of Ambiguity, The 38, 41, 48 n.20, 48 n.21, 78 n.18
Second Sex, The 35, 38–41, 48 n.15, 48 n.21, 54, 77 n.5, 177, 185
Beiser, Frederick 151, 156
Benjamin, Walter 13, 15–16, 83, 91–2, 95, 100–1, 109–18, 123 n.7, 125 n.25, 125 n.26, 125 n.27, 126 n.28, 127, 162, 176, 179, 181
Arcades Project, The 113, 115–16, 118, 125 n.25
and art 15, 109–13, 115–16, 125 n.27, 126 n.28
'Author as Producer, The' 110, 179
'Little History of Photography' 112–13
and messianism 15–16, 83, 110–11, 114–18, 179
'Newspaper, The' 15, 110
'On the Concept of History' 15, 115–17
'Paris of the Second Empire in Baudelaire, The' 111
on technology 15, 111–14, 126 n.28, 179
'Work of Art in the Age of Its Technological Reproducibility, The' 113, 125 n.27
Blanqui, Auguste 54, 59, 65, 69, 75

Bordo, Susan 31
Bosteels, Bruno 68–9
Bourdieu, Pierre 42, 108–9, 125 n.23, 148, 171 n.18
bourgeoisie 15, 29–30, 41, 46, 47 n.5, 47 n.7, 88, 102, 105–9, 118, 121, 124 n.20, 145, 151 171 n.18, 179
Brecht, Bertolt 130, 139, 170 n.3, 171 n.15
Breton, André 122 n.3, 142
Burial at Ornans, A (Courbet) 102–3
Burke, Edmund 70–1

capitalism 3, 8, 52, 58, 60–2, 105, 107, 109, 114, 116–17, 164
categorical imperative 61, 147, 149–50, 157–8 *see also* practical reason
catharsis 13, 95, 140–1, 182
'Cause of the Other, The' (Rancière) 62, 72–6, 77 n.2
Celan, Paul 139, 144
Césaire, Aimé 47 n.7
Chambers, Samuel 9, 20 n.3, 78 n.15
Clark, T. J. 102, 104, 124 n.16, 124 n.17
class 5, 29, 31, 36, 41, 45–6, 53, 69–70, 81 n.31, 89, 102, 106–9, 113–14, 117–18, 121, 122 n.3, 124 n.20, 125 n.23, 152, 171 n.18,
cogito 11, 27–8, 31–4, 37–8, 41, 43–5, 47 n.4, 48 n.18, 116
colonialism 39, 46, 47 n.7, 57, 73, 77 n.9, 80 n.29, 123 n.6, 177
commodification 17, 91–2, 102, 106–9, 118, 132, 168–9
commodity fetishism 100, 110, 116
communism 15, 64, 78 n.14, 85–6, 109, 122 n.3, 162, 171 n.15
consensus 3, 17, 28, 119, 132, 145, 149–51, 164, 166, 168–9
Constructivism 91
contingency 5, 7, 12, 55–6, 58, 62, 65, 67–8, 70, 76
Courbet, Gustave 102–3, 124 n.18
A Burial at Ornans 102–3
Craven, David 114, 123 n.6
culture 15, 18, 39–40, 105–10, 116, 132, 145, 152, 156, 167–8, 172 n.19, 179

Dada 92, 109, 113, 122 n.3, 140
Davis, Oliver 59, 122 n.1, 168

Debord, Guy 130, 170 n.3
deconstruction 9, 19, 23, 30, 66, 98, 139
De Gouges, Olympe 55, 71–2, 80 n.28, 80 n.29
Deleuze, Gilles 53, 101, 122 n.2, 122 n.4, 183–4, 186
De Man, Paul 151
democracy 5–7, 20 n.6, 48 n.19, 89, 97, 99, 108–9, 111, 124 n.21, 128, 164, 186
　molecular democracy 100–11, 112
demos 5–6, 51, 57, 65, 69–70, 74, 86, 182
Deranty, Jean-Philippe 128, 132
Derrida, Jacques 66, 98–9, 135
　'Plato's Pharmacy' 98–9
Descartes, René 1–2, 4, 9, 11, 19, 26–37, 39, 41–5, 46. n.3, 47–8, 51, 86, 120, 175–7 *see also cogito*; good sense
　Discourse on the Method 2, 27, 31–3, 44, 47 n.6, 51
　Meditations 27, 31–4
　Principles of Philosophy, The 29, 33
　'Search for Truth, The' 34
disagreement (*la mésentente*) 4, 7, 10, 59, 85, 88, 94, 114, 122 n.2, 148
Disagreement (Rancière) 2–9, 12, 20 n.3, 20 n.4, 21 n.9, 25–8, 42–4, 51, 53, 56–7, 59, 62, 64–5, 69, 71–5, 77 n.9, 100, 125 n.27, 153, 177–8
disidentification 12, 53, 58, 60, 62, 66, 74, 133, 148, 168, 178, 182
disinterestedness 108–9, 148, 171 n.18 *see also* Kant, aesthetic judgement
dissensus 10, 20, 20 n.4, 28, 30, 56, 59, 62, 69, 71–2, 75, 88, 121, 149, 153, 155, 157–8, 169, 171 n.11, 173 n. 27, 178, 186
distribution of the sensible 3, 5, 10, 13, 17–18, 26–8, 30, 35, 58, 83, 85–6, 88–9, 94, 100–1, 113, 121, 125 n.27, 133, 148, 155, 168, 178–9, 183, 185
division of labour 5, 36, 43–4, 64, 109, 120, 127–8, 151–2
Dobie, Madeleine 80 n.29
Don Quixote (Cervantes) 167

Eagleton, Terry 119–21, 151, 168, 171 n.12
Emancipated Spectator, The (Rancière) 21 n.9, 129–30, 168, 173 n.26, 186

emancipation 2–3, 8–10, 11–12, 14–16, 18, 19, 31, 34, 37, 40–1, 43–6, 52–5, 63–4, 83, 85, 90–1, 93, 100, 102, 104, 108–10, 114–18, 120–1, 126 n.29, 130, 133, 147–9, 153, 169, 175, 178, 181, 184, 186
　aesthetic 10, 14, 15, 18, 104, 133, 147–9, 153, 178, 181
　fragmentary 16, 83, 117–18, 120–1, 149
　intellectual 31, 34, 43–5, 108, 118
equality 2–12, 18–20, 20 n.1, 20 n.4, 20 n.5, 23, 25–33, 35–7, 41–6, 46 n.1, 47 n.8, 49 n.23, 51–9, 62, 65–6, 68–72, 75–6, 78 n.9, 79 n.35, 79 n.26, 80 n.29, 85–6, 90, 92, 100–1, 119–22 125 n.26, 131–2, 148–9, 151, 153, 162–3, 168–9, 171 n.11, 172 n.19, 175–8, 181, 184–6 *see also* aesthetic equality; literary equality
ethical regime of images 13, 16, 18, 87, 127–30, 132, 142, 157, 180–2, 185
exigency 11–12, 53–4, 60–2, 64–5, 75, 148, 182, 184
existentialism 10–12, 23, 39, 41, 51–2, 54–5, 66, 68, 79 n.23, 85, 90, 170 n.9, 176–7
experience
　aesthetic 14, 16–17, 83, 86, 93–4, 96, 148–50, 153–5, 157–8, 169, 179–82, 185–6
　socially lived 14, 19, 38, 79 n.22, 111, 169, 177–8, 181, 183–6

facticity 5, 9, 12, 55–6, 63, 65–70, 76, 78 n.18, 79 n.20
Fanon, Frantz 52, 55, 57, 73, 77 n.7, 80 n.27, 183–4
　Black Skin, White Masks 52
　Wretched of the Earth, The 57, 73, 77 n.7
feminism (and *cartésiennes*) 28, 37, 46 n.3, 48 n.12
Fichte, J. G. 155–8
flâneur 102, 110–11, 125 n.24, 125 n.25
Flaubert, Gustave 88–9, 94, 101, 112
Flynn, Thomas 64, 78 n.11, 79 n.20
Foucault, Michel 3–4, 20 n.3, 23, 47 n.8, 53, 60, 66–7, 86–7, 110, 135, 145

freedom 5, 7, 12, 17, 28–9, 37–42, 48 n.20, 52–6, 63–72, 76, 78 n.18, 78 n.19, 80 n.29, 89, 118, 123 n.5, 131, 147, 149–50, 152–61, 163, 169, 172 n.19, 177–8, 182, 184
French Revolution 63–4, 85–6, 152, 163
Freud, Sigmund 171 n.13 *see also* psychoanalysis
Front de libération nationale 74, 81 n.30
Fuller, Loïe 185
Future of the Image, The (Rancière) 92–3
Futurism 91–2, 123 n.8

Gauny, Gabriel 120, 148, 171 n. 18
good sense (*bon sens*) 2, 9, 11, 20 n.1, 27–8, 31–2, 34, 36, 38, 41–3, 45, 51, 120–1, 131, 169, 175, 177
Gratton, Peter 184
Greenberg, Clement 13–15, 18, 83, 91–2, 95, 101–2, 104–9, 118, 123 n.6, 123 n.8, 124 n.18, 124 n.19, 124 n.20, 124 n.21, 125 n.22, 127, 142, 145, 162, 179–80
  'Avant-Garde and Kitsch' 105–9, 125 n.22
  'Modernist Painting' 105–7, 124 n.19
  'Toward a Newer Laocoon' 102, 104–5, 180
Guyer, Paul 119, 126 n.30

Habermas, Jürgen 151
haecceity 89, 122 n.4, 183–4
Hallward, Peter 6, 59, 69, 72, 77 n.8, 170 n.5
Hatred of Democracy (Rancière) 21 n.9, 70–2
Hegel, G. W. F. 78 n.17, 93, 103, 131, 146–7, 152, 166–9
Heidegger, Martin 30, 47 n.4, 47 n.5, 68, 90, 122 n.28, 137, 139, 141, 173 n.31
Heideggerian and post-Heideggerian philosophy 11, 19, 21 n.9, 23, 29, 53, 122 n.1, 126 n.28, 140
heterotopia 134, 154, 157, 166–9
Hobbes, Thomas 2, 7, 20 n.1
Hölderlin, Friedrich 90, 131, 139, 144, 152, 171 n.17
homonymy 63, 69–70, 72, 79 n.22, 121, 143, 169

Howells, Christina 66, 87–8
Hunt, Lynn 79 n.26

identity 6, 11–12, 53–6, 58–63, 65–6, 68, 71, 73–6, 81 n.31, 93, 151–2, 157, 178 *see also* Schelling, on identity
ideological state apparatus 58
ideology 3, 8, 29, 47 n.5, 54, 58, 102, 107, 117, 119, 121, 124 n.20, 151, 168, 176
Ignorant Schoolmaster, The (Rancière) 21 n.9, 29, 43–5, 49 n.23, 108, 130
imperialism 71, 80 n.27, 114
impossible identification 56, 72–5
inaesthetics *see* Badiou
interest 6–8, 11–12, 26, 28, 35–6, 53, 59–62, 65, 75, 121, 148, 154, 182, 184
interpellation 20 n.3, 40, 58, 119, 121, 168
Ishay, Micheline 80 n.27

Jacotot, Joseph 11, 27, 42–5, 176
Jones, Donna 183
Juno Ludovisi 95, 154

Kail, Michel 39–40
Kant, Immanuel 43, 61, 86–7, 90, 92, 105–6, 108–9, 114, 118–21, 147–50, 153, 155–8, 161, 171 n.18, 175–6, 182
  aesthetic judgement 92, 108–9, 118–19, 121, 147–9, 171 n.18
  aesthetic *sensus communis* 43, 114, 118–20, 126 n.30, 131, 148–9, 175, 182
  Critique of the Power of Judgment 118–20, 148, 150, 171 n.14, 172 n.19, 126 n.30
  Critique of Practical Reason 150, 156
  Critique of Pure Reason 105–6
  practical reason 147–50, 153, 155–8, 161
kitsch 14–15, 18, 91–2, 104–9, 118, 124 n.21, 125 n.22, 145, 168, 179

Lacan, Jacques 20 n.3, 164–6
Lacoue-Labarthe, Philippe 122, 139, 171 n.17
Lane, Jeremy 109, 171 n.18

La Peau de chagrin (Balzac) 116
Lecercle, Jean-Jacques 145–6
Lehman, Robert 171 n.14
Let Us Now Praise Famous Men (Agee and Evans) 108
Lévinas, Emmanuel 40, 135, 166
life
　art and life 14–16, 18, 83, 88, 91, 95, 97, 100–5, 107, 110–16, 118, 132–3, 140–1, 143–4, 148, 161–4, 175, 178–86
　politics of 18, 181–6
　social life 18, 26, 38, 40, 57–9, 63, 70–2, 175, 183
literary equality 97–8, 100–1
literary revolution 13, 15, 104–5, 112, 122 n.1, 183
literature 9, 15, 85–90, 94–5, 97–8, 100–1, 104–5, 107, 110–13, 118, 123 n.6, 123 n.11, 123 n.12, 125 n.22, 139, 144–5, 147, 178, 181
Lloyd, Genevieve 38
logic of equality 4, 6–7, 25–6, 57–9, 69–70, 72, 76
logos 25–6, 35, 57–8, 69, 148
Lost Illusions 101, 124 n.15
Lyotard, Jean-François 90, 129, 135, 166

Macherey, Pierre 122 n.1
Malevich, Kazimir 90, 165
　White on White 165
Mallarmé, Stéphane 90, 144–5, 165, 185
Manet, Edouard 14, 90–1, 102, 106–7, 124 n.17, 124 n.21, 180
　Olympia 102, 124 n.16
　Un Bar aux Folies Bergère 124 n.17
Maoism 76
Marinetti, F. T. 125 n.27
Marx, Karl 8, 42, 45–6, 53, 61–2, 78 n.12, 100, 105–6, 115–16
　Communist Manifesto, The 15, 106, 109
　Economic and Philosophic Manuscripts 61, 78 n.12
　'On the Jewish Question' 8
　'Preface to *A Critique of Political Economy*' 8, 105
Marxism 3, 19, 21 n.9, 29, 46, 47 n.5, 52, 63, 92, 100–1, 105, 115, 122 n.1, 126 n.28, 139–41, 176

Maschino, Maurice 73
May 1968 74–5, 76 n.1, 81 n.31, 135, 137
May, Todd 20 n.5, 56–8, 67, 70–1, 76, 77 n.8
Mecchia, Giuseppina 46 n.1,
metapolitics 5, 8, 15–16, 63–4, 79 n.25, 100–1, 111, 114–17, 132, 153, 171 n.13, 181
Miller, Jacques-Alain 140
mimesis 6, 13–14, 92–100, 105, 118, 127, 140, 143–4, 169, 179–82, 184
　norms of 13–14, 92–100, 105, 118, 127, 143–4, 169, 179–82, 184
　principle of fiction 95, 97–8
　principle of genre 95–8
　principle of decorum 95–8
　principle of presence 95–100
misinterpretation 16, 79 n.22, 83, 114, 119, 121, 148
misunderstanding
　literary 9, 16, 83, 85, 88–90, 94, 97, 101, 110, 114, 121, 122 n.2, 122 n.3, 133, 148, 157, 169
　philosophical 9, 11, 45
modern art 10, 14–15, 90–1, 102–4, 109, 123 n.8, 133
modernism 10, 13–15, 18, 83, 90–2, 101–9, 114, 118, 123 n.6, 123 n.8, 124 n.19, 124 n.20, 124 n.21, 127, 135, 142–7, 165, 170 n.4, 179–80
modernity 10, 13–14, 83, 90–2, 101, 110–11, 114–18, 123 n.6, 123 n.8, 126 n.28, 127, 133, 162
Moi, Toril 49 n.22, 77 n.5
Montaigne, Michel de 2, 20 n.1, 31
Moore, Lisa 124 n.16
mute speech 97–101, 123 n.11
Mute Speech (Rancière) 94–7, 99–100

Names of History, The (Rancière) 79 n.22, 94
Nancy, Jean-Luc 23, 53, 77 n.3, 122 n.1, 135, 139, 171 n.17
Negri, Antonio 29, 31, 47 n.5, 53, 77 n.3
Negritude 55, 89–90, 123 n.6
Newmark, Kevin 125 n.26
new mythology 17, 113, 131–2, 153, 161, 163
Ngũgĩ wa Thiong'o 123 n.12

Nochlin, Linda 102–4
novel, the 123 n.6, 132, 161, 167
Noys, Benjamin 17, 132, 135, 143

Oedipus at Colonus (Sophocles) 161
Olympia (Manet) 102, 124 n.16
On the Shores of Politics (Rancière) 21 n.9, 65
ontology 9, 19, 67, 126 n.28, 136–8, 171 n.11, 176, 184
Our Mutual Friend (Dickens) 183–4

paradox of the spectator, the 129–31, 170 n.3
parapolitics 5–7, 86
patriarchial femininity 40–1, 49 n.22
people 5–7, 17, 41, 51, 55, 57, 65, 69–71, 74, 86, 182
    demos 5–6, 51, 57, 65, 69–70, 74, 86, 182
    ethnos 74–5
Philosopher and His Poor, The (Rancière) 1, 4–6, 11–12, 21 n.9, 42–3, 51–4, 57, 62–4, 76 n.1, 79 n.22, 87, 99–100, 108–10, 118, 120–1, 124 n.13, 148, 172 n.20, 176, 182
philosophy (as a discipline) 8–11, 19, 86, 175–6
    political philosophy 2–3, 5–9, 26, 49 n.23, 56–7, 70, 72, 153
Plato 2–3, 5–6, 16–17, 42–3, 51, 57, 69, 86, 98–100, 120, 124 n.13, 127–31, 138–9, 142, 157, 170 n.10, 182
    Phaedrus 98–100
    Republic 5–6, 16, 42–3, 127–9, 138, 142, 157, 182
Platonic Regime of art 16–18, 83, 87, 129, 131–6, 142, 146, 161–3, 167–9, 170 n.3, 170 n.4, 170 n.6, 170 n.7
poetry 16, 89–90, 95–6, 111, 128–9, 131, 138–41, 144–6, 163, 167–8
poiesis 93, 100, 139
police (and policing) 3–8, 11–14, 18–19, 20 n.4, 25–6, 28, 30, 34, 36, 40, 51–3, 55–60, 62, 64–5, 69–76, 85, 88, 93, 97, 100, 135, 143, 151–5, 162–3, 166, 168–9, 172 n.22, 175, 178–82, 185
politics (micropolitics) of aesthetics 13–18, 76, 83, 85–8, 90–4, 97–102, 111–15, 117, 121–2, 122 n.2, 125 n.27, 132–5, 142–4, 148, 150–3, 157, 161–2, 166–9, 170 n.6, 175, 178–86
Politics of Aesthetics, The (Rancière) 14, 16, 18, 21 n.9, 85–97, 90–1, 93–5, 112, 125 n.27, 126 n.28, 127, 134, 176, 184
politics of art 16–17, 83, 94, 132–5, 149, 153, 161–2, 164, 169, 170 n.6, 185
politics of equality 2–13, 15, 18–19, 20 n.4, 25–31, 37–9, 41–2, 44–6, 46 n.1, 51–60, 62–6, 68–76, 77 n.9, 78 n.15, 79 n.24, 80 n.28, 81 n.31, 85–8, 90, 94, 100–1, 114, 121, 122 n.2, 125 n.26, 125 n.27, 126 n.29, 129, 133–5, 153, 161–2, 166, 168–9, 171 n.11, 172 n.22, 175–9, 185–6
Politics of Literature, The (Rancière) 9, 13, 21 n.9, 88–9, 94–5, 97–8, 100–1, 112–14, 116, 145, 170 n. 10
Pollock, Griselda 125 n.24
postcolonialism 68, 123 n.6
poststructuralism 23, 53, 66, 85, 90
Poullain de la Barre, François 11, 27–9, 35–7, 39, 41–2, 46, 46 n.3, 48 n.14, 48 n.15, 48 n.18, 48 n.21, 176–7
practico-inert 11–13, 16, 18, 52–3, 60–4, 75, 78 n.11, 83, 85, 88, 94, 107, 121, 148, 154–5, 162, 168, 178–9, 181, 184–5
Proletarian Nights (Rancière) 94, 110, 120, 168–9, 172 n.18
proletariat, the 8, 15, 29, 41, 45–6, 52, 54–5, 59, 64–5, 70, 75, 85, 88–9, 106, 108–11, 115, 118, 122 n.3, 145, 179
psychoanalysis 19, 21 n.9, 48 n.21, 87, 90, 101, 140, 142, 166, 171 n.12, 171 n.13
Pugh, David 151

Rancière, Jacques *see individual works*
Red and Black (Stendhal) 183
Rembrantsz, Dirk 1–2, 4, 42
representative regime of the arts 13–14, 16, 18, 87, 91–8, 100–1, 103–5, 111–12, 127, 129, 133–4, 142–4, 154, 169, 171 n.13, 179–82, 185 *see also* mimesis

repressive state apparatus 58
rights 3, 7, 46 n.3, 55–7, 59, 70–2, 79 n.24, 79 n.25, 79 n.26, 79 n.27, 79 n.28, 79 n.29, 135
Ristelhueber, Sophie 186
Rockhill, Gabriel 20 n.3, 130, 134, 170 n.2, 172 n.22
Rodis-Lewis, Geneviève 1–2, 20 n.1
Romans of the Decadence, The (Thomas Couture) 103
Romanticism 90, 104, 138–44, 147–8, 171 n.16, 171 n.17
Rose, Julie 20 n.3, 79 n.23

Sartre, Jean-Paul 11–12, 23, 29, 32–3, 37–8, 41–2, 48 n.21, 51–6, 60–9, 71, 73, 75, 76–9, 85, 87–9, 107, 122 n.3, 123 n.5, 135, 173 n.31, 176–8, 183–4
  authenticity 56, 68, 173 n.31
  bad faith 38, 54–5, 67–8, 76, 77 n.5
  Being and Nothingness 12, 48 n.21, 52–6, 63, 65–8, 71, 73, 76
  'Black Orpheus' 52, 77 n.7, 89–90
  consciousness 52, 55–6, 66–7, 71, 76, 77 n.2, 78 n.16
  contingency 12, 55–6, 58, 62, 65, 67–8, 70, 76
  Critique of Dialectical Reason 11–12, 23, 52–4, 60–5, 73, 77 n.9
  exigency 11–12, 53–4, 60–2, 64–5, 75
  facticity 12, 55–6, 63, 65–70, 76, 78 n.18, 79 n.20
  fatigue 51–2, 55, 63
  for-itself 66–8, 78 n.16, 79 n.20
  freedom 12, 37–8, 48 n.20, 52–6, 63–72, 76, 78 n.18, 78 n.19, 80 n.29, 89, 123 n.5, 177–8
  in-itself 66–8, 78 n.16
  organization 54, 63–6, 178
  party, the 52, 54–5, 63–4
  pledge, the 54, 64–5, 178
  practico-inert 11–13, 52–3, 60–4, 75, 78 n.11, 85, 107
  scarcity 60, 77 n.9, 77 n.12
  seriality 11–12, 52–3, 60–3, 78 n.13
  sincerity 76
  transcendence 55, 68, 76
  What is Literature? 87–9, 122 n.3, 123 n.5

Schelling, F. W. J. 16–17, 83, 113, 129, 131–2, 134, 146–50, 152–3, 158–61, 163–4, 166–7, 169, 171 n.17, 173 n.28, 173 n.29
Schiller, Friedrich 17–18, 93, 95–6, 108, 134, 143, 146–7, 149–58, 161, 166–7, 169, 172 n.20, 172 n.21, 172 n.23, 172 n.24, 172 n.25, 172 n.26, 172 n.27, 176, 182
Schmitt, Carl 126 n.29
Scott, Joan Wallach 80 n.28
seriality *see* Sartre
Sharpe, Lesley 150
Short Voyages to the Land of the People (Rancière) 176
Situationism 140–1
sociology 13, 15, 18, 47 n.7, 59, 92, 99, 104, 108–9, 127, 176
solidarity 29, 41, 46, 51, 72, 119, 175
Still, Clyfford 14, 124 n.21
stultification 15, 36, 44, 49, 104, 108, 135, 152, 162, 179
Stuurman, Siep 48 n.17
subjectivation 4–6, 9–12, 16–17, 19, 20 n.3, 20 n.4, 23, 26–33, 35, 38–42, 44–6, 47 n.5, 48 n.20, 51–6, 58–62, 65–7, 69–76, 77 n.3, 81 n.31, 85–8, 90, 100–1, 122 n.2, 135–9, 142, 145, 147–8, 164–6, 168–9, 175–8
Surrealism 88, 91–2, 109, 116, 122 n.3, 123 n.8, 141
Swenson, James 3, 44
symptomology *see* metapolitics

Tanke, Joseph 86, 92, 134, 162
theatre 129, 130, 139, 145
tragedy 13–14, 95–6, 161, 163, 171 n.12
trust 70, 79 n.25

Un Bar aux Folies Bergère (Manet) 124 n.17

Vallury, Raji 122 n.2
Vaneigem, Raoul 141
Village Burial, A (Augustin Roger) 103
vitalism 183–4
Voltaire, 95–6

'WB' (Ristelhueber) 186
White on White (Malevich) 165

Whitman, Walt 108, 124 n.21, 183, 186
Wilhelm Meister's Apprenticeship (Goethe) 167
Williams, Raymond 122 n.1
Winckelmann, Johann 95, 108
Wohlfarth, Irving 125 n.25
Wollstonecraft, Mary 40–1
Wordsworth, William 169
work 2, 4, 6, 8, 36, 43, 52, 59, 61–3, 72, 98, 108, 111, 118, 120–1, 127, 152, 157, 168–9, 182–3

workers 6, 43, 51–2, 55, 58–9, 61–3, 69, 72, 75, 98–9, 109–10, 114, 118, 120–1, 137, 152, 168–9, 171 n.18, 176, 182–3
writing 18, 80 n.28, 89, 94, 97–100, 139, 168, 175–6, 184–5
wrong 4–9, 11, 26, 28–9, 35, 39–46, 59, 69, 73–4, 168, 175, 177

Žižek, Slavoj 23, 30, 140

Lightning Source UK Ltd.
Milton Keynes UK
UKHW02f2350180618
324449UK00003B/212/P